Negotiation and Conflict Resolution in Organizations
Theories, Skills, and Applications

Andrew J. DuBrin
Professor of Management, Emeritus
College of Business
Rochester Institute of Technology

Academic Media Solutions
Affordable - Quality Textbooks, Study Aids, & Custom Publishing

Cover photos: *metamorworks/Shutterstock*
Negotiation and Conflict Resolution in Organizations: Theories, Skills, and Applications, Andrew J. DuBrin

Paperback (black/white):	ISBN–13: 978-1-942041-94-8
	ISBN–10: 1-942041-94-2
Paperback (color):	ISBN–13: 978-1-942041-93-1
	ISBN–10: 1-942041-93-4
Loose-leaf version:	ISBN–13: 978-1-942041-95-5
	ISBN–10: 1-942041-95-0
Online version:	ISBN–13: 978-1-942041-96-2
	ISBN–10: 1-942041-96-9

Printed in the United States of America by Academic Media Solutions.

Brief Contents

Contents

6 International and Cross-Cultural Negotiation 81

7 Ethics in Negotiation 97

8 Major Sources and Types of Conflict 113

9 Basic Techniques for Resolving Conflict 129

10 Advanced Techniques for Resolving Conflict 145

11 Dealing with Incivility, Difficult People, and Criticism 161

12 Third-Party Resolution of Conflict 177

Preface

Welcome the first edition of *Negotiation and Conflict Resolution in Organizations*, designed for courses in negotiation or conflict resolution, or a combination of the two, that have a strong applied focus. Both negotiation and conflict resolution are growing fields of interest, with more courses on these topics being added regularly at several levels of higher education. Many students who take this course have taken courses in management, organizational behavior, or psychology. Negotiation and/or conflict-resolution courses are typically housed in colleges of business, management, public policy, or law. Furthermore, there are hundreds of workshops about negotiation and conflict resolution offered by institutions of higher learning as well as training organizations.

The emphasis of this book is on information, self-quizzes, cases, and skill-building exercises that translate into skill development in negotiation and conflict resolution. We incorporate relevant theory and research findings where appropriate, but the major thrust of the book is the direct application of knowledge. The size and scope of the book are well suited to college courses that supplement a core textbook with journal articles, major projects, and online information or other instructional media.

THE FEATURES

Negotiation and Conflict Resolution in Organizations summarizes and synthesizes relevant information about negotiation and conflict-resolution topics and provides concrete examples of strategies and tactics in action. In addition, the book incorporates many useful features to make the material more accessible, collaborative, and incisive. A key emphasis of the features of the book is to present information that is helpful in developing negotiation and conflict resolution skills, backed by theory and research when feasible.

- *Learning Objectives* introduce the major themes of each chapter and provide a framework for study.
- *Boldfaced key terms* are defined in the margins, listed at the end of each chapter, and reinforced in an end-of-book glossary.
- *Negotiation and Conflict Resolution in Action* boxes describe the actions of managers and professionals in dealing with negotiations and conflict resolution, usually illustrating techniques described in the chapter.
- *Self-quizzes* provide the opportunity for the reader to reflect on where he or she stands on a dimension of behavior related to negotiation or conflict resolution, such as negotiating style or disposition to engage in interpersonal conflict. The self-quizzes therefore personalize the discussion of the behaviors or attitudes under study. The quizzes are designed for self-reflection and are not presented as validated personality tests.
- *Skill-Building Exercises* allow for direct practice of the skills necessary for becoming an effective negotiator or resolver of conflict. The exercises take about ten minutes to run and usually involve role playing. A few of the exercises are designed for the student to collect live data about a topic under study.

- *Summaries*, located toward the end of each chapter, integrate all key topics and concepts into several cogent paragraphs, providing an overview of the chapter that can be used as a framework for studying,
- *Key Terms and Phrases* provide a useful review of each chapter's terminology.
- *Discussion Questions and Activities*, located toward the end of each chapter, are suitable for individual or group analysis. An occasional question asks the student to consult with a manager or professional to obtain input on an activity related to negotiation or conflict resolution.
- *Case Problems*, located at the end of each chapter, are suitable for individual or group analysis. The cases are uniquely designed to complement the textbook, and they include relevant follow-up discussion questions.
- *Associated Role Plays* accompany each case, with the case providing the scenario or script for the role plays. The role plays are therefore another opportunity for skill development, particularly when students apply concepts from the chapter to their role-playing activity.

THE FRAMEWORK

Negotiation and Conflict Resolution in Organizations is a blend of description, theory, skill development, insight, and prescription. Divided into 12 chapters, the book deals mostly with negotiation in the first seven chapters and mostly with conflict resolution in the next five chapters. Negotiation is conceptualized here as a major approach to resolving conflict. Chapter 1 provides an overview of negotiation and conflict resolution, including definitions of negotiation and conflict management. The chapter describes situations suitable for negotiation and conflict resolution, as well as characteristics of effective negotiation and conflict resolution.

Chapter 2 presents suggestions for successful negotiations, with an emphasis on planning, political astuteness, effective use of emotion, and empathy. Chapter 3 concentrates on skills important for negotiation, such as persuasion skills and emotional intelligence. Personality and cognitive traits associated with negotiation skills are described, as well as gender differences in negotiation skills. Chapter 4 deals with a variety of basic negotiation tactics, including those helpful in preparing for negotiation and those used in face-to-face negotiating. Chapter 5 moves on to more advanced negotiation tactics, including those dealing mostly with facts and information and those dealing mostly with behavior and emotions.

Chapter 6 is about international and cross-cultural negotiation, covering such topics as the influence of cultural factors on negotiation and cross-cultural negotiation tactics. Chapter 7 describes the vital topic of ethics in negotiation, including pressures toward unethical behavior, guidelines for ethical decision making in negotiation, and a description of many unethical tactics. Suggestions are presented for being an ethical negotiator. Chapter 8 describes major sources and types of conflict in the workplace, as well as the evolution of conflict theory and the positive and negative consequences of conflict.

Chapter 9 describes basic techniques for resolving conflict, plus behaviors and attitudes suited to resolving conflict. Chapter 10 presents advanced techniques for resolving conflict and also includes the characteristics of an effective conflict-management system and guidelines for resolving conflicts of interests. Chapter 11 is about a major workplace challenge: dealing with incivility, difficult people, and criticism. Chapter 12 covers third-party resolution of conflict, a growing trend in organizations and society, and includes the manager's role as a mediator, arbitration, the grievance procedure, and outside mediation.

ONLINE AND IN PRINT

Student Options: Print and Online Versions

Negotiation and Conflict Resolutions in Organizations is available in multiple versions: online, in PDF, and in print as either a paperback or loose-leaf text. The content of each version is identical.

The most affordable version is the online book, with upgrade options including the online version bundled with a print version. What is nice about the print version is that it offers you the freedom of being unplugged—away from your computer. The people at Academic Media Solutions recognize that it is difficult to read from a screen at length and that most of us read much faster from a piece of paper. The print options are particularly useful when you have extended print passages to read.

The online edition allows you to take full advantage of embedded digital features, including search and notes. Use the search feature to locate and jump to discussions anywhere in the book. Use the notes feature to add personal comments or annotations. You can move out of the book to follow Web links. You can navigate within and between chapters using a clickable table of contents. These features allow you to work at your own pace and in your own style, as you read and surf your way through the material. (See "Harnessing the Online Version" for more tips on working with the online version.)

Harnessing the Online Version

The online version of *Negotiation and Conflict Resolution in Organizations* offers the following features to facilitate learning and to make using the book an easy, enjoyable experience:

- *Easy-to-navigate/clickable table of contents*—You can surf through the book quickly by clicking on chapter headings, or first- or second-level section headings. And the Table of Contents can be accessed from anywhere in the book.

- *Key terms search*—Type in a term, and a search engine will return every instance of that term in the book; then jump directly to the selection of your choice with one click.

- *Notes and highlighting*—The online version includes study apps such as notes and highlighting. Each of these apps can be found in the tools icon embedded in the Academic Media Solutions/Textbook Media's online eBook reading platform (www.academicmediasolutions.com).

- *Upgrades*—The online version includes the ability to purchase additional study apps and functionality that enhance the learning experience.

INSTRUCTOR SUPPLEMENTS

In addition to its student-friendly features and pedagogy, the variety of student formats available, and the uniquely affordable pricing options that are designed to provide students with a flexibility that fits any budget and/or learning style, *Negotiation and Conflict Resolution in Organizations* comes with the following teaching and learning aids:

- *Test Item File*— This provides a set of 20 multiple-choice, 20 true/false, and five essay questions for every chapter for creating original quizzes and exams.

- *Instructor's Manual*—This is a condensed version of the book offering assistance in preparing lectures, identifying learning objectives, developing essay exams and assignments, and constructing course syllabi.

- *PowerPoint Presentations*—Key points in each chapter are illustrated in a set of PowerPoint files designed to assist with instruction. In addition to the key points, the slides include all of the numbered figures and tables from each chapter.

■ *Online Video Labs with Student Worksheets*—A collection of high-quality, dynamic, and sometimes humorous video segments (contemporary and classic) produced by a variety of media, academic, and entertainment sources, accessed via the web. Organized by chapter, the video segments illustrate key topics/ issues discussed in the chapters. Each video segment is accompanied by a student worksheet that consists of a series of discussion questions that helps students connect the themes presented in the video segment with key topics discussed in the specific chapter.

STUDENT SUPPLEMENTS AND UPGRADES (ADDITIONAL PURCHASE REQUIRED)

■ *Lecture Guide*—This printable lecture guide is designed for student use and is available as an in-class resource or study tool. Note: Instructors can request the PowerPoint version of these slides either to use as developed or to customize.

■ *Quizlet Study Set*—Quizlet is an easy-to-use online learning tool built from all the key terms from the textbook. Students can turbo charge their studying via digital flashcards and other types of study apps, including tests and games. Students are able to listen to audio, as well as create their own flashcards. Quizlet is a cross-platform application and can be used on a desktop, tablet, or smartphone.

Acknowledgments

Thank you to the several college professors who provided me some insight into a new type of textbook that would facilitate knowledge and skill development in both negotiation and conflict resolution. Thanks also to the staff at Academic Media Solutions (AMS) who worked with me to publish *Negotiation and Conflict Resolution in Organizations*, including Daniel C. Luciano, the president/founder of AMS, and Victoria Putman and Lori Bradshaw of Putman Productions. Also receiving my appreciation are the people I have encountered over the years who gave me the opportunity to negotiate and resolve conflict. These encounters helped me develop skills in and insights into negotiation and conflict resolution.

Finally, writing without loved ones would be a lonely task. My thanks therefore go to my family: Drew, Heidi, Douglas, Gizella, Melanie, Rosie, Clare, Camila, Sofia, Eliana, Julian, Carson, and Owen. I also thank Stefanie, the woman in my life, and her daughter Sofia for their contribution to my well-being.

About the Author

Andrew J. DuBrin is professor emeritus of management in the College of Business at the Rochester Institute of Technology, where he has taught courses and conducts research in management, organizational behavior, leadership, and influence processes. He has served the college as chairman of the management department and as team leader. He received his PhD in industrial psychology from Michigan State University. His business experience is in human resource management, and he consults with organizations and with individuals. His specialties include leadership and political behavior in organizations.

Professor DuBrin is an established author of textbooks, scholarly books, and trade titles. He has also written for professional journals and magazines. He has written textbooks on leadership, the principles of management, political behavior in organizations, organizational behavior, and human relations. His scholarly books include the subjects of crisis leadership impression management, narcissism, and the proactive personality. His trade titles cover many current issues, including coaching and mentoring, team play, office politics, coping with adversity, and tolerating ambiguity.

An Overview of Negotiation and Conflict Resolution

CHAPTER 1

Source: ProStockStudio/Shutterstock.

Chapter Outline

The Concepts of Negotiation
and Conflict Management

Situations Suitable for Negotiation
*Characteristics of Effective
Negotiation*

Situations Suitable for Conflict
Resolution
*Characteristics of Effective
Conflict Resolution*

Learning Objectives

**After reading and studying this chapter and doing the exercises, you
should be able to:**

1. Understand and differentiate the concepts of negotiation and conflict
   resolution.
2. Describe situations suitable for negotiation.
3. Identify several characteristics of an effective negotiation situation.
4. Describe situations suitable for conflict resolution.
5. Identify several characteristics of effective conflict resolution.

During the last 35 years, negotiation has become recognized as a subject of scholarly research and a useful set of workplace skills.[1] Almost all managerial and professional positions in organizations require knowledge of and skill in negotiating as well as managing conflict. A basic example is the sales representative at an automobile dealership who negotiates a price for a vehicle that is fair to the customer yet also allows a reasonable profit for the dealership. Should the customer find a flaw in the newly purchased vehicle, the rep must now manage the conflict with the customer. In the executive suite, the chief executive officer (CEO) negotiates with major customers, suppliers, union leaders, and representatives of government agencies over such matters as prices, costs, working conditions, and compliance with laws, including environmental regulations.

This textbook is about negotiation and conflict management—addressed from several perspectives and with an emphasis on conflict resolution. Throughout the book, we discuss relevant theory, research findings, and skill development. Our intention is not merely to describe negotiation and conflict management but also to explain how to become more effective at negotiating and resolving conflict.

You are invited to take Self-Quiz 1-1 to think about your present attitudes toward dealing with workplace situations that require negotiation and other forms of conflict management. As with all other self-quizzes presented in this book, the quiz is designed for self-reflection. The scoring and interpretations offered are to help you think about the issues and are not intended to be scientifically based diagnoses of the concept being measured. Self-quizzes that provide accurate diagnoses are based on extensive psychometric research involving thousands of people who take preliminary versions of the quiz.

The Concepts of Negotiation and Conflict Management

The concepts of negotiation and conflict management are intertwined because negotiation is typically used to resolve conflict, or differences in positions. A useful general definition of negotiation is that it refers to a situation in which two or more parties confer with each other to resolve their differences. Both parties want to gain an advantage from the negotiation but not necessarily to exploit or disadvantage the other side. Several other definitions of negotiation are presented in Table 1.1 to help you appreciate the complexity of the topic.

negotiation A situation in which two or more parties confer with each other to resolve their differences.

Two basic types of negotiation are widely recognized. In distributive negotiation, the basic task is to allocate a resource between the two parties. Because the resources are allocated to one side at the expense of the other, distributive negotiation is also referred to as *win–lose* negotiation. If the amount of resources, such as money or equipment, is fixed, it is possible for only one party to win, and the other party loses. Two other terms for distributive negotiation are *zero-sum* and *fixed-pie* negotiation.

distributive negotiation A type of negotiation in which the basic task is to allocate a resource between two or more parties.

The other type of negotiation is integrative negotiation, in which both sides attempt to attain mutually beneficial results. Integrative negotiation has two steps. First, the two negotiating parties attempt to identify additional items or resources that could be added to the overall mix of what is being negotiated. You might refer to this as a collaborative problem-solving activity. In negotiating the price of a new vehicle, a couple of extra items that might enter the pie are service warranties, a subscription to satellite radio, or free oil changes and engine lubrications for a specified time period. The first step adds the total potential value to the negotiation.

integrative negotiation A type of negotiation in which both sides attempt to attain mutually beneficial results.

The second step of integrative negotiation allocates resources in a way favorable to both parties and is therefore frequently referred to as *win-win* negotiation.[2] As you probably recognize, the term *win-win* has become part of everyday language. Because the list of items being negotiated has expanded, both sides can receive something of value. In the new-vehicle situation, the dealer might receive another $750 for the

My Approach to Dealing with Workplace Problems

Indicate the extent to which the following statements describe your behavior or attitude by circling one number. If you have not encountered the situation mentioned, imagine what your behavior or attitude would likely be. The numbers refer to very inaccurate (VI), moderately inaccurate (MI), neither accurate nor inaccurate (N), moderately accurate (MA), and very accurate.

Statement Related to Workplace Problems	VI	MI	N	MA	VA
1. Getting involved in disagreements is fun.	1	2	3	4	5
2. I back away from differences of opinion.	5	4	3	2	1
3. When you have a disagreement with a coworker, the manager should solve the problem.	5	4	3	2	1
4. Dealing with disagreements on the job usually leads to constructive change.	1	2	3	4	5
5. Most differences of opinion about how to get work accomplished can be negotiated.	1	2	3	4	5
6. An effective manager should focus on results, not invest time in resolving disputes.	5	4	3	2	1
7. The old saying "If you can't stand the heat, stay out of the kitchen" applies well to the workplace.	1	2	3	4	5
8. If a coworker started yelling at me, I would immediately walk away from the situation.	5	4	3	2	1
9. It is acceptable to offer your boss constructive criticism.	1	2	3	4	5
10. If I were angry with my manager, I would express my feelings.	1	2	3	4	5
11. If I were angry with a coworker, I would hide my feelings.	5	4	3	2	1
12. A well-managed workplace has very few conflicts or differences of opinion.	5	4	3	2	1
13. If I were made a job offer, I would attempt to negotiate the starting salary and benefits in my favor.	1	2	3	4	5
14. Dealing with differences of opinions on work-related issues gives me a surge of mental energy.	1	2	3	4	5
15. I would welcome having to negotiate a price for goods or services with a supplier.	1	2	3	4	5

Scoring and Interpretation: Calculate your score by adding up the numbers circled.

60–75: You show a strong willingness to negotiate differences and manage conflict in the workplace. At times, you might even be too willing to get involved in conflict.

45–59: You have an average degree of willingness to get involved in negotiations and conflict management in the workplace.

15–44: You appear to back away from workplace situations that require negotiations or other ways of managing conflict. You might benefit from developing a more proactive approach to negotiation and conflict management.

purchase price, whereas the buyer receives free satellite radio for three years plus a couple of free oil changes and lubrications.

A valuable feature of integrative bargaining is that it helps build a good working relationship between the two parties, who may choose to conduct business with each other again. Both sides leave the bargaining session with an item of value. For example, a home developer negotiates the price of building the foundation for a house with a minority-owned business. Although the price is 5 percent lower than what the owner of the foundation company wants, he consents. The win he receives in exchange is the assurance that he will receive the contract to build the foundation for the home developer's next project.

TABLE 1.1 Several Representative Definitions of Negotiation

- "A method by which people settle differences."[3]

- "The process of communicating back and forth for the purpose of reaching a joint agreement about differing needs or ideas."[4]

- "A process by which we attempt to persuade people to give us something we want in exchange for something else."[5]

- "A process of potentially opportunistic interaction by which two or more parties, with some apparent conflict, seek to do better through jointly decided action than they could do otherwise."[6]

- "The basic idea behind a negotiation is that the agents make offers that they judge 'good' and respond to the offers made to them until a compromise is reached."[7]

- "An ancient craft, a delicate mix of art and sciences, style and substance. It prizes intuition as highly as intellect, good sense as much as hard numbers. It requires emotional detachment and a high aspiration level. It can be a game of power, real as well as imagined. Some people play the game masterfully while others only dimly understand it."[8]

conflict management
A proactive approach of handling conflict by managers, supervisors, and union representatives.

Conflict management refers to the idea that workplace conflict is dealt with constructively, including its resolution. David B. Lipsky and Ariel C. Avgar, two professors who specialize in conflict resolution, define conflict management as the adoption of a proactive approach to handling conflict by managers, supervisors, and union representatives. In organizations that have a systematic approach to conflict management, members don't just wait for workplace disputes to occur and then decide, case by case, which techniques to use. Instead, these organizations develop conflict-management policies and procedures that are consistent with their broader objectives. These broader goals might include retaining top talent and enhancing creativity.[9]

For conflict management to be successful, it is also important that managers and professionals be skilled in resolving conflict. Conflict-resolution skills are of major importance because it is consistently estimated that managers spend about 20 percent of their time resolving conflict. This includes conflicts in which managers are directly involved and situations where they intervene to resolve conflict between two individuals or groups.[10]

Situations Suitable for Negotiation

A frequent popular saying is that "everything is negotiable," which has an element of truth because many situations in the workplace and personal life are negotiable. Many people first heard about the value of negotiation when purchasing a vehicle. It is also true that many situations are not negotiable. If the price of plum tomatoes at your local grocery store is $2.79 per pound, it is highly doubtful that you can bargain for a better price. Similarly, you cannot negotiate the price of a cloud backup service for your own computer—unless, perhaps, you are the owner or CEO of a large enterprise.

Here we list and describe briefly a variety of workplace situations that are negotiable, which, taken collectively, underscore the relevance of negotiation and bargaining. We will present more details about several of these negotiating situations at various places in the book.

1. *Sales negotiations.* Professional sales representatives must be skilled negotiators because the prices of business-to-business goods and services are typically negotiable. According to content marketer Francis Cyriac, negotiations are successful when the real and perceived differences between the two parties are adjusted while maintaining credibility, customer value, and profit margins. Even when the sales representative has properly qualified the prospect and met his or her expectations, the final deal often ends up in negotiation.[11]

2. *Negotiating a starting salary or salary increase.* Starting salaries and raises are often negotiable, yet they may not be negotiable for many local, state, and federal government positions. For example, the starting salary for a beginning police officer position would rarely be negotiable, and government regulations might dictate a fixed percentage for salary increases in a given year. A widely recommended negotiating tactic for obtaining a higher starting salary or raise is to emphasize the contribution you will make or are making to the organization. As wealth advisor Ramit Sethi explains, in terms of getting a better-than-average salary increase, "The key to getting a raise to remembering that it's not about *you*. It's about what you can do for your *employer*." Few managers care that your expenses are high and that you need more money. Instead, show how your work has been contributing to the company's financial success, and ask to be compensated fairly because of this contribution.[12]

3. *Negotiating with venture capitalists (VCs).* An advanced and sophisticated form of negotiation takes place when the founders of a business attempt to make a deal with VCs, individuals who invest in a start-up and also become business partners and provide guidance. (Many readers have likely watched the television show *Shark Tank*, which is hosted by VCs.)

   Deepak Malhotra, a Harvard Business School professor of business administration, explains that few business negotiations contain the degree of high-stakes ambiguity and emotion that is present when company founders negotiate with VCs. These negotiations are not exclusively about the amount of money the VC will invest in the start-up. VCs and founders will need to work together jointly over the years for which the *term sheet* has been signed. (A term sheet is a document that specifies how much equity and control a VC will have in return for the VC's cash investment.) Both sides must therefore focus on multiple outcome scenarios and discuss how each party can help the other create value over the long term.[13]

4. *Purchasing an existing business.* Rather than start from scratch or become a franchisee, many people purchase an existing business. Business firms are often sold to former corporate executives who would like to try their hand at being a business owner. Richard Parker, president of the Business Buyer Resource Center, explains that the most exciting and anxious moments are likely to be experienced at the point of entering into negotiations and making an offer. Negotiating a sale price involves many personality and emotional factors. Business owners find that selling their business is a highly emotional time. They are attempting to sell a business in which they have invested years of physical and emotional energy, and the enterprise is often part of the business owner's self-image.

   The successful negotiator, whether buyer or seller, identifies the factor or factors that will make or break the deal. For example, the seller might need a big enough down payment to provide him or her a specific amount of money after paying off debt and the business broker's commission. In return, the buyer might obtain a concession, such as a lower interest rate on the balance owed to the seller after the down payment.[14]

5. *Negotiating heavy workloads.* At times, management may find it necessary to assign workloads that are perceived to be excessive, leading to considerable employee stress. Hourly workers might be required to work more overtime than they want during a peak in business activity. The peak might stem from a surge in customer demand or from negative reasons, such as a product recall. During the height of the tax season, members of the professional staff might work 60 hours per week. When company leadership observes too much complaining about the workload or too many employee absences due to illness, it would be an appropriate time to negotiate a better way of handling the workload. The options would include providing more opportunities for remote work or hiring a larger number of temporary workers during the peak period.

At times management may find it necessary to assign workloads that are perceived as excessive, leading to considerable employee stress.

Workload negotiations might also be initiated by a labor union or an employee group. The labor-union negotiation usually takes place at the beginning of a contract, but union leadership might seize the opportunity for an impromptu negotiation for the unanticipated heavy workload.

6. *Changes to retiree health-care benefits.* In recent years, many employers have dropped retirees from group health plans as a way of saving the company money. The changes represent a major financial challenge for retirees under age 65 because they are not eligible for Medicare, the government health insurance program. An example is Arconic, a New York-based manufacturer that split off from the Pittsburgh-based Alcoa in 2016. Arconic terminated its pre-Medicare medical and prescription coverage for retirees at the end of 2018. Employees who wanted to continue with health insurance could then purchase insurance through a private insurer or through the individual marketplace created by the Affordable Care Act. Retirees older than age 65 can also be affected because many health insurance programs for this group have also been terminated.[15]

The link between changes to retiree health-care benefits and negotiation is that sometimes it is possible for an employee group or a labor union to negotiate the changes. We emphasize *sometimes* because company management holds most of the power and authority with respect to changes. The exception is when the retiree benefits were originally established in a collective bargaining agreement. For example, in 2018, Xerox Corp. ended company-sponsored health benefits for nonunion retirees. The previously established collective bargaining agreement forbid changing retiree benefits, so the health benefits of union retirees were not affected.[16]

7. *Patent infringements.* A situation calling for negotiation that is of major importance to industry is settling accusations of patent infringements, as illustrated later in the chapter in the Negotiation and Conflict Resolution in Action feature. High-technology firms such as Apple, Samsung, Alphabet (parent of Google), and Facebook appear in court frequently to settle major patent disputes. A notable patent-infringement negotiation took place between Apple and Samsung when they ended their long-running patent battle. The central question was whether Samsung copied the iPhone. In a court filing, the two companies informed the judge that they had reached a settlement without disclosing the terms of the settlement.

The patent battle first surfaced in 2011 and initially resulted in a $1 billion ruling in favor of Apple. A series of appeals pushed the dispute to the U.S. Supreme Court and back to the lower courts. The battle was ultimately about whether Samsung copied Apple during the early days of the smartphone to be competitive. A key part of the patent infringement was whether Samsung copied the iPhone design. Apple contends that the case was never really about money but protecting the hard work and innovation of Apple employees.[17]

8. *Collective bargaining agreements.* Collective bargaining refers to the negotiations that take place between an employer and a group of employees to agree on work-related issues. The employees are represented by a labor union during the bargaining process. Among the myriad issues dealt with in a collective bargaining agreement are working conditions, employee safety, training, wages, layoffs, dealing with sexual harassment, job discrimination, health insurance, and retiree benefits. Wages, layoff procedures, and working hours are examples of mandatory topics for collective bargaining. When a negotiated agreement is reached, the collective bargaining agreement (CBA) becomes a legal contract governing employment issues.[18] Collective bargaining is at the heart of labor relations and is a field of study within itself.

9. *Amount of group-member input in decision making.* Participative decision making has become widespread as leaders have shifted to a more collaborative and democratic approach to leadership. A negotiable issue in participative decision making, however, is how much employee input is required and in relation to which types of decisions. Some group members want to be involved in as many decisions as possible, whereas others would prefer to be left alone so that they can better concentrate on their individual work. A strategy specialist in the department might say, for example, "Let somebody else decide where to hold the year-end party; I want to focus on our strategic plan."

   Group members and the manager might conduct several meetings, both in person and virtual, about which types of decisions should require employee input. The agreement would be informal, in contrast to a legally binding collective bargaining agreement. Agreed-upon topics for group-member input might include the selection of new group members, questions of product design, and the frequency of standing meetings. Agreed-upon topics that do not require group-member input might be allocation of salary increases, repainting the office, and employee benefits.

10. *Dealing with a difficult coworker.* A workplace reality is that in addition to accomplishing tasks and collaborating with group members, at times it is necessary to deal with an annoying, irritating, and interruptive coworker. An alternative to referring the problem to the manager or the human resources department is to negotiate directly with the coworker whom you perceive to be a difficult person. (Case 1A is about negotiating with a difficult coworker.) For example, a frequent and somewhat humorous coworker problem is that of an employee who uses the office microwave oven for heating up fish or other foods that coworkers find unpleasant. A negotiated solution might be to purchase a dedicated small microwave oven for the fish lover.

Characteristics of Effective Negotiation

As suggested previously, a wide variety of workplace situations are suitable for negotiation. Another key consideration is the characteristics of the situation, including the parties involved, that influence whether or not the negotiation will have a successful outcome. The following list identifies seven characteristics of effective negotiation, as outlined in Figure 1.1:

1. *Information is shared.* When negotiators share information, an atmosphere of mutual trust between or among the negotiators will most likely exist. The information shared does not have to reveal private financial data or underlying worries, but it

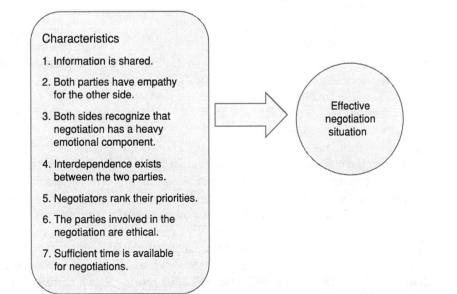

FIGURE 1.1 Characteristics of an Effective Negotiation Situation

should add to the situation. For example, a negotiator who is looking for a lower price from a supplier might share this information (if true): "I am happy to report that we are having a profitable year, but our profit margins are being squeezed. That is why we need to negotiate price with you." A *Forbes* reporter writes, "Studies have shown that revealing some information, even when it's unrelated to the negotiation, increases the outcome." All sensitive data do not have to be revealed. Simply mentioning something interesting about yourself, including your pastimes and career aspirations, can set a positive tone conducive to attaining a workable agreement.[19]

2. *Both sides have empathy for the other side.* Empathy is about understanding another's experience, perspective, and feelings.[20] During a negotiation, both sides want to feel understood, particularly with respect to the position they are taking. If you feel that the opposing party understands the rationale for your demands, you are more likely to be amenable to a compromise that meets some of your demands.

Source: Kazzland Inc/Shutterstock.

During negotiation both sides want to feel understood, particularly with respect to the position they are taking.

Visualize a purchasing manager for a large retail chain. She needs a 5 percent reduction in the cost of a popular brand of television receivers in order to eke out a profit in consumer electronic sales. She pleads, "If we do not have a profitable holiday season, we might have to close another 60 stores." If the vendor shows some empathy about her predicament, the purchasing manager might be willing to accept a 3 percent reduction. An empathetic statement from the vendor representative might be, "Closing another 60 stores would be a terrible blow for your chain." The purchasing manager thinks that the cost of the television receiver is negotiable because one of her alternatives is to find a supplier with a less valued brand name.

3. *Both parties recognize that negotiation about serious issues has a heavy emotional component.* Negotiating is an emotional experience for most people, therefore making it helpful to recognize the emotional component in order to have a successful outcome. It may not be necessary to uncover most of the emotions contained in the negotiation, but it is helpful to acknowledge the feelings that underlie the negotiation. Acknowledgment of emotions makes each side feel better understood, as in the previous point on empathy.

Imagine that an investor is negotiating the purchase of a furniture store that has been a family-operated business for over 75 years. A strictly facts-based approach by the investor would be to talk about how traditional furniture stores are less valuable than in the past because of online furniture stores and competition from low-price outlets. A better approach would be for the investor to first mention that he knows how much the family has loved this business for so many years, then state that he wants to give the business a viable future. Acknowledging the deep emotion built into the family business will give the investor a negotiating edge. The furniture store owner might recognize the investor's emotion with a statement such as, "I understand that you want to feel pride that you have made an acquisition at a very good price."

4. *Interdependence exists between the two parties.* Negotiations are taken the most seriously when the parties need each other in order to attain their objectives.[21] The more the dependent each party is on the other side, the more urgent is the negotiation, and the greater is the likelihood that a workable solution to the problem will be found. Imagine the situation of an American automobile manufacturer who sells 20 percent of its luxury vehicles in China, and this large quantity of vehicles accounts for most of the company's profit margin. The American company is therefore dependent on the Chinese market. In turn, the Chinese dealership that sells the American vehicles is dependent on these vehicles for 25 percent of its profits. When representatives from the American company and the Chinese dealership arrive at the negotiating table,

they both know they need each other. As a result, the probability increases that they will arrive at a satisfactory price for selling next year's model in the Chinese market.

5. *The negotiators rank their priorities.* The research of Adam Grant and Adam Galinsky suggests that ranking priorities, leaving all the issues on the table, and being transparent about it are likely to achieve favorable outcomes. Both parties can then compare their rankings and decide on what the true set of options is.[22] In negotiating with a parts supplier, for example, a head of manufacturing might establish these priorities: quality of the parts, cost, on-time delivery, and technical support. The head of marketing at the supplier might establish these priorities: price, lead time to provide the parts, the possibility for repeat business, and reasonable demands for tech support. Both sides would then have plenty to discuss and negotiate.

Ranking priorities and leaving all the issues on the table, and being transparent about it, is likely to achieve favorable outcomes.

6. *The parties involved in the negotiation are ethical.* When both sides in the negotiation have high ethical standards, a solution to the problem or conflict that will lead to a long-term constructive working relationship is more likely to be reached. Behaving ethically also involves taking into account all stakeholders in the deal, not just the two parties negotiating. The term *stakeholders* refers to the entire community that may be affected by the long-term consequences of the negotiation. A historically important example is when, in 2004, Johnson & Johnson permitted its Belgian subsidiary Tibotec Pharmaceuticals to distribute an experimental AIDS medication to people in poorer nations. Johnson & Johnson lost money by giving the medicine away, but it also shortened the development time for a drug that could prevent more AIDS deaths, which was more important than negotiating a deal to make money in countries where few people could afford the drug at the time.[23]

7. *Sufficient time is available for negotiations.* An obvious, but often overlooked, characteristic of effective negotiation is that ample time is allowed for the negotiation. Each negotiating party needs sufficient time to present his or her side of the story, and both sides must take the time to listen to each other. The more complex the negotiation, the more time is needed. An example of a complex negotiating situation is when a company is forced to deal with a supplier that is powerful because the supplier has no, or almost no, competition. In 1900, North America had 35 suppliers of cast rail wheels, so railway builders had plenty of options for purchasing the wheels. One hundred and fifteen years later, there was only one supplier of cast rail wheels.

Considerable thought, and therefore time, has to be invested in developing a negotiating strategy when the supplier has most of the negotiating power. A suggestion offered by a team of procurement specialists is to bring new value to the supplier. One such approach is to be a gateway to a new market for the supplier, as illustrated in the following scenario:

A beverage company was dealing with annual price hikes from a beverage-packaging supplier. No alternative was evident. The supplier had secured a patent for its manufacturing process, and its packaging was offered at a lower price compared with other sources. By chance, the buyer was about to enter two large developing markets in which the supplier had tried but failed to make much progress. The procurement manager recognized that she could give the supplier a foothold in these markets. She and her team worked with the marketing team and presented the supplier with an attractive offer. In exchange for the concession of a 10 percent price reduction globally, the company would use the supplier's cans in the new market.[24]

Situations Suitable for Conflict Resolution

Situations suitable for conflict management, including conflict resolution, overlap with situations suitable for negotiation because negotiation is one way to resolve conflict. Here we present a sampling of conflict situations that are often dealt with by means other than negotiation. Figure 1.2 outlines these favorable situations. All of these conflict-prone situations will be mentioned again later in the book. Techniques for resolving conflict other than through negotiation are emphasized in Chapters 9 through 12.

1. *Turf wars (or territorial disputes).* A turf war occurs when two different organizational units believe that they have responsibility for the same problem or are unwilling to share resources.[25] Another group might be performing the same task as another group, or it might be an intentional power grab. For example, two different cross-functional teams might think it is their responsibility to develop a new-product idea in the same general field. A resource turf war might take place when two different project managers claim they have the authority to invite the same talented person to join their respective projects. People tend to be quite emotional about what they perceive to be their responsibility or property, so conflict is likely to emerge.

2. *Workplace incivility.* Incivility and rudeness in the workplace are rampant and on the rise. Incivility specialist Christine Porath observes that the accumulation of thoughtless actions leaves employees feeling disrespected because of being intentionally ignored, undermined by coworkers, or publicly belittled by an insensitive manager. Harsh electronic messages and narcissistic coworkers add to incivility.[26] Uncivil treatment of workers leads to conflict as those treated uncivilly fight back.

3. *Sexual harassment.* Workers who commit sexual harassment against other workers frequently enter into conflict with the harassed person. More conflict arises if the person harassed reports the incident to the manager or human resources department. The accused harasser might then enter into conflict with the manager or human resources representative. False accusations of sexual harassment also trigger conflict. Sexual harassment is a major source of conflict because it is so widespread, taking place in the most lucrative industries, in minimum-wage jobs, in glamorous fields, and in ordinary workplaces.[27]

4. *Employee desire to balance work and family demands.* Many workers, especially those with young children, want to attain what they perceive to be a balance between the demands of work and those of family or personal life. Quite often, they hope to receive a flexible work schedule, including working remotely, as a way to

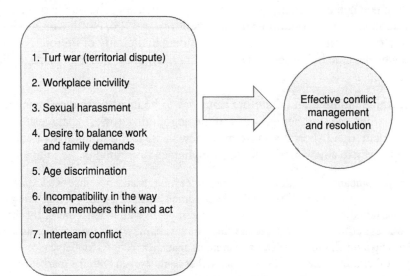

1. Turf war (territorial dispute)

2. Workplace incivility

3. Sexual harassment

4. Desire to balance work and family demands

5. Age discrimination

6. Incompatibility in the way team members think and act

7. Interteam conflict

Effective conflict management and resolution

FIGURE 1.2 Situations Suitable for Effective Conflict Management and Resolution

attain this balance. When the employer does not provide for flexible working hours, the employee is likely to experience conflict and its accompanying stress.

5. *Age discrimination.* Many workers in their mid-50s and older feel discriminated against because of their age, and these employees might therefore enter into conflict in such ways as filing age-discrimination complaints with a federal, state, or local government agency. Even during the 2018–2019 period of historically low unemployment, nearly 8 million older Americans were out of work. Many of those still employed were stuck in minor job roles with little opportunity to prepare for retirement.[28] The root of the challenge for older workers in finding new employment is that many recruiters place a premium on finding higher performers with proven experience. Paradoxically, at the same time, they emphasize searching for *digital natives*, most of whom are too new to the workforce to have established a track record.[29]

6. *Incompatibility in the way different team members think and act.* Destructive team conflict often arises from a perceived incompatibility in the way various team members function. Such incompatibility may be based on many factors, including personality, industry experience, personality, ethnicity, sex or gender, and age. When team members are unable to get past their differences, the resulting clashes can lower productivity and stifle innovation.[30]

7. *Interteam conflict.* Teams within organizations frequently enter into conflict with one another over limited resources. A key factor behind this conflict is that the organization usually lacks the funding needed to allocate all the funds and other resources that the teams request. For example, company leadership might decide to give one product group a much bigger advertising budget than another. Traditional theories about intergroup conflict suggest that disputes over resources tend to enhance group cohesiveness within the teams and reduce intragroup power struggles.

However, recent research with both laboratory negotiation teams and organization work teams indicates that intergroup conflict will sometimes also increase the occurrence of performance-distracting power struggles in hierarchical teams.[31] The explanation given for these findings is that the threat posed by the interteam conflict provokes fights over resources within the team. Perhaps conflict is contagious! To the extent that the new research is valid, intergroup conflict therefore spills over into conflict within teams.

Characteristics of Effective Conflict Resolution

The characteristics of effective conflict resolution overlap considerably with the characteristics of effective negotiation. Two key characteristics are the parties having empathy for each other and recognizing that conflict has a heavy emotional component. Conflict management, including its resolution, is also more likely to be successful when the organizational culture favors managing rather than suppressing conflict. For example, leadership at a company with a culture favoring conflict management would act quickly to investigate allegations of racial harassment, sexual harassment, and age discrimination.

Conflict is more likely to be resolved when it is not entirely personal and vindictive but instead contains some task elements. If the sales manager and credit manager are involved in intense conflict mostly because they detest each other, the conflict will be very difficult to resolve. Yet if the conflict involves objective issues about the difficulty in getting customers approved for credit, this problem is more likely to be resolved.

A strategic factor contributing to effective conflict management is to have systems and procedures in place for resolving conflict. These procedures might include a grievance procedure, a hotline for listening to various complaints, and a designated union representative who listens to employee conflicts. Lipsky and Avgar refer to these methods or procedures as *multiple access points*. Employees should be able to identify the company representative or organizational unit that has the authority, knowledge, and relevant experience to give advice about how to manage the problem in question.[32]

Cisco Systems and Arista Networks Settle Their Dispute

Cisco Systems Inc., the leading manufacturer of network equipment, and a smaller competitor, Arista Networks Inc., resolved a long-standing dispute in 2018. Arista agreed to pay Cisco $400 million on the day that a jury trial for the dispute was scheduled. The settlement finally resolved lawsuits filed by Cisco alleging that Arista copied its intellectual property. Another component of the settlement was for Arista to drop its lawsuit alleging that Cisco engaged in anticompetitive behavior to hold on to its dominant share of the ethernet-switch market. Arista agreed to maintain the product modifications required by previous International Trade Commission rulings and to make limited changes to further differentiate its user interface from that of Cisco.

Cisco and Arista also agreed to observe a five-year stand-down period for any utility-patent-infringement claims either party might have against features currently implemented in their products and services. Furthermore, they agreed to a three-year dispute-resolution process for allegations over new or modified features in their products. According to the settlement statement, "Cisco and Arista have come to an agreement which resolves existing litigation and demonstrates their commitment to the principles intellectual property (IP) protection."

Arista's major allegation was that Cisco monopolized or attempted to monopolize several markets for ethernet switches. Arista contended that Cisco encouraged customers and competitors to adopt its command line interface (CLI) for many years, thereby making it the industry standard for configuring and maintaining network equipment, including switches. Cisco had sued Arista in 2014 for infringing its rights in the CLI. Mark Chandler, the general counsel for Cisco, declared in his blog that "the patented and copyrighted Cisco features and implementations being used by Arista are not industry standards." The lawsuit filed by Cisco accused Arista of copying technology, infringing on 14 patents, and using copyrighted material.

Considerable human drama was behind the final negotiated legal settlement of the conflict between Cisco and Arista. The seeds for the conflict began when star executive Jayshree Ullal left Cisco to become the CEO of Arista Networks, a small start-up that would soon sell to key Cisco customers such as Microsoft and Facebook. John Chambers, the founder of Cisco and the CEO at the time, intensely disliked losing sales, especially to someone he considered to be family.

A bitter rivalry soon developed between Chambers and Ullal, and defeating Arista became a priority for Chambers and Cisco. Over the next five years, Cisco struggled to regain the market share snared by Arista. The threat from Arista intensified when the rival was poised to win about $2 million of business from Microsoft, one of Cisco's biggest customers. With this win, Microsoft became Arista's biggest customer.

Chambers felt betrayed by Ullal and wondered how she could do such a thing as entering into head-to-head competition with him. He told his executive team to keep Arista from winning any new business from Cisco customers. Chambers's animosity toward Ullal became so strong that in 2012, her photo appeared in an internal Cisco presentation—pasted onto a bull's-eye target pierced with arrows. The accompanying message was, "Arm the field, stop the bleeding, and fire back."

Questions

1. Why couldn't the management teams at Cisco and Arista settle their differences without having to spend enormous amounts of time and money fighting a legal battle?
2. Cisco won a $400 million settlement in this case. Does this mean that Cisco was totally innocent, and Arista totally guilty?
3. To what extent do you think Chambers was being immature in his rivalry with Ullal?

Source: Original story based on facts and observations in the following sources: Scott Graham, "Cisco, Arista Settle IP, Antitrust Dispute with Arista Paying $400M," *The Recorder* (www.law.com/therecorder/2018), August 7, 2018, pp. 1–2; Jan Wolfe, "Arista to Pay $400 Million to Cisco to Resolve Court Fight," *Reuters* (https://in-reuters.com), August 6, 2018, pp. 1–2; "Cisco, Arista Agree to Dismiss All Patent Litigation," *Seeking Alpha* (https://seeking alpha.com), August 6, 2018, p. 1; Rachael King, "Cisco's Costly Feud," *Wall Street Journal*, August 18, 2017, pp. A1, A9.

Summary

Negotiation refers to a situation in which two or more parties confer with each other to resolve their differences. In distributive bargaining, the basic task is to allocate a resource between the parties (zero-sum negotiation). In integrative negotiation, both sides attempt to attain mutually beneficial results (win-win negotiation). Conflict management is the adoption of a proactive approach to handling conflict by managers, supervisors, and union representatives. Conflict resolution is a key part of conflict management.

Among the many situations suitable for negotiations are (1) sales negotiations, (2) negotiating a starting salary or salary increase, (3) negotiating with venture capitalists, (4) purchasing an existing business, (5) negotiating heavy workloads, (6) changes to retiree health-care benefits, (7) patent infringements, (8) collective bargaining agreements, (9) amount of group-member input on decision making, and (10) dealing with a difficult coworker.

Characteristics of effective negotiation include (1) information is shared, (2) both sides have empathy for the other side, (3) both sides recognize that negotiation about serious issues has a heavy emotional component, (4) interdependence exists between the two parties, (5) the negotiators rank their priorities, (6) the parties involved in the negotiation are ethical, and (7) sufficient time is available for negotiations.

Situations suitable for conflict management and resolution include (1) turf wars, (2) workplace incivility, (3) sexual harassment, (4) employee desire to balance work and family demands, (5) age discrimination, (6) incompatibility in the way different team members think and act, and (7) interteam conflict.

The characteristics of effective conflict management and resolution overlap considerably with those of effective negotiation. Two key characteristics are the parties having empathy for each other and recognizing the heavy emotional component of conflict. Resolution is more likely when the conflict is not entirely personal and vindictive but contains task elements. A strategic factor contributing to effective conflict management is to have systems and procedures for resolving conflict.

Key Terms and Phrases

Conflict management, p. 4
Distributive negotiation, p. 2

Integrative negotiation, p. 2
Negotiation, p. 2

Discussion Questions and Activities

1. Identify a situation in your personal life that you negotiated successfully. What made the negotiation successful?
2. Why are the agents for professional athletes able to negotiate such lucrative contracts for the athletes they represent?
3. Some students think that the final grade they receive in a course can be negotiated if they think the grade is too low. What is your opinion on this issue?
4. Item 7 on the self-quiz in this chapter includes the following statement: "If you can't stand the heat, stay out of the kitchen." How does this statement relate to negotiation and conflict resolution?
5. How does the familiar saying "My way or the highway" relate to negotiation and conflict management?
6. Describe anything you have ever done for an employer that you think would justify a good salary increase.

7. A frequent lament of a CEO who has spearheaded his or her company's purchase of another company is that the company paid too much. What do you think might have gone wrong in the negotiations to purchase the other company?
8. Why bother resolving conflict with an uncivil coworker? Why not just send a text to the manager stating that the coworker should be fired?
9. Esthetic (plastic or cosmetic) surgeons have experienced a surge in demand from middle-aged people who want to look younger. How is this surge in demand linked to workplace age discrimination?
10. How about settling the Apple versus Samsung dispute in class? Compare a couple of iPhones and Galaxy phones in class to make a judgment about whether Samsung has copied the design of the iPhone.

Skills-Building Exercise: Examples of Real-Life Negotiations

Each student in the classroom or taking the course online will identify a situation in work or personal life in which he or she entered into negotiation. Students in a traditional classroom will come to the front of the class one by one to describe their negotiation situations. Online students will communicate their situations electronically, such as by e-mail or submission to a common class website. After the presentations, students should spend about 10 minutes drawing conclusions about what types of situations in life have been negotiated by class members and which factors were advantageous in those negotiations.

Samantha, a business analyst, works for a large real-estate-development company in downtown Kansas City, Missouri. The company is thriving and expanding, including entering into major new deals. A current project is turning a few abandoned waterfront properties into office, residential, and retail space. Even though the company is prospering, top-level management continues to look for ways to reduce costs in order to enhance profits.

A major initiative for cost reduction is to decrease the amount of money spent to lease office space by reducing the amount of office space needed to operate the company. Management decided to shift to an open-office plan to reduce the amount of office space needed. To replace employee cubicles and almost all private offices, workers and their managers are assembled into huge open areas and sit at tables. Coworkers are typically situated about one foot from each other. The open-office plan has reduced the amount of office space required to conduct company business by about 25 percent. In addition, top management bought into the idea that an open-office plan facilitates better collaboration and creativity because workers can have face-to-face interactions so readily.

The shift to the open-office plan was implemented about 10 months after Samantha began working with the company. Samantha was skeptical about how well she would be able to concentrate on analytical work if placed in close physical proximity to her coworkers. Yet she wanted to be a good corporate citizen, so she decided to shrug off any inconveniences she experienced.

By the fourth week of the open-office arrangement, Samantha was worried that she could not work in such a noisy environment with virtually no privacy. The company had installed a few telephone-booth-like structures for workers to use when they needed a few minutes to make a confidential phone call. The booths could also be used when a worker wanted to work on a problem in solitude for a brief period of time. Samantha, however, felt that a few moments of privacy were insufficient for getting important tasks accomplished.

In addition to the general noise of voices and electronic beeps, Samantha thought that a couple of coworkers were violating the very limited privacy she had at the office. One coworker, Mark, would come over to her table area several times a day, with the lead-in statement, "Got a minute?" He would then want to chat for up to 10 minutes about some work-related or personal issue he was facing.

Avery, a coworker who sat about two feet from Samantha, was even more disruptive to her ability to concentrate on work. Avery would frequently snap her chewing gum while working and would often eat snacks, such as an apple, in a loud manner. During her many phone conversations, Avery would often shriek in laughter.

Samantha was reaching the point where she could not tolerate the open-office plan much longer, but she was perplexed as to what to do about her dilemma. She wasn't sure whether to bring the problem to her manager's attention or to confront Mark and Avery about their distracting behavior.

Samantha thought, "I'm in a horrible bind, but I don't know how to deal with my problem."

Case Questions

1. To what extent does Samantha's situation call for conflict resolution?
2. To what extent does Samantha's situation call for negotiation?
3. What advice might you offer Samantha to have a more peaceful and productive work environment at her company?

Associated Role Play

Confrontation with an Annoying Coworker

Samantha decides that she has to do something soon to deal with her disruptive workplace. She decides to start small by dealing with one of her two most disruptive coworkers, Mark. Samantha plans to confront Mark about his disruptive behavior the next time he approaches her to engage in a non-work-related discussion.

One student plays the role of Samantha, who wants to substantially reduce the frequency of Mark's interruptions without triggering an adverse relationship with him. Another student plays the role of Mark, who thinks he is a friendly coworker whose goal is to make the workday more enjoyable for others with his friendly chats. Run the role play for about 10 minutes, with the rest of the class, or members of a small group, providing feedback about the effectiveness of the confrontation.

Speed Photonics is a six-year-old company involved in the research and development of photonics for diverse applications, including manufacturing and surgery. Photonics is an emerging field that essentially substitutes light for electrons. Because light travels at approximately 10 times the speed of electricity, light offers a speed advantage for data transmission. Although the field of photonics is relatively new, many competitors have jumped into the field in hopes of being part of a major scientific revolution.

As a result of both heavy competition and being in a rapidly changing field, leadership at Speed Photonics places heavy work demands on its employees. The technical and administrative staff hired into the company are expected to work fast and hard without complaining. CEO Todd expresses it this way: "Working for Speed Photonics should be a calling, not just one step on a career path. Yes, we have relatively traditional working hours, but to succeed at Speed Photonics, you have to be willing to stay connected to the company most of the time. I am not suggesting that our workers have to tuck their smartphones under their pillows. But they have to stay connected to the office most of the time, just in case their input is needed."

Todd, as well as other members of the management staff, including project managers, therefore feel free to get in touch with workers about important problems almost any time after standard working hours. The professional staff is reached after hours through phone calls, text messages, and e-mails and sometimes through collaborative software.

Jocelyn, a purchasing manager, was having a quick lunch in the Speed Photonics company cafeteria, along with a few software engineers and accountants. Jocelyn said to the group, "I know that members of this group and many other employees are getting discouraged with how many times we have to communicate with each other and management after normal working hours. Just last Saturday morning, I was watching my daughter play softball when I saw a message labeled "urgent" from the head of manufacturing. He wanted to know right away if I could find a lower-priced supplier for a fiberglass component."

Jake, an accountant, added: "How about getting a call from my boss late in the afternoon on a Sunday, just in the closing minute of a key NFL game? My boss said she found a discrepancy in my tax report."

Jocelyn said to the group, "I think we should approach Todd and other members of his team about what has become a burdensome workload. We don't get paid extra for being on call 24/7."

Case Questions

1. How might this case relate to negotiation or conflict management?
2. In what way should Jocelyn and her coworkers approach the top-management team about what they consider to be an intrusion on their private lives?
3. Employees at Speed Photonics knew when they were hired that they were entering a highly competitive field. Are they therefore justified in complaining about their expected connectivity to the office?

Associated Role Play

Jocelyn and three of her coworkers decide that a frank discussion with Todd about off-hours demands made by the company is warranted. At the same time, the four professionals do not want to communicate the message that they are not dedicated employees. Jocelyn sends a polite e-mail message to Todd requesting a group meeting on the topic of after-hours connectivity. He agrees to a 30-minute meeting at 4:45 on a Thursday afternoon in a conference room.

Four students play the roles of Jocelyn and her coworkers, who are looking for fewer after-hours communication demands from Speed Photonics. Another student plays the role of Todd, who is willing to listen but believes strongly that his demands for after-hours connectivity are legitimate. Observers will provide feedback as to how much progress the workers and the CEO are making in resolving conflict during this 30-minute session.

1. Updated from Hal Movius, "The Effectiveness of Negotiation Training," *Negotiation Journal*, December 2008, p. 509.

2. William T. Craddock, "Five Things Every Project Manager Should Know about Negotiation," paper presented at PMI® Global Congress 2010, Washington, DC (Newton Square, PA: Project Management Institute, 2010), pp. 1–2.

3. "What Is Negotiation?" *Skills You Need* (www.skillsyouneed.com), p. 1.

4. Frank L. Acuff, *How to Negotiate Anything with Anyone around the World* (New York: AMACOM, 2008), p. 8.

5. Michael Kublin, *International Negotiating: A Primer for American Business Professionals* (New York: International Business Press, 1995), p. 18.

6. David A. Lax and James K. Sebenius, *The Manager as Negotiator: Bargaining for Cooperation and Competitive Gain* (New York: The Free Press, 1986), p. 11.

7. Leila Amgoud and Souhila Kaei, "On the Study of Negotiation Strategies," AC, 2006, p. 150.

8. Jim Murray, quoted in "10 Winning Characteristics of Successful/Effective (Win/Win) Negotiators," *Situational Communication* (www.situationalommunication.com), September 15, 2015, p. 1.

9. David B. Lipsky and Ariel C. Avgar, "The Conflict over Conflict Management" [Electronic version], *Dispute Resolution Journal*, 65 (2–3), 2010, p. 38.

10. Fatemehg Shoa Shargh, Mansour Soufi, and Mohammand Ali Dadashi, "Conflict Management and Negotiation," *International Research Journal of Applied and Basic Science* (www.irjabs.com), 2013, p. 1.

11. Francis Cyriac, "10 Negotiation Skills Every Sales Rep Must Master," *Inside Sales Box* [Blog] (www.insidesalesbox.com/blog), 2018.

12. Ramit Sethi, "How to Negotiate a Raise You Deserve (in 3 Months)," *I Will Teach You to Be Rich* [Blog] (www.Iwillteach youtoberich.com), 2018, p. 2.

13. Deepak Malhotra, "How to Negotiate with VCs," *Harvard Business Review*, May 2013, pp. 83, 87.

14. Richard Parker, "Negotiating Your Way to a Great Deal," *The Business Buyer* (www.diomo.com), p. 103. Copyright 2001–2017. Diomo Corporation. All Rights Reserved.

15. Daniel Moore, "Citing Cost-Cutting Measures, Arconic to End Retiree Health Care," *Pittsburgh Post-Gazette* (www.post-gazette.com), October 4, 2018, pp. 1–5; Eleanor Laise, "New Options for Retiree Health Benefits," *Kiplinger's Retirement Report* (www.kiplinger.com), January 2013, pp. 1–4.

16. Sarah Taddeo, "Xerox to Cut Benefits for Non-Union Retirees," *Rochester Democrat and Chronicle*, October 16, 2018.

17. Jacob Kastrenakes, "Apple and Samsung Settle Seven-Year-Long Patent Fight over Copying the iPhone," *The Verge* (www.theverge.com), June 27, 2018, pp. 1–3.

18. "Collective Bargaining," *Legal Dictionary* (https://legaldictionary.net/collectivebargaining/), 2018, pp. 1–2.

19. Kristi Hedges, "Six Surprising Negotiation Tactics That Get You the Best Deal," *Forbes* (www.forbes.com), December 5, 2013, p. 2.

20. Prudy Gourguechon, "Empathy Is an Essential Leadership Skill—and There's Nothing Soft about It," *Institute of Leadership and Management* (www.institutelm.com), December 26, 2017, p. 1.

21. Roy J. Lewicki, David M. Saunders, and Bruce Barry, *Negotiation*, 7th ed. (New York: McGraw-Hill Education, 2015), p. 10.

22. Research reported in Adam Grant, *Give and Take: Why Helping Others Drives Our Success* (New York: Penguin, 2014).

23. "Why We Need More Ethics in Business Negotiations," *Business Insider* (www.businessinsider.com), July 27, 2011, p. 1.

24. Petros Parinkas, Grace Puma Whiteford, Bob Tevelson, and Dan Belz, "How to Negotiate with Powerful Suppliers," *Harvard Business Review*, July–August 2015, pp. 92–93.

25. Amy Gallo, "How to Navigate a Turf War at Work," *Harvard Business Review* (https://hbr.org), September 27, 2017, pp. 1–9.

26. Christine Porath, "The Hidden Toll of Workplace Incivility," *McKinsey & Company* (www.mckinsey.com), December 2016, p. 1.

27. Colleen Ammerman and Boris Groysberg, "Why Sexual Harassment Persists and What Organizations Can Do to Stop It," *Harvard Business Review* (https://hbr.org), December 21, 2017. P. 2.

28. Ruth Simon, "Booming Job Market Can't Fill Retirement Shortfall," *Wall Street Journal*, December 21, 2018, p. A1.

29. Kate Rockwood, "More Than a Number," *HR Magazine*, February 2018, p. 26.

30. Ginka Toegel and Jean-Louis Barsoux, "How to Preempt Team Conflict." *Harvard Business Review*, June 2016, pp. 78–83.

31. Lisanne Van Bunderen, Lindred L. Greer, and Daan Van Knippenberg, "When Interteam Conflict Spirals into Intrateam Power Struggles: The Pivotal Role of Team Power Structures," *Academy of Management Journal*, June 2018, pp. 1100–1130.

32. Lipsky and Avgar, "The Conflict over Conflict Management," p. 38.

Suggestions for Productive Negotiation

CHAPTER 2

Source: Monkey Business Images/Shutterstock.

Chapter Outline

Planning for Negotiation

Politically Astute Negotiation

Appropriate Use of Emotion

   *The Impact of Emotion
       on Negotiation*

   *The Effects of Anger
       in Negotiation*

Negotiating with Empathy

Learning Objectives

After reading and studying this chapter and doing the exercises, you should be able to:

1. Understand the basics of planning for negotiation.
2. Be aware of the importance of political astuteness in negotiation.
3. Understand the appropriate use of emotion in negotiation.
4. Know how to negotiate with empathy.

Negotiating successfully involves far more than an awareness of and an ability to implement tactics of negotiation. Successful negotiators plan for the actual negotiating sessions, and they are also aware of factors that often influence the outcome of negotiation. Three such major factors covered in this chapter are political astuteness, empathy for the other side, and using emotion appropriately.

The observations of negotiation specialist Michael Blanding point to the relevance of the information presented in this chapter. He writes that a simple view of negotiation describes a cold transaction between what one person possesses and what the other person is willing to pay for it. At the right price, the deal is done. In reality, negotiations are rarely so dispassionate. As soon as the checkbook or credit card comes out, a flood of emotions will surface at the same time—fear, anxiety, competitiveness, anger, and annoyance—all of which can influence what either side considers to be acceptable.[1]

Planning for Negotiation

Planning is strongly recommended before entering into the negotiating session, either in person or virtually. By planning, the negotiator avoids having to rely almost entirely on impromptu responses and intuition while dealing with the other side. As described in the Harvard Law School Program on Negotiation, planning before the negotiation will focus the parties on the most important issues to be dealt with and help the negotiators concentrate on how the agreed-upon deal can be implemented.[2] Here we provide a list of representative suggestions for negotiation planning based on the observations of negotiation practitioners and researchers.[3]

1. *Think through whether your situation requires negotiation.* A negotiation situation generally exists when you are in a problem-solving situation with others that can work to your advantage. If you have no negotiating power, and the other side holds all the power, negotiation is not worthwhile. Also, if there is no potential advantage to you, do not negotiate. Take the case of Paisley, who freelances home repairs of computers. Her minimum hourly price is $60 per hour for her time on the customer's premises, but she does not charge for travel time. Paisley says, "I will not do home computer repairs for less than $60 per hour. I have to travel, and I have to receive a phone call or e-mail describing the problem before I take on the assignment. I see no reason to negotiate."

   As will be described in Chapter 4, part of advance planning is to establish a best alternative to a negotiated agreement (BATNA). If you can identify an alternative deal with another party, you will feel less pressure to accept a deal that is not in your best interest. Assume that a chief executive officer (CEO) wants to build new facilities in New Jersey and expects to receive a substantial tax abatement in return. If the CEO knows that state officials in Maryland will grant the company a favorable tax abatement, he can establish the lower limits for the tax abatement New Jersey offers.

2. *Decide on what you hope to attain from negotiation.* It is helpful to think through the best possible outcome for you from the negotiation, perhaps by preparing a list of possible goals and a ranking of the importance of each item on the list. A department head might be planning to negotiate a new budget for the upcoming fiscal year. Among the items on his or her list might be money for new equipment; the addition of two staff members; new furniture; and entertainment, including a department dinner. Money for hiring staff members might receive the highest priority, with money for entertainment receiving the lowest priority.

"I will not do home computer repairs for less than $60 per hour. I have to travel, and I have to receive a phone call or e-mail describing the problem before I take on the assignment. I see no reason to negotiate."

Goals established in preparation for negotiation tend to be more effective when they are specific and measurable. In the case of the department head just mentioned, "money" should be translated into a specific currency amount, such as $300,000 for the first year to cover the costs of recruiting, training, salary, and benefits.

3. *Clarify the extent of your authority.* If you are representing your organization, you need to know in advance the extent of your authority in the negotiation. The more authority you have in the negotiation, the more effective you can be during negotiations. The limits to your authority include at what point another representative from the organization has to step in to continue the negotiation. During a price negotiation with a customer, an industrial sales representative might be asked to grant a 15 percent price reduction and a 60-day payment option. With limited authority, the sales representative might be forced to say, "I will have to check with my manager." With more negotiating authority, the sales representative would be able to respond, "I can grant those concessions if you are prepared to increase your order by one-third."

4. *Negotiate process before substance.* An advanced approach to negotiation planning is to plan for the process of the deal as well as the substance. *Substance* is the terms that make up the final agreement and should be planned as much as possible, still recognizing that the negotiation is likely to change the final outcome. *Process* refers to how you will get from where you are today to the final agreement. Among the factors involved in the process are the number of people who will have to improve the final deal and the amount of time you have to make the deal. It is also good to know who the deal's final decision maker will be when negotiating with another company.

5. *Think in advance of what concessions you are willing to make.* A manufacturer of housings for desktop computers might be able to concede up to 10 percent in price because, if pressed, he could incorporate less expensive materials into the metal housings. The same manufacturer might not be able to go below a certain quantity of desktop housings because very short production runs are not profitable. Another possible concession might be the delivery date because the manufacturer might be able to allocate an additional assembly line to producing the housings in the short run.

6. *Gather relevant information.* It is helpful to know in advance what the other side is offering or demanding so that you can refine what you are offering or demanding. It is not always easy to obtain this information, but it might be possible. A caterer might have the opportunity to cater a luncheon for 500 people at a business conference. The head of the company would need to know what kind of cash advance she might be receiving for preparing the meal and would need to have some idea of what the customer might be willing to pay before she enters into negotiation.

As the caterer said to her key chef, "If they are talking about a maximum of $10 per person, they will need to find someone to cater in a macaroni-and-cheese luncheon." On the other hand, if the company is thinking of around $16 per person, the caterer might know what type of menu offerings to bring to the negotiating table.

Gathering relevant information often involves finding out the market value of similar deals. Knowing the market value is especially important when the negotiator and his or her firm is negotiating in unfamiliar territory. For example, if the caterer just mentioned had never catered a meal for more than 100 people, she would need information about the range of prices charged for catering similar luncheons for 500 people.

Gather relevant information.

7. *Prepare yourself mentally.* Having the right frame of mind and the right attitude toward negotiation can help facilitate success during negotiation. Getting into the right frame of mind should therefore be part of your negotiation planning. Consider these suggestions:
   - Aim to be business-like, firm, and realistically demanding.
   - Do not feel you owe the other side anything. Both sides need each other.
   - Do not grant yourself higher or lower status than the other side.
   - Stay as focused on the negotiation as possible by giving it a high priority.
   - Stay relaxed and unhurried.

8. *Deemphasize the importance of winning.* At its best, negotiation is about collaboration rather than competition. Be more concerned about attaining your goals than winning. Define your true principal goal in the negotiations, and then be as certain as possible that your actions help you attain that goal. Team leader Melissa is negotiating with her manager, with the goal of adding two more team members. Instead of focusing on the idea that if she is authorized two more team members, she *wins*, Melissa might gather convincing data. She could demonstrate that the two added team members would contribute twice their value in terms of salary and benefits. The reason is that a major activity of Melissa's team is to find ways to reduce costs throughout the organization.

9. *Plan what you can do for the other person.* Wharton School professor Stuart Diamond advises that negotiation should be a give-and-take proposition. When you ask the other side what you can do for him or her, it goes a long way toward a successful negotiation.[4] Planning is involved because you need to identify in advance what your potential contribution would be to the other side.

10. *Identify the bargaining mix in advance.* Before entering into a negotiation, it is highly recommended that you identify in advance the variables or factors that can be discussed during negotiation. Assume that a high-tech company representative, or team of representatives, is going to negotiate building the driver interfaces (or touch screens) for an automobile manufacturer. The team holds a couple of planning sessions with representatives of the finance and manufacturing groups of its own company. As a result of these discussions, the bargaining mix includes price within a 15 percent band, delivery dates, the quantity of driver interfaces for the first order, the number of features on the interface, and the interface décor. What the bargaining mix does *not* include is who the subcontractors for the interfaces will be, the quality of the interface components, and the wages paid to the personnel assigned to the driver interface project.

11. *Formulate in advance which negotiation techniques you think will be effective.* Dozens of negotiation techniques will be described in this book, particularly in Chapters 4 and 5. It will most likely prove helpful to estimate in advance which tactic or tactics will gain you the most advantage in the upcoming negotiation. Assume that you will be entering into negotiations for the purchase of a family business, and you know that the owners are emotionally attached to their business. At the same time, they appear to be ethical people. You might therefore conclude that a highly effective technique would be, "Establish a positive negotiating climate." During the negotiation, you would therefore make positive statements about the family business and how much you would like to be its next steward.

Politically Astute Negotiation

political astuteness
Understanding the lay of the land, and using it to your advantage.

A major contributor to being an effective negotiator is political astuteness, understanding the lay of the land and using it to your advantage.[5] Political astuteness has also been defined more simply as being street smart.[6] While negotiating, you size up the situation and apply common sense and intuition to help you gain advantage yet while still being fair. The tactic just mentioned of establishing a positive negotiation climate illustrates political astuteness.

The application of political astuteness to negotiation has been framed in terms of the expectancy theory of motivation. (The theory is based on the premise that the amount of effort people expend depends on how much of a reward they can expect in return and the value of that reward.) The proposed model interprets an individual's propensity to initiate negotiations. A person evaluates the desirability, attractiveness, and importance of the goal sought to be attained. The astute person also evaluates the benefits associated with the action that satisfies these goals and the hunch that the actions will result in the anticipated outcomes. If the negotiation situation offers sufficient reward, and the reward is attainable and valuable enough to warrant the effort, the person will initiate negotiation.[7]

A helpful way of personalizing the link between political astuteness and negotiation is to take Self-Quiz 2-1.

The research of Jean Hartley suggests that when people acquire formal knowledge of political astuteness, it is most likely in a course about negotiation. The most frequent opportunities for learning political astuteness, however, come about through failure or mismanagement.[8] (Getting fired for insulting people in negotiations is a quick way to learn about political astuteness.) Several of the tactics of political astuteness that fit negotiations are described in the following paragraphs and summarized in Figure 2.1. The emphasis is on positive and ethical tactics.[9]

1. *Verify your assumptions about the other party or parties.* A political mistake some negotiators commit is to make assumptions about the other people involved in the negotiation without verifying the validity of the assumptions. Such false assumptions could backfire. For example, Teresa assumes that the opposing side in a negotiation is a pushover. She therefore does very little preparation with respect to justifying her demands. After introducing her terms regarding contract length, Teresa simply says, "In this industry, a three-year contract is typical." The other party is not a pushover, however, and knows that a three-year contract is not typical. As a result, this lowers her trust in Teresa as a negotiator.

2. *Adapt your style to the negotiating situation.* It requires considerable political astuteness or sensitivity to size up which negotiating style best fits the situation and then to adapt your style accordingly. A major dimension in negotiating style is assertiveness, ranging from being laid back to highly aggressive. The *smash-mouth* negotiator might win in an organizational culture that favors aggressive behavior. Yet in another situation, a winning style would include careful listening, acknowledging when the other side has a good point, and frequent smiling. In negotiating a government contract, the smash-mouth approach is frequently rejected by the government representatives. The discussion about empathy in negotiation presented later in the chapter provides additional insight into the genteel approach to business negotiation.

3. *Develop an effective opening stance.* The first impression you create in a negotiation will often influence the final outcome. It is therefore helpful to think of what you need to do to create a positive impression in the negotiation at hand. Negotiation specialist Kathleen Kelley Reardon observes that sometimes this means beginning with an apology to decrease any anticipated animosity.[10] For example, "I apologize for our company being two weeks late with delivery, but it will not happen again."

   At other times, an effective opening stance means making a firm statement about expectations to indicate to the other side that you are serious. For example, a representative of a company that offers cloud computing services might use this opening line in speaking to the representatives of a bank: "I think that my company offers one of the best value propositions in the industry."

   In terms of an effective opening stance, it is helpful to remember that in negotiation, it is usually better to think before you speak. As the somewhat exaggerated adage states: "It's better to be silent and to be thought a fool than to speak and remove all doubt."

My Political Astuteness about Negotiation

Indicate whether you tend to agree or disagree with the following statements in relation to the process of negotiation. Think about how you have behaved or thought in negotiation or how you might behave or think during negotiation.

Statement Related to Political Sensitivity	Mostly Agree	Mostly Disagree
1. In order to gain control, it is a good idea to insult the other party.		
2. An effective opening statement would be something like, "Thanks for agreeing to meet to negotiate our different positions."		
3. It is a good idea to find something to compliment about the other party.		
4. During negotiation, I attempt to figure out what issues are really important to the other side.		
5. A good way to start a negotiation is to ask for about three times as much as you are expecting to receive.		
6. A good way to start a negotiation is to offer about one-third of what you are really willing to pay.		
7. Occasionally smiling at the other side is an effective way of building a relationship during negotiation.		
8. You gain a lot of advantage during negotiation by staying angry with the other side.		
9. It gives you an edge in negotiation to display so much knowledge that the other side feels stupid.		
10. If reasonably true, at some point in the negotiation, I would be willing to say to the other party, "I am enjoying working out these problems together."		
11. Early in negotiation, it helps your side if you point out that you are desperate to get the issues resolved quickly.		
12. I like the idea of arriving about 10 minutes late for a negotiation session just to keep the other side on edge.		
13. A sincere handshake or fist bump helps set the right atmosphere for negotiation.		
14. If I were negotiating something such as a vehicle purchase, I would be willing to take out my checkbook or credit card to suggest that I was willing to close the deal.		
15. It is a good idea to treat the other party as a business partner, rather than an adversary.		

Scoring and Interpretation: The more of your answers that are in agreement with the following key, the greater is your political astuteness a negotiator. At the same time, the higher your score, the more likely it is that you are skilled at setting up a positive negotiating climate.

1. Mostly disagree	6. Mostly disagree	11. Mostly disagree
2. Mostly agree	7. Mostly agree	12. Mostly disagree
3. Mostly agree	8. Mostly disagree	13. Mostly agree
4. Mostly agree	9. Mostly disagree	14. Mostly agree
5. Mostly disagree	10. Mostly agree	15. Mostly agree

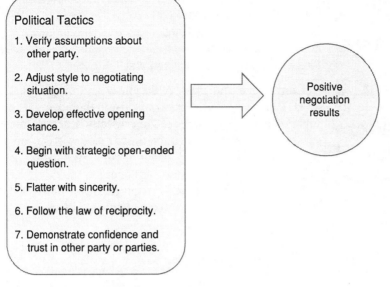

FIGURE 2.1 Politically Astute Negotiation

4. *Begin with a strategic open-ended question.* A frequently effective way to be politically astute is to begin negotiations with an open-ended question that could frame the purpose of the negotiation. In this way, you gather useful information that you can use to make a winning presentation. Three such questions are as follows: "What would you like to accomplish at this meeting today?"; "How could our company be of the best help to your company?"; and "What would be an ideal outcome of today's negotiation for you?"

5. *Flatter with sincerity.* A powerful technique for ingratiating yourself with the other party in a negotiation is to flatter that person. Although one meaning of the term *flattery* is "insincere praise," another meaning refers to a sincere compliment. Effective flattery has at least a modicum of credibility, implying that you say something about the target person that is plausible. Credibility is also increased when you point to a person's tangible accomplishments. If a buyer was negotiating the price of a large piece of earth-moving equipment, he or he might say, "The reason I am here is that I know that your earth-moving equipment has a worldwide reputation for power and dependability." One reason this flattering statement might work is that people prefer to conduct business with an ally rather than an adversary.

6. *Follow the law of reciprocity.* According to organizational behavior scholar Allen Cohen, the law of reciprocity governs relationships in organizations. He says, "The secret of the universe lies in six words: Everyone expects to be paid back."[11] The payback to the opposing party in a negotiation is not always easy to identify, but let's take a basic example. Visualize Buck, who is negotiating the price of a high-end sports-utility vehicle (SUV) with a sticker price of $98,500. He is looking for a discount from the sticker price, and he knows that it is difficult for the dealer to sell many of these vehicles. During the negotiation, Buck injects the suggestion of reciprocity by saying, "My sister is also in the market for a top-end SUV, and if we strike a deal, you can expect a visit from her." Buck is behaving ethically if his sister is indeed looking to purchase a similar SUV.

law of reciprocity Everyone expects to be paid back.

7. *Demonstrate confidence and trust in the other party or parties.* Under ideal circumstances, the opposing parties in a negotiation trust each other and believe that the other side is ethical. Trusting the other people present in negotiations includes believing that they are presenting a factual argument and that their ideas are technically sound. For example, one negotiator might say to the other, "The reason we are unwilling to pay a high price for your thermal gloves is that the previous batch tended

Demonstrate confidence and trust in the other party or parties.

to melt a 1,500°F." A trusting response would be, "I am not aware of the melting problem, but I certainly will have our lab technician look into it." Expressing confidence and trust is reciprocal. If you demonstrate trust and confidence in the other side, he, she, or they are more likely to express confidence in you.

Confidence and trust in the other side might have an optimal level. Too much confidence and trust in the other side could be dysfunctional because you would uncritically accept whatever he or she says. A negotiating point sometimes made is, "We can get the same product from another vendor for one-half of what you are asking." If this were true, the other side might not have invited you to negotiate.

The accompanying Negotiation and Conflict Resolution in Action feature illustrates politically astute negotiation.

NEGOTIATION AND CONFLICT RESOLUTION IN ACTION

Garth Negotiates Successfully with His Demanding Boss

Garth is the logistics manager at a trucking company that delivers across the United States, as well as making deliveries into Canada and Mexico. He senses that his career is moving along well and that he has a future as a member of the executive team at his present company or another nationwide trucker. About one year ago, however, Garth encountered a career hurdle. His boss, Carter, the vice president of logistics, was making such heavy demands on his time that Garth thought his career was in jeopardy. Garth's reasoning was that if he could not meet these demands, he would fall out of favor with his boss.

Garth decided that instead of entering into conflict with Carter in relation to the latter's most outrageous demands, he would look to negotiate a favorable solution. Garth describes what happened:

> Our company was facing a tough period because of increased competition. Even worse, the company was being investigated for underpaying truckers, even if the charges were unfounded. Carter said that "All hands must be on deck," requiring that I work all day on Saturdays until pressures on the company eased. I told Carter that I understood the seriousness of his concerns and that I, too, felt personally responsible for the company's success. I also

explained that I had many family commitments on Saturdays, including being a coach on my daughter's basketball team.

> As a possible compromise, I told Carter that I would work four nights a week between 9 and 10, from home, as a substitute for Saturday work. My night work would include research into making our routes even more efficient and finding more ways to at least partially load trucks on their return trips.

> To Carter's credit, he listened to my offer and said he would give my alternative to working Saturdays a try. My late-night reports proved to be useful in both saving money for the company and generating additional revenue. It appeared that I did get back on Carter's good side.

Questions

1. What did Garth do that you would classify as being politically astute?
2. To what extent do you think that by working from 9 to 10 four nights a week, Garth was giving in too much to company demands?

Source: A couple of observations in this story are based on Sue Shellenbarger, "How to Manage a Demanding Boss," *Wall Street Journal*, January 18, 2017, p. A13.

Appropriate Use of Emotion

Up until about the year 2000, scholarly inquiry in the field of negotiation focused on the rational, or cognitive, side of negotiators. Since then, a new generation of researchers has added the key role of emotion in negotiation. It is now recognized that emotions are important at the negotiating table and that the display or expression of emotion can be an important negotiating tactic.[12]

The Impact of Emotion on Negotiation

Emotion has a profound impact on negotiation in a variety of ways, such as intense anger making it difficult to negotiate rationally, or intense joy prompting you to be too generous in your offer. Even feelings unrelated to the negotiation itself, such as having bumped another vehicle while getting out of a tight parking space, can affect negotiating skill.[13] Andy Wasnyczuk, a lecturer at the Harvard Business School and former chief operating officer for the professional football team the New England Patriots, says, "I can't imagine a good negotiator who doesn't either have an explicit understanding about emotions or is highly intuitive about the process."[14]

The appropriate use of emotions in negotiation is part of being emotionally intelligent. Although the concept of emotional intelligence has been popularized and defined in many casual ways, its original technical definition, formulated by Peter Salovey and John Mayer, is highly useful for negotiation: "the ability to monitor one's own and others' feelings and emotions, to discriminate among them and to use this information to guide one's thinking and actions."[15] An emotionally intelligent negotiator would therefore observe when the other party appears to have a surge of positive emotion, and then ask to close the deal.

emotional intelligence The ability to monitor one's own and others' feeling and emotions, to discriminate among them and to use this information to guide one's thinking and action.

Even when the negotiator thinks the process might go smoothly, he or she needs to be emotionally prepared to negotiate. A frequent problem is that anxieties and petty resentments may lurk beneath the surface. If you let these feelings fester, or if you annoy the other party, the deliberations can fail.[16]

If you decide to express your emotions to the other side, it is best to express them appropriately. Instead of venting, attempt to express how you feel concisely and declaratively, such as, "I am upset with the frequent requests for modifications of my offer. I am doing my best to please your side." It can be helpful to develop a range of emotional expression—from entirely rational discussion to more emotional content, to full expression of emotion.[17]

No matter what emotions are brought to the bargaining table, an astute negotiator recognizes his or her emotions and works to emphasize the positive emotions that help facilitate the deal. At the same time, he or she works to downplay the negative emotions that might scuttle the deal.[18] Three experiments were with conducted about the effects of positive, negative, and neutral emotions during negotiation with 274 executive master of business administration (MBA) students enrolled in a negotiation course. All three experiments found that the display of positive emotions had beneficial effects. Experiment 1 found that negotiators who displayed positive rather than neutral or negative emotion were more likely to incorporate a future business relationship in a future contract. Experiment 2 found that negotiators who displayed positive emotions were more likely to close a deal. Experiment 3 found that the display of positive emotion was a more effective strategy for gaining concessions from the other party in a distributive setting.[19]

The Effects of Anger in Negotiation

Anger is one of the most potentially destructive emotions during negotiation, often causing the deal-making progress to break down as each side neglects its needs in order to save face. Anger will even cause people to walk away from a deal they need. Research suggests that the general effect of feeling angry while negotiating is to harm the process by escalating conflict, biasing perceptions, and increasing the likelihood of an impasse. Anger often reduces joint gains, decreases cooperation, and intensifies competitive behavior. Furthermore, anger increases the rate at which offers are rejected. Angry negotiators will sometimes look for ways to harm or retaliate against the other side even when a more cooperative approach might increase the value that might accrue to both sides from negotiating.[20]

Yet, when anger is deployed effectively, it can demonstrate passion and conviction that are likely to sway the other side to accept less or offer more. The required skill is to direct the anger at the situation or problem, not the other party.[21] A moderate amount of anger, however, can help people perform better in negotiation, especially when they think in advance that anger will be helpful.[22]

Negotiations specialist Alison Wood Brooks of the Harvard Business School recommends that the best way to deal with anger in negotiations is to recognize that many negotiations take place over several meetings. As a consequence, if tempers are flaring, ask for a break, cool down, and regroup. Resist the urge to fight back, and give yourself time for your anger to dissipate.[23]

Negotiating with Empathy

One characteristic of a situation favorable for negotiation is when both sides have empathy for each other, as mentioned in Chapter 1. Negotiation theory suggests that understanding one's opponent is valuable for success in competitive interactions. Empathy has been shown to motivate social understanding across a variety of situations. From a technical standpoint, empathy is an emotional response focused on another person that allows one person to affectively connect with another. Empathy has also been framed as an emotion of concern experienced when witnessing another person's distress.[24] In practice, empathy is a behavior fueled by the emotion of compassion. For example, if you have empathy for the other party, you listen attentively to that person. Here we look at several observations about empathy and effective negotiation.[25]

> **empathy** An emotional response focused on another person that allows one person to affectively connect with another.

1. *Displays of empathy enhance positive social behavior.* Displaying empathy during negotiation often enhances positive social behavior. Conversely, a lack of empathy can trigger antisocial behavior that leads to a breakdown in negotiations. During negotiation, an agency head of a might say to a director: "This is getting embarrassing. We haven't been authorized to give merit increases to any worker in four years." With empathy, the director might respond, "I understand that almost all workers would prefer to receive a merit increase, but our budget is quite limited." The agency head might then feel that at least there is an opportunity for productive negotiation.

   Suppose that, instead, the director had shown no empathy by responding, "Your people are lucky to have a job at all with so many cuts in government spending." The agency head might have then made the antisocial response, "More than one-half our workers could easily find a job in the private sector. Then you would look like a very weak leader."

2. *Empathy during negotiation can lead to value creation.* When people are stuck in the bargaining mode during negotiation, they often tend to calculate costs and benefits in the short term. They do not want the other side to gain most of the advantage. But when the negotiation is treated like a friendship, including the display of empathy, more information is exchanged, and new ways of meeting each other's need are explored. A pet-food company representative might be negotiating with a supermarket chain manager about the price of a new line of food for cats and dogs. If, instead of "fighting like cats and dogs," the two sides express empathy for each other's position, creative alternatives might emerge. For example, the pet-food company representative might be able to offer a lower price if the grocery chain representative allows for a few in-aisle displays.

3. *Asking questions can facilitate the development of empathy.* Having a natural disposition toward being empathetic facilitates expressing during negotiation. Yet asking the right questions is often a more direct route to displaying empathy. An atmosphere of information gathering and sharing is created by asking appropriate open-ended questions. The idea is that the answers to the questions furnish the data for situations in which empathy can be expressed. Here is a sampling of questions

suited to displaying empathy, provided that the responses are processed carefully:

- "Why do you need 60 days to process an order?'
- "Which features of our service create problems for you?"
- "What types of pressures are you facing?"
- "What have we talked about so far that will work well for you?"
- "What do we need to do to satisfy your most important demands?"

4. *Actively listening to the responses helps you to acquire the understanding necessary for empathy.* As hinted at in the point just made, asking open-ended questions during negotiation is not sufficient for empathy to be communicated. It is necessary to carefully process the answers to understand the

Asking questions can facilitate developing empathy.

other person's point of view. If negotiations are conducted online, you have to carefully process the written response. Genuineness and sincerity are essential parts of the development of empathy. Suppose you ask, "What type of pressures are you facing?" You then receive this answer: "We know that our product is successful and very useful. Yet our margins are being squeezed more than we can handle." You could demonstrate empathy by responding, "Making a decent profit on this product is therefore an important consideration for you." Your response will probably facilitate negotiations proceeding more smoothly.

Empathy, as with any variable related to negotiation, has an optimum point. With too much empathy for the other side, you might neglect your own interests. In the scenario just presented, you might have so much empathy for the small profit margins of the other side that you neglect your own profit margins.

Summary

Successful negotiators plan for the actual negotiating sessions, and they are also aware of factors that often influence the outcome of negotiations. Representative suggestions for negotiation planning include the following: (1) think through whether your situation requires negotiation, (2) decide on what you hope to attain from negotiation, (3) clarify the extent of your authority, (4) negotiate process before substance, (5) think in advance of what concessions you are willing to make, (6) gather relevant information, (7) prepare yourself mentally, (8) deemphasize the importance of winning, (9) plan what you can do for the other person, (10) identify the bargaining mix in advance, and (11) formulate in advance which negotiating techniques you think will be successful.

A major contributor to being an effective negotiator is political astuteness, or understanding the lay of the land and using it to your advantage. The application of political astuteness to negotiation has been framed in terms of the expectancy theory of motivation, which includes evaluating the desirability, attractiveness, and importance of the goal sought in negotiation.

Tactics of political astuteness in negotiation include the following: (1) verify your assumptions about the other party or parties, (2) adapt your style to the negotiating situation, (3) develop an effective opening stance, (4) begin with a strategic open-ended question, (5) flatter with sincerity, (6) follow the law of reciprocity, and (7) demonstrate confidence and trust in the other party or parties.

Emotions are important at the negotiating table, and the display or expression of emotions can be an important negotiating tactic. The appropriate use of emotions in negotiation is part of being emotionally intelligent. If you decide to express emotions to the other side, express them appropriately.

Anger is one of the most potentially destructive emotions during negotiation, often causing the deal to break down. The general effect of feeling angry while negotiating is to harm the process by escalating conflict, biasing perceptions, and increasing the likelihood of an impasse. Yet, when anger is deployed effectively, it can demonstrate passion and conviction that are likely to sway the other side to accept less or offer more. Because most negotiations take place over several meetings, the angry person has time to cool down.

One characteristic of a situation favorable for negotiation is when both sides have empathy for each other. Several observations about empathy and effective negotiation are as follows: (1) displays of empathy enhance positive social behavior, (2) empathy during negotiation can lead to value creation, (3) asking questions can facilitate empathy, and (4) actively listening to the responses helps you to acquire the understanding necessary for empathy.

Key Terms and Phrases

Emotional intelligence, p. 25
Empathy, p. 26

Law of reciprocity, p. 23
Political astuteness, p. 20

Discussion Questions and Activities

1. Provide an example of a work-related situation that you would not be willing to negotiate, and explain your reasoning.
2. How would you find out how much authority you had in a given negotiating situation?
3. If you were purchasing a home, what concessions could you make to the other side in order to reduce the asking price?
4. What link do you perceive between being politically astute and being street smart?
5. You enter the office of a company vice president to negotiate a huge contract for your firm. You notice that she has several banners and decorations that relate to Notre Dame football. What is a politically astute comment you might make to the vice president?
6. What problems might a negotiator who scored zero on Self-Quiz 2-1 encounter in negotiations?
7. Give an example of a flattering statement you might make to the other side in negotiating a budget for your department.
8. What reciprocity might you offer your instructor for providing a stimulating course about negotiation and conflict management?
9. Give an example of how strong emotion might lead someone to "act like a jerk" during negotiations.
10. You are negotiating to purchase some office equipment for a company that has entered bankruptcy. Give an example of a statement reflecting empathy that you can offer the business owner.

Skill-Building Exercise: Responding to a Heavy Work Demand

Your assignment in this skill-building exercise is to respond in two ways to a heavy work demand from your immediate manager. Your hope is to arrive at a negotiated solution to the request. For each of the following scenarios, first respond in a positive, politically astute manner that will help you preserve a good working relationship with the boss. Then respond in a negative, politically naïve manner that would probably trigger a poor relationship with the boss.

Scenario 1: Tax Season

You are a tax accountant in an accounting firm of 150 employees. Your boss informs you that she expects you to work about 65 hours per week from now until the end of the tax season. You have two children under 10 years of age. Give your positive and negative responses to your boss's directive.

Scenario 2: The Weekend Proposal

You are a content specialist at an advertising agency. At 3:30 p.m. on a Friday, your boss asks you to prepare a proposal for an advertising account for a company that specializes in food supplements for seniors. He needs the proposal by 10 a.m. Monday. You and your spouse already have plans for a weekend vacation, and you have nonrefundable hotel reservations that you purchased online. Provide your positive and negative responses to what appears to be an unrealistic demand on your time.

Scenario 3: An Outside-of-Job-Description Request

You are a merchandising specialist for a large online retail firm. Your boss knows that you are a skilled carpenter off the job. Your boss asks you if you would be willing to help her rebuild an old staircase in her house, a job that would probably require a month of weekend days on your part to accomplish. Provide your positive and negative responses to your boss's outside-of-job-description request.

Your response to the three demands can now be compared with those of other class members to sharpen your insight into what constitutes an effective response versus an ineffective response.

Pamela is an experienced real estate agent who works for the upscale real estate broker Sadlinger-Ross Properties in Chicago. Recently, one of the deals she was attempting to finalize was the sale of a $4 million brownstone situated near Lake Michigan. During the time of the sale, many properties were selling for more than the asking price because it was a seller's market (a market in which there are more interested buyers than homes for sale). The seller was a couple who were retiring and moving to North Carolina.

The second potential buyer who visited the property was Donna, a successful entrepreneur who founded and operated an online marketplace for antique jewelry. Pamela was joyful when Donna offered $3.8 million for the property on her second visit to the brownstone. The couple weighed the offer, but they decided that they would definitely not let the property go for less than the asking price and that they really wanted more money. Fearing that she would lose out on the property because of another potential buyer's higher bid, Donna made what she called her "last and final offer" of $4.1 million.

The couple was pleased with the final offer and instructed Pamela to promptly close the deal. Donna, accompanied by a close friend, asked to arrange a final walk-through of the brownstone before making a $350,000 down payment. Immediately after opening the door to the terrace, Donna became enraged. "Where is that cast-iron terrace furniture that was here before? Does the couple think I'm a pushover who can be tricked? The iron furniture was part of the deal."

Pamela went downstairs to speak to the couple, who were waiting on the first floor. The husband said, with the wife in apparent agreement, "We didn't say that the cast-iron terrace furniture was included with the deal. We promised that to my wife's sister. Go tell Donna that she is being small-minded. The big picture is that we are letting go of a property that will increase rapidly in value."

Pamela rushed back upstairs to relay the couple's reaction to Donna. Donna replied, "The couple is small-minded, not me. I have the right to the iron terrace furniture. I don't think they are serious about selling this property. Maybe you can show me another property."

Pamela thought to herself, "Here we are again in the real estate business, dealing with senseless anger. Now I have to act fast to salvage this deal. I've already invested loads of time, energy, and advertising money in this deal."

Case Questions

1. In what specific ways are emotions threatening to prevent the deal for the Chicago brownstone being completed?
2. Explain who you think is being unreasonable (or reasonable) in this deal.
3. What advice can you offer Pamela to negotiate a way to salvage this deal?

Associated Role Play

Two students play the role of the couple who want to close the deal on the brownstone building for the offered price of $4.1 million. Yet they believe strongly that they should not have to include the cast-iron terrace furniture that they have already promised to give to the wife's sister. Another student plays the role of Donna, who wants to close the deal on the brownstone building, yet she is adamant that the terrace furniture in question be included in the deal. The three students will engage in a spirited negotiation for about 15 minutes to reach a solution. A fourth student plays the role of the real estate agent Pamela, who will attempt to facilitate the negotiation. Other class members might provide feedback about how well the negotiations are proceeding or whether a workable solution to the problem has been reached.

Camden is the director of human resources (HR) at a high-tech firm located in Seattle, Washington. He is convinced that too many managers, as well as other workers in the company, have biases that can result in discrimination and other unfavorable actions against certain demographic groups. Camden's proposed solution to the problem of both conscious and unconscious bias is to conduct anti-bias training throughout the company. He has written many e-mails to the CEO, Marvin, about the subject of anti-bias training but has usually received a lukewarm response. Yet finally, the CEO and several members of the top-management team have agreed to meet in person for one hour with Camden to discuss his proposal. A partial transcript of the meeting is as follows:

Camden: Thanks, Marvin, to you and the rest of the executive team for meeting with me to discuss my proposal for anti-bias training. Other high-tech firms, as well as Starbucks, have already launched anti-bias training. We are behind the curve.

Marvin: What convinces you that we need anti-bias training?

Camden: It's because we are all a little bit biased—including you, Marvin. For example, I only see one woman and no African Americans on our executive team. Also, I see very few wheelchair users in professional positions in our company.

Melody (director of marketing): Nice try, Camden, but your thinking is too superficial. I have worked with Marvin on several searches for key staff members. We look for the best-qualified person without respect to the candidate's demographic group. In fact, as you know, our company has reached out to several traditionally black schools in the South that graduate many computer science and business graduates. In a few years, one of these bright graduates is likely to be situated in the executive suite.

Camden: I hear some good intention, but we still need to overcome our biases, including you, Melody.

Bruce (director of cloud services): Camden, could you please give us one example of how bias has entered into a personnel decision in our company?

Camden: A sales representative came to visit me practically in tears. She told me she was turned down for a promotion into a lucrative territory because her boss thought that her ability to travel was limited. The boss cited the fact that she was a single parent with two children in elementary school.

Max (director of finance): Camden, please tell us exactly how much money you are talking about for this anti-bias training.

Camden: I estimate that the direct costs would be about $2 million per year, including the hiring of anti-bias consultants and travel.

Max: And what about the indirect costs, such as time lost from productive work?

Camden: I think that people would put in extra hours to make up for the training time, and perhaps they will work even more efficiently to compensate for the time invested in training. But the fact that you do not think anti-bias training is "productive work" suggests your biases.

Conrad (director of operations): Could you sum up in a sentence or two why we should invest in anti-bias training throughout the company?

Camden: We are one of the best companies in our field from a technology and operations standpoint. I want us to also be one of the best companies from the standpoint of management of human resources. A bias-free company is an ideal worth striving for.

Case Questions

1. Which of Camden's comments would you regard as politically astute? Explain your reasoning.
2. Which of Camden's comments would you regard as lacking political astuteness? Explain your reasoning.

Associated Role Play

One student plays the role of Camden, who, during the meeting with the executive team, wants to point out to one member of the team that he or she has some biases. Yet Camden wants to be politically astute and diplomatic. Camden thinks that if he cannot demonstrate biases in other people, he will be in a weak negotiating position to obtain funding for his program. Another student plays the role of an executive who interacts with Camden but is not aware of any personal bias that he or she might have. Other students can provide feedback on the effectiveness of Camden's techniques.

Notes

1. Michael Blanding, "The Role of Emotions in Effective Negotiation," *Harvard Business School Working Knowledge* (https://hbswk.hbs.edu), June 30, 2014, p. 1.

2. Program on Negotiation (PON) Staff, "Putting Your Negotiated Agreement into Action," *Harvard Law School Program on Negotiation* (www.pon.harvard.edu), October 22, 2018, p. 1.

3. Deepak Malhorta, "Control the Negotiation Before It Begins," *Harvard Business Review*, December 2015, pp. 66–72; Elizabeth Harrin, "Effective Step in Planning Negotiation," *iMindQ* (www.imindq.com), 2018, pp. 1–4; "4 Ways to Win Workplace Negotiations," *Glassdoor* [Blog] (www.glassdor.com/blog), January 4, 2013, p. 2; Abhishek Sharma, "Negotiations Planning Template," *SlideShare* (www.slideshare.net), October 25, 2012; Eric Garner, "7 Strategies That Boost Negotiation Success," *Business Know-How* (www.businessknow-how.com), December 13, 2017, pp. 1–2.

4. Cited in "4 Ways to Win at Workplace Negotiations," p. 2.

5. Jean Hartley, "Political Astuteness: An Essential Skill in the Workplace," *Open University Business School* (http://business-school.open.ac.uk), 2019.

6. Kathleen Kelley Reardon, "Politically Astute Negotiating," in *Management Skills: A Jossey-Bass Reader* (San Francisco: Jossey Bass, 2005), pp. 546–563.

7. Ilias Kapoutsis, "Playing the Political Game at Work: The Roles of Political Will, Political Prudence and Political Skill," in Eran Vigoda-Gadot and Amos Drory, editors, *Handbook of Organizational Politics* (Cheltenham, UK: Edward Elgar, 2016), p. 49.

8. Hartley, "Political Astuteness," p. 2.

9. Reardon, "Politically Astute Negotiating," pp. 546–563; Andrew J. DuBrin, *Political Behavior in Organizations* (Thousands Oak, CA: Sage, 2009), pp. 118–139.

10. Reardon, "Politically Astute Negotiations," pp. 555–556.

11. Quoted in Michael Warsaw, "The Good Guy's (and Gal's) Guide to Office Politics," *Fast Company*, April 1998, p. 160.

12. Shirli Kolpelman, Ashleigh Shelby Rosette, and Leigh Thompson, "The Three Faces of Eve: Strategic Displays of Positive, Negative, and Neutral Emotions in Negotiations," *Organizational Behavior and Human Decision Processes*, 99, 2006, pp. 81–100.

13. Program on Negotiation (PON) Staff, "Emotional Triggers: How Emotions Affect Your Negotiating Ability," *Harvard Law School Program on Negotiation* (www.pon.harvard.edu), December 13, 2018, pp. 1–2.

14. Quoted in Blanding, "The Role of Emotions in Effective Negotiation," p. 2.

15. Peter Salovey and John D. Mayer, "Emotional Intelligence: New Ability or Eclectic Traits?" *American Psychologist*, September 2008, p. 503.

16. Kimberlyn Leary, Julianna Pillemer, and Michael Wheeler, "Negotiating with Emotion," *Harvard Business Review*, January–February 2013, p. 3.

17. "Dealing with Your Emotions in Negotiation," *Negotiation Experts* (www.negotiations.com), September 24, 2018, p. 3.

18. Blanding, "The Role of Emotions in Effective Negotiation," p. 4.

19. Kolpelman, Rosette, and Thompson, "The Three Faces of Eve," pp. 81–100.

20. Alison Wood Brooks, "Emotion and the Art of Negotiation," *Harvard Business Review*, December 2015, pp. 60–61.

21. Blanding, "The Role of Emotions in Effective Negotiation," p. 3.

22. Elizabeth Bernstein, "To Win a Negotiation? Get Mad: New Studies Show Anger Can Be Highly Motivating in Competition," *Wall Street Journal*, November 7, 2017, p. A13.

23. Wood Brooks, "Emotion and the Art of Negotiation," pp. 61–62.

24. Adam D. Galinsky, William W. Maddox, Debra Gilin, and Judith B. White, "Why It Pays to Get Inside the Head of Your Opponent: The Differential Effects of Perspective Taking and Empathy in Strategic Interactions," *Psychological Science*, 4, 2008, p. 1.

25. Jeffery Krivis, "Can We Call a Truce? Ten Tips for Negotiating Workplace Conflicts," *Mediate* (www.mediate.com), pp. 1–7. Copyright 1996–2018 © Resourceful Internet Solutions, Inc.; Roy J. Lewicki, David M. Saunders, and Bruce Barry, *Negotiation*, 7th ed. (New York: McGraw-Hill Education, 2015), p. 112; Deepak Malhorta, "Control the Negotiation before It Begins," *Harvard Business Review*, December 2015, pp. 66–72; "6 Ways to Improve Empathy in Negotiations," *ENS International* (www.negotiate.org), 2019; Eric Barker, "The Secret to Smart Negotiations Is Simply Empathy," *Success* (www.success.com), May 18, 2017, pp. 1–11.

Negotiation Skills

Source: ASDF_MEDIA/Shutterstock.

Chapter Outline

Learning Objectives

**After reading and studying this chapter and doing the exercises,
you should be able to:**

1. Apply your persuasion skills to negotiation.

2. Understand how to apply emotional intelligence to negotiation.

3. Emphasize your most appropriate personality and cognitive traits during
   negotiation.

4. Explain how gender differences could have an impact on negotiation
   skill.

Understanding and applying negotiation strategies and tactics are essential to being an effective negotiator. At the same time, you need negotiating skills that enable you to apply the strategies and tactics. A basic example is that it would be difficult to apply the tactic of "make a last and final offer" unless you were able to communicate your position convincingly.

A research report concluded that negotiation involves a complex mix of cognitive reasoning and communication abilities that require practice to hone into successful tools to attain professional and organizational goals. The Society for Human Resource Management regards negotiation as a core workplace competency, further attesting to the importance of skills to support negotiating ability.[1]

In this chapter we focus on two groups of skills that underlie effective negotiation—persuasion skills and emotional intelligence—followed by a description of personality and cognitive traits that support negotiation skills. We also describe gender differences in negotiation skills because they incorporate several subsets of skills.

Persuasion Skills and Negotiation

The ability to persuade others is an essential negotiation skill, with persuasion skills being composed of a wide variety of attitudes and behaviors. Our purpose is served here by describing 10 skills directly related to negotiation effectiveness.[2] Skills 4 through 10 are from the widely accepted persuasion theory developed by Robert Cialdini.[3] The 10 skills are outlined in Figure 3.1.

1. *State your position.* An obvious starting point in a negotiation is to state your position clearly. Assume Derek believes that if riding mowers are offered in three different colors rather than one, the mowers will attract more attention and therefore generate more sales. In negotiating a budget for the added expense of two additional colors, he states, "I kind of like the idea of three colors. It would be catchy to potential buyers." Derek's position would be clearer if he stated, "I want money to offer our riding mowers in three colors in order to attract more buyers who visit our dealers or purchase online."

> **Ten Persuasion Skills for Negotiation**
>
> 1. State your position.
> 2. State your reasons.
> 3. State your evidence for your reasons.
> 4. Liking: People like those who like them.
> 5. Reciprocity: People repay in kind.
> 6. Social proof: People follow the lead of similar others.
> 7. Consistency: People align with their clear commitments.
> 8. Authority: People defer to experts.
> 9. Scarcity: People want more of what they can have less of.
> 10. Pre-suasion: Put people in a receptive mood before asking them for something.

FIGURE 3.1 Ten Persuasion Skills for Negotiation

2. *State your reasons.* The reasons answer the *why* behind your position, such as why a manager thinks that offering pet health insurance to employees would be a good investment for the company. In Derek's case, he has incorporated his reasons into the statement of his position: offering two more colors might attract more potential customers. He might also add that the traditional red riding mowers are disliked by homeowners who might prefer a more subdued color, such as green.

3. *State your evidence for your reasons.* Especially when dealing with logical and fact-oriented negotiating counterparts, it is helpful to provide supporting evidence for your reason or reasons. Perhaps Derek could dig up evidence about how product offerings for major purchases sell better when multiple colors are offered. He might document the fact that more new vehicles are sold on dealer lots when a given model is offered in several colors. Derek might also provide data indicating that when smartphones are offered in multiple colors, sales increase an average of 10 percent. (He must be able to provide proof of his evidence if asked. Otherwise, his credibility as a negotiator will diminish.)

4. *Liking: People like those who like them.* As a negotiator, you have a better chance of persuading the other side if those people or that person likes you. Emphasizing similarities between you and the other person and offering praise are the two most reliable techniques for getting another person to like you. The negotiator should therefore emphasize similarities, such as common interests or background with the other negotiators—for example, "I notice that we are both supply-chain specialists." Praising others is a powerful persuasion technique and can be used effectively even when the negotiator finds something relatively small to compliment—for example, "I notice that you have a Lenovo desktop computer. I know that they are great workhorses in offices and factories even if they are less well known in this country than Dell or Apple."

5. *Reciprocity: People repay in kind.* Negotiators can often influence the other party to act in a certain way by displaying the behavior first. (This concept is different from the law of reciprocity described in Chapter 2.) The negotiator might therefore serve as a model of openness, good ethics, and a sincere desire to bargain in good faith. A negotiator might say, for example, "I know that we both have to make a profit, and we both want a good deal."

6. *Social proof: People follow the lead of similar others.* The point of this principle is that persuasion can have high impact when it comes from peers, such as a coworker telling the other party that what you are offering is a good deal. It would therefore be quite difficult for the negotiator to use this principle directly. An indirect use of the principle would be to mention how a person in a position similar to that of your counterpart capitalized on your offer. For example, "Our 5 percent discount for automatic reordering has been popular with many purchasing managers this year."

7. *Consistency: People align with their clear commitments.* People need to feel committed to what you want them to do. After people take a stand or go on record in favor of a position, they prefer to stay with the commitment. This principle of persuasion would therefore be an ideal situation for the negotiator because his or her counterpart would feel committed to the proposition offered. The idea of building a long-term relationship with a supplier fits the principle of commitment. A vendor representative might say, for example, "Our company has been in the stored-energy business for over 50 years. If we become your supplier for lithium batteries, you know that we will be around to serve you as needed."

8. *Authority: People defer to experts.* The action plan here is to make the other party aware of your expertise to enhance the probability that you will persuade them. Reference to specialized education, certification, or experience can help establish expertise. A project manager in a telecommunications company negotiating for more time to complete a project might explain to the CEO, "As a PMP [project manager professional], I have a good fix on how much time is needed to complete a project when a major new demand is placed on us." Because the PMP designation is

well respected in high-tech and manufacturing settings, mention of the certification connotes expertise.

9. *Scarcity: People want more of what they can have less of.* An application of this principle is that the negotiator can persuade his or her counterpart to act in a particular direction if the counterpart or counterparts believe the resource being negotiated is shrinking rapidly. The scarcity principle is widely used in negotiation, such as the negotiator stating, "Our supplies of aluminum are shrinking rapidly, so I urge you to take advantage of the low price per ton we can offer you this week." In advertising, you have probably heard ad nauseum the persuasion attempt, "Supplies won't last long."

10. *Pre-suasion: Put people in a receptive mood before asking them for something.* Persuasion is likely to be the most effective when you get the other parties to agree with you before the negotiating session. You attempt to get the other side in a receptive mood before making your actual demand or offer. A practical approach to pre-suasion is to solicit the other party's advice before offering your proposition. Assume that corporate trainer Mia is going to negotiate a budget for retraining workers currently in jobs that are becoming obsolete. Mia's program will help these workers acquire new job skills needed by the company. She consults in advance with managers throughout the company to solicit their opinions on what job skills are needed most by the company. At the point of negotiation for a budget, Mia is requesting money to do what the managers already want to accomplish.

A caution about the 10 principles just described is that they don't always work smoothly. An effective approach is to think through the negotiating situation in advance, choose several of the techniques that seem best suited to the situation, and then use them in combination. For example, in negotiating with representatives of a company for the first time, you might emphasize the principles of stating your evidence for your reasons, authority, and scarcity.

Emotional Intelligence and Negotiation

In Chapter 2 we described how emotional intelligence contributes to the empathy required for effective negotiation. Emotional intelligence is also an asset for other aspects of negotiation as well as conflict resolution. The effective negotiator or resolver of conflict must take into account not only the economic, political, and physical aspects of the process but also his or her own emotional responses and those of the other parties.[4] The following example of how emotions complicate negotiation took place in a medical setting:

> *In a day-long settlement discussion of a personal injury claim involving medical malpractice, a mediator was able to reach what she considered an equitable settlement from the defendants—a physician, a nurse, a medical resident, and the hospital where the surgery was performed. When the mediator presented the settlement offer to the plaintiff, the plaintiff became visibly agitated. In a rambling flow of words, he asserted repeatedly that "No one ever said they were sorry!" The mediation failed. The case went to trial, then an appeal. Finally, three years after the mediation, the plaintiff received a settlement of less than 50 percent of the amount offered at mediation. All of the parties had to cope with excessive legal fees.[5]*

The Four Domains of Emotional Intelligence and Negotiation Skill

A widely used categorization of emotional intelligence is to divide it into four domains or components.[6] Each one of these domains contributes to negotiation skill, as explained next.

self-awareness A domain of emotional intelligence that allows people to know their strengths and limitations and have high self-esteem.

1. *Self-awareness.* The ability to understand one's own emotions is the most essential of the four domains and contributes directly to skill in negotiation. Having high self-awareness allows people to know their strengths and limitations and have high self-esteem. In preparing for negotiation, a person with high self-awareness might

think, "I know that I am weak in financial analysis, so I will work extra hard to prepare the financial side of the picture."

Self-awareness includes an awareness of one's emotional responses to situations, such as the likely level of self-confidence during negotiation and whether or not emotional control can be exercised. As the negotiation session nears, the self-aware person might reflect, "I know that I get nervous when dealing with a person of much higher rank and status than I have, so I will work extra hard at projecting self-confidence." The person might also mentally prepare him- or herself not to display visible signs of being upset and discouraged if the negotiation does not proceed smoothly.

2. *Self-management.* The ability to control one's emotions and act with honesty and integrity in a consistent and adaptable manner is important in general and also in negotiation. The right degree of self-management helps prevent the negotiator from throwing temper tantrums when negotiations do not proceed as planned. Self-management would also help the negotiator refrain from making progress-hindering statements such as, "I hate negotiating with fools," or "You are getting me so angry that I am ready to walk out right now."

   Self-management can also help the negotiator release positive emotion strategically— that is, when it will do the most good. If the other side grants a couple of small concessions, the negotiator might say, "I am so happy with the way negotiations are proceeding," or "I am really enjoying working with you folks."

   Effective self-management also helps to shield the negotiator from the negative effects of suppressing emotion. Suppressing resentment, anger, or other strong emotions can impair a negotiator's cognitive and behavioral functioning in several ways. Internal tension may result, putting the negotiator on edge. The effort to suppress emotional displays might drain cognitive energy, leading to factual mistakes while negotiating. A more remote theoretical observation is that negotiators who suppress emotion may be more likely to perceive the other side as an adversary, triggering intense competitiveness rather than cooperation or collaboration.[7]

self-management A domain of emotional intelligence that helps prevent the negotiator from throwing temper tantrums when negotiations do not proceed as planned.

3. *Social awareness.* Having empathy for others and having intuition about organizational problems, including political forces, are key aspects of the social awareness component of emotional intelligence. The socially aware negotiator shows empathy for the other side without totally neglecting his or her own needs, a point worth repeating. Sizing up organizational problems and political disputes can be a valuable negotiating skill. One example is that the sales negotiator might sense that the customer is facing a cash-flow problem and would therefore offer generous credit terms as a negotiating point. A politically astute negotiator might see that two members of the other side are rivals. As a result, the negotiator might be careful not to defer to or praise one of the members and not the other.

social awareness A domain of emotional intelligence that enables the negotiator show empathy for other side without totally neglecting his or her own needs, a point worth repeating.

4. *Relationship management.* The relationship management domain of emotional intelligence includes the interpersonal skills of being able to communicate clearly and convincingly, disarm conflicts, and build strong personal bonds. Relationship management has also been defined as the ability to inspire, influence, and develop others while managing conflict. Because the interpersonal demands of negotiation are so heavy, relationship management is essential for negotiation effectiveness. A basic reality is that if the other side likes you, the probability of you gaining concessions increases.

relationship management A domain of emotional intelligence includes the interpersonal skills of being able to communicate clearly and convincingly, disarm conflicts, and build strong personal bonds. Relationship management has also been defined as the ability to inspire, influence, and develop others while managing conflict.

Perhaps the negotiator who wants to be effective should study the Dale Carnegie classic *How to Win Friends and Influence People*, first published in 1936, that has sold over 15 million copies. Among the dozens of negotiating behaviors leading to being liked are smiling, complimenting the other side, listening, and remembering the names of the other negotiators. Among the behaviors leading to being disliked are insulting the other side, swearing, showing up late for the meeting, dominating the discussion, and finishing other people's sentences for them.

Emotion Recognition for Effective Negotiation

In order to implement emotional intelligence at an advanced level in negotiation, it is necessary to understand, or "pick up on," the emotional cues of the other party or parties. For example, what does it mean if your counterpart begins to breathe heavily and speak rapidly? Is the person excited enough to strike a deal? Or are your demands or offer irritating that person? Expressions of emotion provide a pathway for understanding the other party's reactions and intentions and what the person is likely to do next.

The process of working through a settlement in negotiation can be infused with a wide range of emotions, including pleasure and displeasure, surprise, fear, and anger. During negotiation, a person's emotions might be interpreted correctly or incorrectly by the other side. During negotiation, success often depends on the ability to communicate, exchange information, and make judgments about other people.[8]

A group of researchers tested the hypothesis that accuracy in emotion recognition is associated with objectively better performance in a goal-directed interpersonal interaction. The participants in the study were students of Chinese descent, attending a business school in Singapore. The stated goal of the exercise was to complete a simulated transaction for the purchase of industrial light bulbs. The participants played the roles of a purchasing manager or a sales manager. Students engaged in both the cooperative and competitive aspects of negotiation. Two weeks after the exercise, the students returned to the laboratory to complete a test, developed in Singapore, of emotion-recognition accuracy using facial photos.

The key result of the study was that students who had high scores in emotional-recognition accuracy cooperated more effectively to create greater value for the buyer and seller. Furthermore, the buyer and seller pairs also competed more effectively to capture a greater proportion of the value for themselves. In short, this complex laboratory experiment demonstrated that being able to read emotional cues from facial expressions was associated with better negotiation results. The study therefore supports the idea that emotion-recognition accuracy is an individual difference that predicts the ability to perform well in negotiations.[9]

The accompanying Negotiation and Conflict Resolution in Action feature illustrates how a business executive used negotiation skills effectively to purchase a professional basketball team.

NEGOTIATION AND CONFLICT RESOLUTION IN ACTION

Former Microsoft CEO Negotiates a Deal to Purchase the LA Clippers for $2 Billion

In 2014, former Microsoft CEO Steve Ballmer successfully negotiated the purchase of the Los Angeles Clippers, a professional basketball team, for $2 billion, the second-highest price ever paid for a sports team. Ballmer had risen to the top of Microsoft through the sales function, and he had negotiated many sales contracts along the way. After his time at Microsoft, a major fantasy goal of Ballmer's was to own a professional sports team. Ballmer told a sports reporter that buying the Clippers was not the craziest purchase he had ever made. Ballmer's comments included the following:

> Lots of people run lots of numbers. I feel like I paid a price I'm excited about. It was obviously a price that was negotiated and I feel very good about it. It's not a cheap price, but when you're used to looking at tech companies with huge risk, no earnings, and

no multiples, this doesn't look like the craziest thing I've ever acquired. . . . There are real earnings in this business. There's real upside opportunity.

To finalize the deal, Ballmer and his legal team had to deal with many legal challenges. A California court confirmed the authority of Shelly Sterling, the wife of the owner Donald Sterling, to sell the team on behalf of the family trust. Donald Sterling had been accused of making racist remarks about the fans his girlfriend was encouraging to attend Clippers games. As a result, he was stripped of his ownership by the National Basketball Association (NBA) and fined $2.5 million. Evidence had also been presented to the court by his wife that Mr. Sterling was experiencing Alzheimer's disease and was therefore not mentally competent to block the sale of the team.

Source: Aleksandar Grozdanovski/Shutterstock.

In 2014, former Microsoft CEO Steve Ballmer successfully negotiated the purchase of the Los Angeles Clippers, a professional basketball team, for $2 billion, the second-highest price ever paid for a sports team.

Ballmer revealed the negotiating tricks he used to beat out other bidders in a podcast prepared by *Business Insider*. (The other bidders included movie producer and philanthropist David Geffen, television celebrity and businesswoman Oprah Winfrey, and a group from the Mideast.)

1. *Do your research and learn the landscape.* After leaving Microsoft, Ballmer met with the commissioners of the NBA and the National Football League (NFL) to see if any team was for sale. No team was available, but when Sterling was banned from the NBA, Ballmer was ready to pounce.
2. *Find a mutual connection to introduce you to the seller.* Ballmer had never met the Sterlings, but Disney CEO Michael Eisner, whom Ballmer knew, had a Clippers box adjacent to that of the Sterlings. Eisner gave Ballmer the contact information for Shelly Sterling.
3. *Make the seller get to know you so that the deal feels more personal.* Ballmer spent an entire day befriending Shelly Sterling, and he even brought along a bank statement to prove his ability to make an enormous bid for the Clippers.
4. *Make the bid as hassle-free as possible, and don't try to nickel and dime.* Given that Ballmer was an independent bidder and not part of a group, he was easier to deal with as a negotiator. Ballmer did not want to overpay, but he also did not want to haggle over minor dollar differences in his bid. He told Sterling and her lawyer that he wasn't a great negotiator. Ballmer also said, "This is what I'd like to pay, this is the maximum I'd pay, and, oh, by the way, you have to understand, I don't want to look stupid to my wife for being a guy who dramatically overpays. I wasn't trying to be some tough getting the last 3 percent to 5 percent out of the deal. I just wanted to own the team."

Questions

1. In addition to the four points Ballmer makes about his successful negotiating tricks, what other points about successful negotiation does Ballmer's approach indicate?
2. What do you think motivated Ballmer to use $2 billion of family assets to purchase a professional sports team?

Source: Original story based on information in the following sources: Anna Mazarkis and Alyson Shotell, "4 Negotiating Tricks to Win a Highly-Competitive Deal, According to Steve Balmer—Who Beat Out Oprah and Larry Ellison to Buy the LA Clippers," *Business Insider* (www.businessinsider.com), July 28, 2017, pp. 1–4; CNBC with Associated Press (AP), "Done Deal: Ballmer Gets the LA Clippers," *CNBC* (www.cnbc.com), August 12, 2014, pp. 1–2; Nick Schwartz, "Steve Ballmer Explains Why He Paid $2 Billion for the Clippers," *For the Win* (http://ftw.usatoday.com), August 12, 2014, p. 1.

Personality and Cognitive Traits Associated with Effective Negotiation Skills

The cognitive trait of mental ability is not exactly a skill, but it drives many negotiation skills, such as problem solving, dealing with complexity, and making calculations. Similarly, a personality trait itself is not a skill, but personality traits facilitate many of the skills needed for effective negotiation. Consider these two examples: Melissa scores high on the personality trait of conscientiousness. During negotiation, she will therefore most likely engage in such skills and behaviors as carefully planning her activities, respecting deadlines, and preparing written summaries of key points that transpired during the

Source: stockfour/Shutterstock.

Melissa scores high on the personality trait of conscientiousness. During negotiation, she will therefore most likely engage in such skills and behaviors as carefully planning her activities, respecting deadlines, and preparing written summaries of key points that transpired during the negotiation.

Source: AVAVA/Shutterstock.

Confidence in one's abilities is a basic personality trait that has been linked to leadership effectiveness in research studies for over 100 years.

practical intelligence Adapting the environment to suit an individual's needs, and includes wisdom and common sense.

negotiation. Sanjay scores high on the personality trait of extraversion. During negotiation, he will therefore engage in constructive negotiation behaviors such as being assertive about his demands, reaching out to build relationships with negotiating partners, and smiling appropriately.

In this section, we describe how certain personality and cognitive traits facilitate effective negotiation, as outlined in Figure 3.2. Our intent is not to list all the best-known personality traits and how each one could possibly be related to negotiation effectiveness. Emotional intelligence is classified as a personality trait by some scholars and management writers but is really a combination of personality and cognitive traits.

1. *Self-confidence.* Confidence in one's abilities is a basic personality trait that has been linked to leadership effectiveness in research studies for over 100 years. Self-confidence also contributes to negotiation effectiveness, particularly because you have to deal with the other side disagreeing with you or often being on the attack. Self-confidence, however, is most effective for negotiation when it is mixed with some humility. Admitting a mistake or stating that you do not have a complete answer can help develop sympathy for your negotiating demands. Self-confidence should also not reach the point that you display arrogance, condescension, or narcissism during negotiation. Former Microsoft CEO Steve Ballmer, as described in the earlier feature, is a highly self-confident individual, yet he also displayed humility by focusing on building a relationship and not bragging about his power and wealth. He also said that he was not a great negotiator.

2. *Problem-solving ability and cognitive intelligence.* Almost any analysis done during negotiation requires good problem-solving ability, even if there is not a completely linear relationship between traditional intelligence and negotiation success. Practical intelligence also contributes heavily to being an effective negotiator. The concept of practical intelligence refers to adapting the environment to suit an individual's needs, and it includes wisdom and common sense.[10] Experience helps a person develop practical intelligence, so an experienced negotiator would bring more practical intelligence to the table. He or she might size up the situation and conclude, "It appears

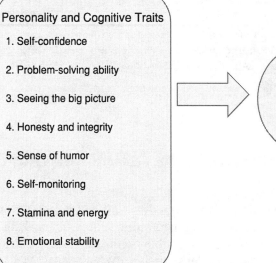

FIGURE 3.2 Personality and Cognitive Traits Associated with Effective Negotiation Skills

that these people are more concerned about quality than price. My strategy then will be to emphasize how well our call center workers are trained and the dependability of our service."

3. *Seeing the big picture without neglecting the details.* Seeing the big picture, or overall viewpoint, versus focusing on details is mostly a cognitive trait, yet it is also framed as a personality trait in the Myers–Briggs Type Indicator, one of the most well-known personality tests. Business writer Michael Kaplan notes that the ability to operate at both the broad and detail levels enables negotiators to see beyond the immediate needs and wants of their counterparts and use their intuitive skills to understand the interests driving the conversation.[11] A big-picture viewpoint during negotiation is that a supplier wants to establish a long-term, mutually profitable relationship with the company making the purchase. A big-picture perspective would also be that too much haggling about this particular transaction could damage a long-term relationship. One detail for this particular negotiation is that the sale should be profitable.

4. *Honesty and integrity.* Being trusted by your counterparts in negotiation is a big asset in the aim of attaining your goals. Imagine that Sam, a digital marketing specialist, is negotiating with his manager to be permitted a flexible work schedule that would include about one day a week of working remotely. If Sam comes across as being honest and having integrity (or has developed such a reputation), his manager will be convinced that Sam will actually conduct company business while working remotely. The topic of honesty and integrity will be treated at length in Chapter 7, which covers ethics in negotiation.

5. *Sense of humor.* From a scientific point of view, a sense of humor might not be considered a pure personality trait because it is composed of other traits as well as cognitive skills. Nevertheless, a sense of humor resembles a trait because it is a stable disposition of a person. Negotiation expert Alison Wood Brooks notes that a well-timed, sincere, successful joke can help reduce tension, increase feelings of closeness among people, build rapport, and foster an enjoyable atmosphere during negotiation. Humor might also be used to divert answers to difficult questions, such as a question you do not want to answer or shouldn't answer.[12] For example, when asked if his company had received any unfavorable reviews on Yelp, a negotiator replied, "Sorry, I don't look at Yelp. It's too depressing."

6. *Self-monitoring.* According to a meta-analysis of 5,000 studies, one of the strongest drivers of negotiation success is self-monitoring, the process of observing and controlling how we appear to others.[13] High self-monitors are pragmatic and are even chameleon-like actors in social groups. They often say what others want to hear. A representative for a labor union might pick up on the hint that the company representative was concerned about how few Muslim workers were hired by the company. During negotiations about a new labor contract, the labor-union representative might casually mention the union's outreach program for training Muslim people in high-skilled trades.

self-monitoring The process of observing and controlling how we appear to others.

7. *Stamina and energy.* Attaining a successful outcome to negotiation requires considerable effort and time, with a willingness to keep coming back with a revised offer or demand if necessary.[14] Many sessions are required to negotiate a major deal, and negotiating sessions might last hours, requiring considerable stamina and energy not to feel and appear fatigued. A team of negotiators might have to work for three years to sell a fleet of airplanes to an airline or the federal government.

8. *Emotional stability (low neuroticism).* People with high neuroticism are prone to psychological distress and coping with problems in unproductive ways. Emotional stability is usually an asset in negotiations because when under the pressure of a high-stakes negotiation, a neurotic negotiator might become anxious, swear at the other side, and throw a temper tantrum. A more emotionally stable negotiator might remain calm, yet still express appropriate emotion. For example, he or she might say, "This last-minute price increase really upsets me. Let's get down to the real reason for the increase."

Gender Differences in Negotiation Skill

Gender differences in negotiation skill refer to differences between men and women in their approach to negotiation based on their roles. Despite the widespread misuse of the terms, *gender* and *sex* are not synonymous from a technical standpoint. Gender is about typical roles, such as women being more polite and conciliatory than men. Sex is about biological differences, such as men generally having much more facial hair than women. Gender differences in negotiation style and skill are group stereotypes that might be true about one-half of the time.

As men and women increasingly occupy similar roles in the workplace, gender differences continue to decrease. The presence of more transgender people in professional and managerial positions is another factor that decreases gender differences in negotiation skills. Assume that Gloria negotiated for 10 years as a man named Gus and is now negotiating as a woman; Gloria's gender differences in negotiating style would be obscured.

Here we look at some of the evidence and opinions about how gender can influence negotiating style and skill. A major factor obscuring these differences is that an emphasis on listening and building a collaborative atmosphere is a more accepted negotiating style today for both men and women. Jenni Pereira, a principal in private equity at an investment company, recalls starting out in professional negotiations with an attitude that reflected, "I have to win, I have to be right, I have to show that I'm right." What she quickly learned is that there is more than one way to be right. "At the end of the day, it's about being open and collaborating," Pereira said.[15]

Source: LightField Studios/Shutterstock.

As men and women increasingly occupy similar roles in the workplace, gender differences continue to decrease. The presence of more transgender people in professional and managerial positions is another factor that decreases gender differences in negotiation skills. Assume that Gloria negotiated for 10 years as a man named Gus and is now negotiating as a woman; Gloria's gender differences in negotiating style would be obscured.

Scientific Evidence about Gender Differences in Negotiation Style

A team of researchers conducted a meta-analysis of available data-based studies about gender differences in negotiation style, as well as what factors (moderators) influence these differences. Fifty-one studies were analyzed that involved 10,888 survey participants or experimental subjects, including undergraduates and graduate students as well as businesspeople. As predicted, men achieved better financial outcomes than women on average, but gender differences depended on the context or situation.

An analysis of the moderating factors revealed that the male advantages were reduced when negotiators had appropriate negotiating experience and when the subjects had information about the bargaining range. Another factor reducing gender differences was when participants in the study negotiated on behalf of another individual. Equally important, the gender difference favoring men was even reversed under the conditions of the lowest *role incongruity* for women.

Role-incongruity theory includes the idea that women are often reluctant to negotiate because initiating negotiations is perceived as a stereotypically male behavior. Women who are behaving consistently with their gender role might not actively seek opportunities to negotiate. Women might therefore only respond to negotiation challenges when necessary, such as when a negotiation exercise is a course requirement. However, if gender-role pressure is not as strong, women may take the initiative to negotiate. (The pressure might be less when people do not endorse traditional gender roles or when it is the norm for men and women to be assertive.) In these cases, women might negotiate more effectively than women who may be more influenced by the female gender role. Gender differences in economic outcomes favoring men should then be reduced when participation in negotiation is voluntary rather than compulsory.

A major conclusion from the meta-analysis is that gender differences in negotiating skill and effectiveness depend on the situation or context and are subject to change.[16] One interpretation of the results of the meta-analysis is that gender roles do not give men an advantage if women are trained in negotiation, if they have information about the bargaining range, and if they are bargaining for other individuals.[17]

Neutralizing Gender Differences in Negotiation Skill

Although gender differences in negotiation skill may be smaller than in years past, it may prove of some value to look at some of the ways that have been suggested for neutralizing these differences. Anticipating gender-related triggers is a good starting point. For example, women might be inspired by reminders that they are representing themselves as well as their colleagues, their organizational unit, the organization as a whole, or customers. (The trigger is negotiating on behalf of others, which tends to lessen the effect of gender.) Gathering relevant information in advance of the negotiation, such as what is possible when heading into a negotiation about maternity leave or working out the details of a contract, will also reduce gender differences.

The opinion has been expressed that compared with men, women are less prone to express their value in dollars and are more uncomfortable in doing so. Going into a salary negotiation with relevant industry data about salary will place women on a more equal footing with men in terms of bargaining about salary. Another potentially fruitful approach is for managers to clearly state performance goals when sending their employees into competitive bargaining situations. Setting high but realistic goals is good for all negotiators but may be especially beneficial for women in ambiguous, competitive negotiations.[18]

Summary

Negotiating skills enable you to apply appropriate negotiating strategies and tactics. Ten persuasion skills directly related to negotiation effectiveness are as follows: (1) State your position. (2) State your reasons. (3) State your evidence for your reasons. (4) Liking: People like those who like them. (5) Reciprocity: People repay in kind. (6) Social proof: People follow the lead of similar others. (7) Consistency: People align with their clear commitments. (8) Authority: People defer to experts. (9) Scarcity: People want more of what they can have less of. (10) Pre-suasion: Put people in a receptive mood before asking them for something.

Emotional intelligence is an asset for many aspects of negotiation and conflict resolution. Four domains, or components, of emotional intelligence contribute to negotiation skills: self-awareness, self-management, social awareness, and relationship management.

In order to implement emotional intelligence at an advanced level in negotiation, it is necessary to understand the emotional cues of the other party or parties. A study conducted in Singapore found that students who had high scores in emotional-recognition accuracy cooperated more effectively to capture a greater proportion of value for themselves.

A variety of personality and cognitive traits can facilitate the skills needed for effective negotiation, including (1) self-confidence, (2) problem-solving ability, (3) seeing the big picture, (4) honesty and integrity, (5) sense of humor, (6) self-monitoring, (7) stamina and energy, and (8) emotional stability.

Gender differences in negotiation skill refer to differences between men and women in their approach to negotiation based on their roles. As men and women increasingly occupy similar roles in the workplace, gender differences tend to decrease. A major conclusion from a meta-analysis is that gender differences in negotiating skill and effectiveness depend on the situation or context and are subject to change. Several suggestions have been advanced for neutralizing whatever gender differences in negotiating skill exist. Anticipating gender-related triggers is one suggestion. Another is for managers to state performance goals clearly when sending their employees into competitive bargaining situations.

Key Terms and Phrases

Practical intelligence, p. 40
Relationship management, p. 37
Self-awareness, p. 36

Self-management, p. 37
Self-monitoring, p. 41
Social awareness, p. 37

Discussion Questions and Activities

1. Imagine yourself negotiating the purchase of a piece of expensive jewelry online. What would you do to show the seller that you like him or her?
2. What do you think of the effectiveness of mentioning your formal education as a way of demonstrating your expertise during negotiation?
3. How effective do you think it would be for an industrial sales representative to send a purchasing manager an expensive gift in advance to put the manager in a receptive mood?
4. Assume that an investor is negotiating to purchase a small business. What might the investor do during the negotiation session to get the other side to like him or her?
5. Which one or two emotional expressions have you found to be the most reliable indicators that another person is accepting your proposition?
6. Which one or two emotional expressions have you found to be the most reliable indicators that another person is rejecting your proposition?
7. When people are negotiating online, how effective would emoticons and emojis be in expressing how they are feeling about the other party or parties?
8. How effective would it be for a woman to cry during negotiation to win an advantage?
9. How effective would it be for a man to cry during negotiation to win an advantage?
10. To what extent do you think men swear more than women in order to attain their goals during negotiation?

Skill-Building Exercise: The Emotionally Intelligent Negotiator

Your assignment is to make emotionally intelligent responses to the incidents that take place during a negotiation as presented in the following scenarios.

Scenario 1: Hot Coffee on the Lap

You are 10 minutes into a negotiation about cost-of-living adjustments. While walking near you, a negotiator from the other side happens to stumble and accidentally spills an entire cup of hot coffee on your lap. The incident displeases you intensely, and you feel compelled to say something. What would be your emotionally intelligent response to the hot coffee spilled on your lap?

Scenario 2: An Insult to Your Company

As the representative of your building custodial services company, you are negotiating a new multi-building contract. As the negotiations get under way, your counterpart says, "I'll be upfront about this. Your company has a reputation for promising great service, but then you often follow through with sloppy work. Sometimes a cleaning crew does not even show up." You feel strongly that you have received an invalid criticism, and you still want to negotiate a favorable contract. What would be your emotionally intelligent response to the criticism your company has received?

Scenario 3: The Recent Recipient of a Kidney Transplant

You are the key representative of a company that makes plastic straws. Today, you are meeting with several representatives of a major fast-food company to negotiate the price of your company shifting from plastic straws to straws made from another material, such as biodegradable paper. The lead negotiator from the restaurant chain opens the session with this comment: "I may look a little fatigued today because I had a kidney transplant two weeks ago. But I'm feeling much better." You feel compassion for the person, but you think his medical problem should not influence negotiations in his or her favor. Make an emotionally intelligent response to the negotiator with the recent kidney transplant.

As time permits, compare your emotionally intelligent responses to the three scenarios with those of several classmates. Look for any possible patterns in the emotionally intelligent responses. Did you find any responses that you would classify as emotionally unintelligent?

Arianna is the employee benefits manager at a financial services company with 5,500 employees. She has already had several successful in-person and online meetings with the top-management team about enhancing employee benefits. Arianna has negotiated with some success a few extra weeks of parental leave for new parents of both biological and adopted children, as well as a limited program of onsite yoga classes.

Today, Arianna feels that she must be at her persuasive best because she is going to make the case for pet medical insurance as a voluntary employee benefit. Arianna thinks it would be ideal if the company paid most of the insurance, but she will even settle for employees being able to purchase pet insurance at a discount through a major pet insurance company.

"Thanks so much for your willingness to discuss a major breakthrough for our company and our employees," began Arianna. "A key purpose of employee benefits is to help employees form a bond with the company. The bond helps keep employees from quitting, and it also drives their productivity. And one of the most powerful possible voluntary benefits is pet insurance. Employees who own dogs or cats that are kept as domestic pets are covered for part of the veterinary care expenses in the case of accident or illness."

Dana, the vice president of finance, asked about the cost of pet insurance. Arianna responded, "Dana, I object to the word *cost*. I am talking about an *investment* of approximately $25 per month per animal, depending on the plan. We could pay the entire fee or part of the fee. A couple of pet insurance companies are willing to charge the company nothing. The employee would pay the premium directly to the insurance company. Because it would be a large group plan, employees would pay less for the pet insurance than if they purchased the plan individually. Receiving a discount on the insurance would be considered an employee benefit."

Malcolm asked Arianna to explain again why the company should bother with pet insurance. She replied, "As I have already described in e-mails sent earlier, many employees are as emotionally attached to their pets as they are to other family members. Pet insurance has become the most frequently requested voluntary benefit today. I emphasize the term *voluntary* because we would not force employees to carry pet insurance like they do with medical insurance for people. With pet insurance, our employees can worry less about the health of their beloved domestic animals and concentrate more on their work."

Katrina, the vice president of marketing, said to Arianna, "Why stop with pet insurance? How about offering an onsite spa and daycare facility for pets? In this way,

our employees could drop by during lunch and breaks to say hello to and hug their pets."

Arianna replied, "I feel your sarcasm coming through, Katrina. I am focusing on a benefit that almost any employee who has a cat or dog at home would love. Pet health care is very expensive. Pet parents can get quite upset when worrying about paying the bills. The right pet insurance can pay up to 90 percent of the veterinary bills. In this way, our employees won't be forced to choose between making a car or mortgage payment and providing vet care for a beloved family member."

Malcom said, "Arianna, what is that you are really negotiating for today?"

Arianna said, "Maybe I will phrase my argument in another way. The Society for Human Resource Management reports that about 10 percent of business organizations currently offer pet health insurance as a voluntary benefit. I am asking the management team to let us join that forward-looking group of companies. I want your permission to give you a formal written proposal for providing pet health insurance to our employees who want such insurance."

Karl, the vice president of wealth management, responded, "But what about our employees who do not have animal pets at home? Won't they feel left out?"

Arianna responded, "Karl, I think you are taking a small-minded view. The big picture is that we will be doing something great for many employees by offering a program for pet health insurance."

Case Questions

1. In ways is Arianna communicating persuasively about the relevance of offering employees pet health insurance?
2. In what ways is Arianna detracting from making a persuasive case about the relevance of offering pet health insurance to company employees?
3. To what extent is Arianna involved in a negotiation with the management team?

Associated Role Play

One student plays the role of Arianna, who is invited back for a 10-minute session with the executive team. The team has decided favorably on offering pet health insurance, but the team wants to move forward with the lowest-priced option. Arianna, however, senses victory and wants to present a persuasive argument for providing an expensive program for pet health insurance. Three other students play the role of members of the executive team who want to control costs on the new benefit and also did not appreciate Arianna's negative comments during the previous session.

Alexis is the program coordinator for a construction trades training program for students from several high schools in upstate New York. The training program is offered through Boards of Cooperative Educational Services (BOCES). BOCES are public organizations that were created by the New York State Legislature in 1948 to provide shared educational programs to school districts. BOCES member schools benefit because they typically could not afford to offer many of these programs with their own resources.

Students enrolled in the program headed by Alexis learn basic construction skills, such as building or reinforcing foundations, inserting plywood, installing windows, and painting both interiors and exteriors. The thrust of the program is for students who learn basic construction skills to find an entry-level job, then develop more skills through on-the-job training. As with most areas of the country, there is a dire shortage of skilled workers available for construction jobs in New York. The graduates from Alexis's program need more experience before they can be classified as skilled workers.

Today, Alexis is meeting with Tony, the owner of Carmel Construction, a firm that specializes in restoring "zombie" houses. These are one-, two-, three-, or four-family buildings that have been foreclosed by a mortgage lender and usually have been vacant for over a year. Most of these houses have been vandalized and are in wretched condition. The investors who purchase the zombie houses attempt to sell them quickly after they are restored. Neighbors, neighborhood associations, and local officials welcome the work of Carmel Construction because blight is removed, and neighboring real estate values increase.

Alexis is meeting with Tony at his office to negotiate for job openings and starting pay for five of her graduates. Tony begins the meeting by saying, "Good to see you, Alexis. You sent me a text saying that you have five nice kids ready to work for Carmel. They will become members of our zombie squad. I hope they are nice because some of those BOCES grads I've seen in the past weren't the sharpest."

With a quizzical expression, Alexis responded, "I hope that you are kidding, Tony, because our graduates have a proven track record of providing beginning talent for construction firms. Do you have a problem or something?"

"Calm down, Alexis. You need to be able to take honest feedback," said Tony. "My only problem is that I need to hire a bunch of beginner construction workers who can bring value to my company. I'm trying to run a profitable business, and I'm not a social agency. Profits in restoring vacated houses are razor thin."

Alexis said, "I am here to help you operate a profitable business by providing you with great beginning talent. Please calm down and focus on why I am here. I am looking to place five talented, eager young workers at Carmel. As you know, all five are certified to have basic construction skills. They are job-ready and eager to get started."

"Who certified them?" asked Tony. "Was it you? Was it a representative from BOCES? Or was it their parents?" Tony said with a laugh. "I know that some of the grads from your program can be pretty good, so I will take your word on their ability to work. I will need the five to start by mid-June. Might I be able to interview the candidates within the next 10 days?"

"Yes, Tony, they will be available for interviews on short notice," said Alexis. "We can arrange transportation for those students who do not have their own means of getting to a job interview."

Tony replied, "If you have to arrange transportation for a job interview, how will they be able to come to work when they are hired?"

Alexis responded, "Have no fear, Tony. The students you hire will become dependable workers who will find a way to get to and from the job. Two more important issues are whether the jobs will be part-time or full-time, and what will be the starting wage?"

Tony answered, "For now, I am offering 40 hours per week at $11 per hour. Anyone who proves to be a good worker will be increased to $15 per hour within 12 months. And the prospects look for year-round work. And I will be adding some health benefits that fit industry standards."

Alexis responded, "An offer of $11 suggests that you are being stingy. Minimum wages are going up in New York State as well as the rest of the country. Remember, you will be hiring certified beginning construction workers. Can you do any better than $11 per hour? Please be a little considerate."

Tony answered, "I will go as high as $11.50 per hour. I would like to be a generous employer, but squeezing a profit out of refurbishing zombie homes is tricky. I don't have a guaranteed salary from the school system."

Alexis said in parting, "Okay, a deal is a deal. I will get in touch with the five students and then contact you to arrange their interviews. I know that you will be proud of our students if you just give them a decent chance."

With a laugh, Tony said, "I hope you are right. And by the way, would you or someone you know like to purchase a rebuilt zombie home, fixed up by certified construction workers?"

Case Questions

1. Which aspects of emotional intelligence is Tony applying (or not applying) in the negotiation session described in the case?
2. Which aspects of emotional intelligence is Alexis applying (or not applying) in the negotiation session described in the case?
3. Explain whether the outcome of the negotiations is an example of distributive or integrative bargaining.

Associated Role Play

One student plays the role of Alexis, and another plays the role of Tony. They have reached the point of negotiating a starting hourly wage for the construction students. Yet, the scenario has changed, because both Tony and Alexis do their best to display the emotional intelligence dimensions of social awareness and relationship management during the negotiation. Observers might provide feedback on how well the role players are able to display social awareness and relationship management.

Notes

1. Troy B. Wiwczaroski, György Szabados, and Anita Pierog, "Developing English Language Skills in Employees," Working paper, Debrecen University (http://acta.bibl.u-szeged.hu/34974/1/vikek_016_017_140-146.pdf), 2014.

2. Skills 1, 2, and 3 are from Jane Thomas, *Guide to Managerial Persuasion and Influence* (Upper Saddle River, NJ: Pearson/Prentice Hall, 2004), pp. 3–9.

3. Robert B. Cialdini, "Harnessing the Science of Persuasion," *Harvard Business Review*, October 2001, pp. 72–79; Robert B. Cialdini, *Pre-suasion: A Revolutionary Way to Influence and Persuade* (New York: Simon & Schuster, 2016).

4. Edward J. Kelly and Natalija Kaminskiene, "Importance of Emotional Intelligence in Negotiation and Mediation," *International Comparative Jurisprudence*, Issue 1, September 2016, p. 55.

5. Ibid.

6. Daniel Goleman, Richard Boyatzis, and Annie McKee, "Primal Leadership: The Hidden Driver of Great Performance," *Harvard Business Review*, December 2001, pp. 42–51; Daniel Goleman and Richard Boyatzis, "Emotional Intelligence Has 12 Elements. Which Do You Need to Work On?" *Harvard Business Review*, February 8, 2017, pp. 1–6.

7. Kelly and Kaminskiene, "Importance of Emotional Intelligence in Negotiation and Mediation," p. 60.

8. Theory reviewed in Hillary Anger Elfenhein, Maw Der Fon, Judith White, Hwee Hoon Tan, and Voon Chuan Aik, "Reading Your Counterpart: The Benefit of Emotion Recognition Accuracy for Effectiveness in Negotiation," *Journal of Nonverbal Behavior*, 2007, pp. 209–210.

9. Ibid, pp. 205–223.

10. Timothy A. Judge, Amy C. Colbert, and Remus Ilies, "Intelligence and Leadership: A Quantitative Review and Test of Theoretical Propositions," *Journal of Applied Psychology*, June 2004, pp. 542–552.

11. Michael Kaplan, "Do You Have These 11 Successful Negotiation Traits?" *Veteran Talent* (www.workofhonor.com), October 10, 2016.

12. Alison Wood Brooks, "In Negotiation, Make 'Em Laugh!" *Leadership Briefings*, January 2018, p. 7.

13. Research reviewed in Tomas Chamorro-Premuzic, "The Personality Traits of Good Negotiators," *Harvard Business Review* (https://hbr.org), August 7, 2017, pp. 1–6.

14. "Ten Personality Traits of Top Negotiators," *Dummies* (www.dummies.com), 2019, pp. 1–3.

15. Quoted in, "Women and Negotiation: Are There Really Gender Differences?" *Knowledge@Wharton* (http:knowledge.wharton.upenn.edu), October 26, 2015, pp. 1–6.

16. Jens Mazel, et al., "A Meta-Analysis on Gender Differences in Negotiation Outcomes and Their Moderators," *Psychological Bulletin*, January 2014, pp. 85–104.

17. "Women Outperform Men in Some Financial Negotiations," *Science Daily* (www.sciencedaily.com), December 1, 2014, pp. 1–4.

18. Dina W. Pradel, Hannah Riley, and Kathleen L. McGinn, "When Does Gender Matter in Negotiation?" *Negotiation*, November 2005, pp. 1–5; Suzanne de Janasz and Beth Cabrera, "How Women Can Get What They Want in a Negotiation," *Harvard Business Review*, August 12, 2018, pp. 1–8.

Basic Negotiation Tactics

Source: adriaticfoto/Shutterstock.

Chapter Outline

Preparing for Negotiation

Deal with Your Anxiety about the Upcoming Negotiation

Establish Negotiation Goals

Create a Positive Negotiation Climate

Understand the Other Party's Perspective

Know Your Target Price and Your Walkaway Terms

Know Your Best Alternative to a Negotiated Agreement (BATNA)

Face-to-Face Tactics during Negotiation

Begin with a Plausible Demand or Offer, yet Allow Room for Negotiation

Be Ready to Compromise

Use Facts More Than Threats

Make Small Concessions Gradually

Impose a Deadline

Make a Last-and-Final Offer

Evaluate the Significance of a Last-Minute Demand

Allow for Face-Saving

Learning Objectives

After reading and studying this chapter and doing the exercises, you should be able to:

1. Prepare for an upcoming negotiation, including the following:
   a. Deal with your anxiety about an upcoming negotiation.
   b. Establish negotiation goals.
   c. Create a positive negotiation climate.
   d. Understand the other party's perspective.
   e. Know your target price and walkaway terms.
   f. Know your best alternative to a negotiated agreement (BATNA).

2. Be ready to implement face-to-face tactics during negotiation, including the following:
   a. Begin with a plausible demand or offer, yet allow room for negotiation.
   b. Compromise when appropriate.
   c. Use facts more than threats.
   d. Make small concessions gradually.
   e. Impose a deadline.
   f. Make a last-and-final offer.
   g. Evaluate the significance of a last-minute demand.
   h. Allow for face-saving.

At the core of becoming an effective negotiator is to be aware of and be able to implement negotiation tactics. Two examples are compromising and establishing goals for the negotiation. The terms *negotiation strategy* and *negotiation tactic* are frequently used interchangeably, but it is helpful to draw a distinction between the two. A negotiation *strategy* is an overall plan to obtain what you want during negotiation, such as doing whatever it takes to gain an advantage. A *tactic* refers more to a method of conducting a favorable negotiation, such as imposing a deadline or granting small concessions gradually.

As described in Chapter 1, two widely recognized general approaches to negotiation are distributive bargaining and **integrative bargaining**. The basic approach of distributive bargaining is to distribute the gains in such a way that one side wins at the expense of the other, also referred to as a zero-sum game. Distributive bargaining is also referred to as personal-gains bargaining, a situation in which the negotiator's aim is to win as much as possible for his or her side at the expense of the other side.

Personal-gains bargaining is the traditional approach to negotiation and is still widely practiced. An example would an employee group attempting to extract as large a minimum wage as possible, whether or not it creates major problems for the employer. In the same scenario, the employer would engage in personal-gains bargaining if top-level management attempted to keep the minimum wage as low as possible in order to enhance profits.

In integrative bargaining, both sides respect each other and want to build a lasting, constructive relationship. Integrative bargaining is also referred to as mutual-gains bargaining to indicate a type of negotiation in which both sides attempt to attain mutually beneficial results.

In the scenario about the minimum wage, the employee group would engage in mutual-gains bargaining if it negotiated for a minimum wage that would help both the employees and the employer. Among the concerns would be whether the company could stay competitive and not have to dismiss valuable employees or replace them with robots. The employer would engage in mutual-gains bargaining if it looked to pay the highest minimum wage possible that would allow the company to stay competitive, keep valuable employees, and provide an adequate return to shareholders.

In most negotiating situations, it is not entirely clear whether each party is more concerned about personal gains or mutual gains. Negotiation theory suggests that the distributive and integrative perspectives are not mutually exclusive. In practice, negotiators rely on both processes either in sequence or at different times during interactions with the other party.[1] Also, the results of the negotiation may take a long time to evaluate. For example, if the company raises the minimum wage to $16 per hour, it may take a couple of years to see if both sides benefit from the increase. The positive results might be a more stable and productive workforce giving better customer service, therefore enhancing company profits. The negative results might be fewer jobs available for entry-level workers and lower profits for the company.

The accompanying self-quiz provides you the opportunity to think through your tendency toward preferring the strategy of personal-gains bargaining versus mutual-gains bargaining.

Preparing for Negotiation

Negotiation is usually a serious activity with consequences for the short term, intermediate term, and long term. It is therefore to your advantage to prepare for an upcoming negotiation. At times, a tactic or strategy employed to prepare for negotiation will also be continued into the negotiation sessions, such as creating a positive negotiation climate. Contained in this section, and outlined in Figure 4.1, is a group of key tactics to help you prepare for negotiation in and outside the workplace. The information in Chapter 2 about planning for negotiation is also relevant when preparing for negotiation.

personal-gains bargaining
A situation in which the negotiator's aim to win as much as possible for his or her side at the expense of the other side.

mutual-gains bargaining
A type of negotiation in which both sides attempt to attain mutually beneficial results.

My Approach to Negotiation

The following quiz is designed to give you tentative insight into your major approach to negotiation. Check whether each statement is mostly true or mostly false as it applies to you now or would apply to you if you were negotiating something important.

Statement about Negotiation	Mostly True	Mostly False
1. I look at negotiations as a time to do battle.		
2. During negotiation, I like to see the other side smile.		
3. The first person to grant a concession in negotiation is acting foolishly.		
4. I like to see the other side squirm during negotiation.		
5. Negotiation is the time to find workable compromises.		
6. An ideal result of negotiation would be for me to get exactly what I want and the other side to get nothing.		
7. To intimidate the other side during negotiation, I like to shout and scream.		
8. A little kindness toward the other side goes a long way in negotiation.		
9. An effective negotiation tactic is to show respect for the other side.		
10. An effective negotiation tactic is to grant a series of small concessions to the other side.		
11. I know that I have been successful when the other side walks away with nothing.		
12. I know that I have been successful when the other side walks away from the negotiation thinking that he or she got a good deal.		
13. When the negotiation session is over, there is one winner and one loser.		
14. As the old saying goes, "The winner takes all."		
15. When negotiations are complete, both sides should walk away with something valuable.		
16. For one side to win in negotiation, the other side has to lose.		
17. If you smile during a negotiation session, the other side will try to take advantage of you.		
18. After both sides have agreed on major issues during a negotiation, it is a good idea for one side to try to grab a last-minute concession.		
19. Negotiation is only fun for me when I win big.		
20. Negotiation is not very complicated: one side wins, and the other side loses.		
21. I like to begin negotiations with an outrageous demand or offer.		
22. An effective negotiator bargains in good faith.		
23. It would make me feel cheap if I offered somebody only one-half of his or her asking price.		
24. Being tactful and diplomatic helps you be a successful negotiator.		
25. After negotiations are completed, I would be willing to shake hands (or exchange fist bumps) with the other side and say, "It was a pleasure doing business with you."		

Scoring and Interpretation: Give yourself 1 point indicating a tendency toward being a mutual-gains negotiator for each question you answered as follows:

1. Mostly False	10. Mostly True	18. Mostly False
2. Mostly True	11. Mostly False	19. Mostly False
3. Mostly False	12. Mostly True	20. Mostly False
4. Mostly False	13. Mostly False	21. Mostly False
5. Mostly True	14. Mostly False	22. Mostly True
6. Mostly False	15. Mostly True	23. Mostly True
7. Mostly False	16. Mostly False	24. Mostly True
8. Mostly True	17. Mostly False	25. Mostly True
9. Mostly True		

If you scored 19 or more points for the 25 statements just listed, you have a strong tendency toward being a negotiator who attempts to find solutions that benefit both sides. You demonstrate genuine concern for the welfare of the other side. This is the nontraditional approach to negotiation, but it goes a long way toward establishing constructive relationships within organizations.

Give yourself 1 point indicating a tendency toward being a maximizing-personal-gains negotiator for each question you answered as follows:

1. Mostly True	10. Mostly False	18. Mostly True
2. Mostly False	11. Mostly True	19. Mostly True
3. Mostly True	12. Mostly False	20. Mostly True
4. Mostly True	13. Mostly True	21. Mostly True
5. Mostly False	14. Mostly True	22. Mostly False
6. Mostly True	15. Mostly False	23. Mostly False
7. Mostly True	16. Mostly True	24. Mostly False
8. Mostly False	17. Mostly True	25. Mostly False
9. Mostly False		

If you scored 19 or more points for the 25 statements just listed, you have a strong tendency toward being a negotiator who attempts to maximize personal gain, with little concern for the welfare of the other side. This is the traditional approach to negotiation, such as that found in civil lawsuits, but it interferes with establishing constructive relationships within organizations.

1. Deal with your anxiety about the upcoming negotiation.

2. Establish negotiation goals.

3. Create a positive negotiation climate.

4. Understand the other party's perspective.

5. Know your target price and your walkaway terms.

6. Know your best alternative to a negotiated agreement (BATNA).

FIGURE 4.1 Tactics Used to Prepare for Negotiation

Deal with Your Anxiety about the Upcoming Negotiation

For many people, the prospects of an upcoming negotiation are anxiety provoking. Professor Alison Wood Brooks of Harvard Business School offers a suggestion for dealing with this challenge that supports all the negotiating tactics described in this and the following chapter. She recommends that you deal with the anxiety that often precedes entering negotiations by reframing anxiety as excitement. (Anxiety does include excitement, but the fact that anxiety also contains dread should not be ignored.) Think of yourself as being excited rather than nervous about the upcoming negotiations.

Also, build your confidence by practicing negotiation when the opportunity presents itself, such as negotiating more time to complete an important project.[2] It is also important to recognize that you will probably experience heavy emotion during negotiation, so be prepared to use your emotional intelligence to advantage.[3] As a basic example, you might be so excited about negotiating the price of a used bicycle that you forget that any bicycle you purchase must include a generator for the lights.

Establish Negotiation Goals

A natural starting point in preparing for negotiation is to establish goals for what you intend to accomplish through negotiation. As G. Richard Shell of the Wharton School explains, you will not know when to say "yes" and when to say "no" if you do not know what you want to attain.[4] The more specific you are about what you hope to achieve in an upcoming negotiation, the greater the probability of success. It is usually helpful to have high but not unrealistic expectations. For example, if you had the opportunity to negotiate the starting salary for an offered promotion, you might establish a negotiating goal of a 15 percent increase over your present salary. A demand of 25 percent might be unrealistic.

An expectation is slightly different from a goal because it points to what we think we can really achieve, whereas a goal is a specific target toward which we strive. In the example just mentioned, the person set a goal of 15 percent but really expected to receive a salary increase of around 10 percent.

Negotiation theory and research suggest that skilled negotiators conceive of their goals as a range, such as the most they think they can get, what they hope to get, and the least they are willing to take. In contrast, unskilled negotiators establish their goals as a fixed point, meaning that they set a single targeted amount. It has also been observed that skilled negotiators engage in *issue planning*, whereas less skilled negotiators favor *sequence planning*. Issue planning involves identifying all of the key issues and their accompanying arguments and positions, yet not thinking ahead about the sequence for presenting the issues. Sequence planning involves thinking through all the issues and planning to present them in a particular order. For example, the sequence planner might decide that available resources (i.e., how much money is available in the pool) must be discussed before considering possible solutions.

Issue planning often provides more flexibility because a negotiator is able to argue a given point at any time during the negotiation. Sequence planning might provide less flexibility because the negotiator might be locked into a chain of arguments that, if disrupted, might make his or her case seem less logical.[5]

A negotiation goal should be established based on research and opinion about what is feasible. Sarah, the owner of a company that manufactures and sells designer covers for mobile devices, decides to subcontract the manufacture of a new line of covers. She looks toward finding a subcontractor in Mexico or Pakistan. Sarah would like to negotiate for a 60-day cycle between sending an order and receiving the merchandise. Yet before establishing the negotiating goal of 60 days, she conducts research about manufacturing cycles for similar products in Mexico and Pakistan. As a result of her research, Sarah decides to negotiate for a 75-day turnaround.

Being passionate, or at least highly enthused, about attaining your negotiation goal facilitates its accomplishment. Sarah might be passionate about getting her artistic cover designs to market quickly, so during negotiation with a subcontractor, she might make a statement such as, "If we can get a 75-day turnaround from you, we can beat our competitors to the market. And that could mean many more repeat orders for you down the road."

A negotiation goal is often higher than the minimum offer you will make or the maximum demand you will accept. Sarah might set the goal of a 75-day turnaround, but if necessary, she will accept 90 days before searching for another subcontractor.

Here are a few additional examples of negotiating goals in practice:

Director of Information Technology (IT) at Bank Headquarters: "Will negotiate for a 15 percent increase in our operating budget for next year based on a heavy increase in demand for our services."

Chief Marketing Officer of Trucking Company: "Will negotiate with all customers for a 5 percent trucking fee next fiscal year to cover our increased energy costs."

Sarah, the owner of a company that manufactures and sells designer covers for mobile devices, decides to subcontract the manufacture of a new line of covers. She looks toward finding a subcontractor in Mexico or Pakistan. Sarah would like to negotiate for a 60-day cycle between sending an order and receiving the merchandise. Yet before establishing the negotiating goal of 60 days, she conducts research about manufacturing cycles for similar products in Mexico and Pakistan. As a result of her research, Sarah decides to negotiate for a 75-day turnaround.

Labor Union Vice President: "Will demand an extra week of paternal leave for our workers based on new developments in human resources throughout the country."

Note carefully that each of the three negotiations has some sensible justification for the negotiation goal. This is important because demands in negotiations should be justifiable.

Create a Positive Negotiation Climate

In recent years, American politicians at the national level (both liberals and conservatives) have employed the tactic of viciously insulting the other side before negotiating a major issue, such as a budget appropriation. The tactic often backfires, with the other side resisting an offer from the insulter. A key reason is that effective negotiation means that the parties collaborate in key decisions and build constructive relationships by working with their counterparts in the dispute.[6]

In recent years, American politicians at the national level (both liberals and conservatives) have employed the tactic of viciously insulting the other side before negotiating a major issue, such as a budget appropriation. The tactic often backfires, with the other side resisting an offer from the insulter.

Acting in good faith is a major contributor to establishing a positive negotiating climate. Good-faith bargaining means that the negotiator is honestly attempting to reach an agreement instead of trying to manipulate the other side to attain maximum gain. The owner of a Mexican restaurant was negotiating a bank loan so that he could open a second restaurant to be constructed in an affluent area. The owner emphasized that he needed a loan with low interest because the rent would be quite high for the new restaurant. He said, "I need the loan, but I do not want to have such high principal and interest payments that my profits will be too small."

Negotiation proceeds much more swiftly and smoothly if a positive tone surrounds the session. An effective opening line is "Thanks for fitting this meeting into your busy schedule." Nonverbal communication such as smiling and making friendly gestures helps create a positive climate. A calm voice helps build the trust necessary for creating a positive climate. Creating a positive negotiation climate may precede the actual negotiations, but for maximum effect, it should continue after negotiations have begun.

In negotiating with coworkers for assistance, a positive climate can often be achieved by phrasing demands as a request for help. Most people will be more accommodating if you say to them, "I have a problem, and I wonder if you could help me with it." The problem might be that you need the person's time and mental energy. By giving the person a choice of offering you help, you have established a much more positive climate than would occur by demanding assistance.

Another way of creating a positive negotiating climate is to validate the other side's position by describing his or her position in your own words (a form of the communication technique of *paraphrasing*). Make a positive comment to the other person that emphasizes the value in the relationship.[7] Assume that you are renting a house and the owner plans to raise the rent 5 percent for the next year. You might state, "I recognize that your costs are rising. You have been a wonderful landlord, but 5 percent more for rent is beyond my budget."

A sense of humor was mentioned in Chapter 3 as an important trait for negotiation, and it can be especially useful in building a climate favorable for negotiation. A well-timed, sincere humorous comment or joke can help reduce tension, increase the feeling of closeness among negotiation participants, build rapport, and foster a positive tone during negotiations. Humor also contributes to a positive negotiation climate by making the interactions more favorable. Finding humor in the negotiation tends to increase your counterpart's feeling of satisfaction and helps you both remember the negotiation sessions in a favorable light.[8]

In general, a humorous comment relevant to the discussion is much more effective than telling a rehearsed joke during negotiation. The joke teller will often be perceived as wasting time and being immature. In contrast, a well-timed, witty comment enhances the moment. For example, a purchasing manager might say to a vendor, "Our company loves doing business with you. But I am authorized to lose only $100 per manufactured unit to meet your minimum price."

Understand the Other Party's Perspective

As in many forms of human interaction, empathy can be an important part of negotiation. Deepak Malhotra and Max H. Bazerman observe that negotiators often channel too much effort into pushing their own position and too little into understanding the other side's perspective.[9] To obtain a good deal, or any deal at all, negotiators should dig for information about *why* the other side wants what it demands or offers. Inaccurate or incomplete assumptions about the other side's motives can lead negotiators to propose solutions to the wrong problems, waste money, or kill a deal.

At the start of 2018, the Teamsters union began negotiating contract talks with United Parcel Services Inc. (UPS). A major negotiating point was that the Teamsters wanted to prohibit UPS from using drones and driverless vehicles to deliver packages in the future. The contract was major because it covered approximately 260,000 employees. The perspective the Teamsters had to understand was that UPS officials were not mean-spirited and simply trying to reduce costs at the expense of union jobs. In contrast, the UPS perspective was that the company wanted a contract that would provide the flexibility to remain highly competitive as smaller delivery business entered the field.[10]

At the same time, the UPS negotiators had to understand the perspective of the Teamsters. Instead of assuming that the union was looking to grab more power for itself, the Teamster officials might have had a genuine interest in the welfare of members. Being replaced by a drone or driverless vehicle is a major blow to worker well-being.

Another key part of understanding the other party's perspective is that you look for common ground. A company representative might be attempting to negotiate the rent for a branch office on a two-year lease at a price that is below market value. The common ground is that the representative of the commercial center wants to have a high occupancy rate, and the office tenant is looking for a stable location.

At the start of 2018, the Teamsters union began negotiating contract talks with United Parcel Services Inc. (UPS). A major negotiating point was that the Teamsters wanted to prohibit UPS from using drones and driverless vehicles to deliver packages in the future.

To understand the other party's perspective, you often have to prepare in advance. Obtain as much information as you can about the other party's side before the negotiation session. With respect to the office lease, for example, the potential renter should research comparable rents in the area before making an offer. Knowing how long the desired space has been vacant is also useful information because vacancies are nonperforming assets.

Know Your Target Price and Your Walkaway Terms

Your *target price* is what you are hoping to attain. Professor Adam Galinsky of Columbia University Business School recommends that before negotiating, you should also know your *walkaway price*, meaning the price that would make you terminate negotiations.[11] It is helpful to walk into negotiation with both your target price and your walkaway terms. Suppose you have inherited a collection of old baseball cards and you want to monetize your inheritance. If you know very little about trading baseball cards, you will need to do considerable research about their value. Your research will help you decide on what is a realistic price for the cards (your target price) and what would be too low of an offer (your walkaway terms).

Know Your Best Alternative to a Negotiated Agreement (BATNA)

BATNA Best alternative to a negotiated agreement.

The reason that you would probably negotiate would be to produce something better than the result obtainable without negotiation. The goal of negotiating is not just to agree but to obtain more valuable results than would otherwise have occurred. When you are aware of your best alternative to a negotiated agreement (BATNA), it sets a floor to the agreement you are willing to accept. The BATNA is a long-standing, well-accepted negotiation tactic.

Your BATNA becomes the standard that can protect both parties from accepting terms that are too unfavorable. It also keeps you from walking away from terms that would be beneficial for you to accept.

What might a BATNA look like in practice? Suppose that you and your partner have been operating an antique furniture store that also sells online. The store is profitable, but both of you have chosen to look for corporate employment, provided you can sell the store. Working with a financial analyst, you set an offering price of $75,000 for the store and the accompanying website. Your BATNA is $60,000 because if you do not receive this minimum price, you have two backup courses of action. First, you can continue to operate the antique furniture store for a while longer and forget about corporate jobs for now. Second, you have a retired family member who would take over responsibility for the store at a salary of $40,000 per year, enabling you to essentially break even.

Knowing the other side's BATNA is also important because it helps define the other side's bargaining zone. Understanding each other's bargaining zone makes it possible to arrive at mutually profitable trade-offs. In the negotiation about the antique store, another prospective buyer could purchase another store for less than $60,000 or perhaps start a store from scratch. The couple's BATNA therefore has to give market conditions some consideration.

An underlying advantage of knowing your BATNA is that it capitalizes on the power of a positive "no." Famous negotiator William Ury reasons that being able to say "no" to a demand places you in a strong position.[12] During negotiations, a statement such as "I am not willing to pay that much for the added feature" can bring you respect because you are standing up for your principles. For the best effect, "no" should be expressed in a friendly and firm manner.

Face-to-Face Tactics during Negotiation

In this section, and outlined in Figure 4.2, are the basic negotiation tactics to be used during the negotiation session. A group of more advanced, or subtle, tactics is presented in Chapter 5.

1. Begin with a plausible demand or offer, yet allow room for negotiation.
2. Be ready to compromise.
3. Use facts more than threats.
4. Make small concessions gradually.
5. Impose a deadline.
6. Make a last-and-final offer.
7. Evaluate the significance of a last-minute demand.
8. Allow for face saving.

FIGURE 4.2 Face-to-Face Tactics during Negotiation

Begin with a Plausible Demand or Offer, yet Allow Room for Negotiation

Common sense suggests that you begin negotiations with an extreme, almost fanciful, demand or offer. The final compromise will therefore be closer to your true demand or offer (target price) than if you opened the negotiations more realistically. An attorney represents a client who broke her pinky finger when she slipped on icy steps leading into a restaurant. The attorney asks for $2 million to compensate her client for pain and suffering and the temporary loss of a fully functioning pinky.

In reality, the attorney is hoping to receive a $50,000 settlement from the restaurant. In contrast, a plausible demand is more useful because it shows that you are bargaining in good faith. Also, if a third party has to settle the case, a plausible demand or offer will receive more sympathy than an implausible one will. In the broken-pinky case, the judge might be disgusted with the gluttony of the attorney and suggest a $5,000 payment by the restaurant.

Although it is advisable to begin with a plausible demand or offer, one must still allow room for negotiation. A basic tactic of negotiation is to begin with a demand that allows for compromise and concession. If you recognize that you are one week behind in preparing a key report for top-level management, you might ask for a four-day deadline extension to give yourself some breathing room. Yet you will agree to a two-day extension and do your best to reach your new deadline. (You also have to recognize, in this case, that top-level management has more power than you even if you are a specialist in the content of the report.)

Be Ready to Compromise

An extension of the negotiation tactic just described is to be ready to compromise, the settlement of differences by mutual concessions. Many people think that the purpose of negotiation is to attain a workable compromise. One party agrees to do something if the other party agrees to do something else. Compromise is a realistic approach to negotiation and conflict resolution, and you have probably used compromise many times in your life. Haggling over the price of a used lawnmower would be an everyday example of compromise. Most labor–management disputes are settled by compromise. For example, the labor union representative may agree to accept a smaller increase in hourly pay if management will subcontract less work to other countries.

compromise The settlement of differences by mutual concessions.

Some people argue that compromise is not a mutual-gain (integrative) tactic. The problem is that the two parties may wind up with a solution that does not solve the problem. A marketing manager might ask for a 25 percent budget increase for digital marketing. His goal is to ultimately sell more goods and services. He winds up receiving a 12.5 percent increase. Top-level management has saved some money, but the increase does not improve digital marketing efforts or noticeably increase company revenue. Nevertheless, compromise is both inevitable and useful in most negotiations.

Use Facts More Than Threats

During negotiation, both sides often become emotional, sometimes to the point of one party threatening the other, such as saying, "If you don't change that feature on your website that you copied from us, I will sue you so heavily that your company will go bankrupt." It is a better negotiating tactic to stick with the facts rather than threatening the other side. In this example, a better approach would be to say, "We want you to remove that feature because the legal interpretation we received is that the feature is our intellectual property."

Joseph Grenny, a social science writer, notes that people want psychological safety within a negotiating session. You should therefore do everything you can to share your understanding of the situation without triggering a perception of hostility or malicious intent on your part. Grenny makes three recommendations[13]:

1. Frame your statement as a natural consequence, not planned revenge. Rather than threatening the other side in the website example, you would state, "I have an obligation to protect our company's intellectual property."

2. Express your reluctance to impose punitive measures. You might say, "I know that we can settle this issue about intellectual property rights without resorting to legal action."
3. Press for continuing dialogue rather than seeking to impose a negative consequence. As in point 2, you are better off continuing to conduct a dialogue about the problem than seeking a way to zap the other party. A constructive comment on your part might be, "Let's talk about this problem some more before deciding on what we have to do right away."

Make Small Concessions Gradually

Making steady concessions leads to more mutually satisfactory agreements in most situations. Gradually, you concede little things to the other side. The hardline approach to bargaining is to make your concession early in the negotiation, then grant no further concessions. The tactic of making small concessions is well suited to purchasing a new car. In order to reach a price you consider acceptable, you might grant a concession such as a willingness to subscribe to the online roadside assistance or finance the car through the deal instead of a third party. A concession the dealer might grant you would be to include the first two servicing trips in the price of the car or vehicle financing at a preferred rate.

Making a few small concessions may contribute to a successful negotiation, but according to experimental evidence, successful negotiators make fewer concessions than unsuccessful negotiators. At the same time, successful negotiators tend to characterize their opponent's concessions as insufficient.[14]

Impose a Deadline

Giving the other side a deadline is often helpful in gaining a satisfactory solution to a negotiation or resolving a conflict. Deadlines often propel people into action because they require some type of external control or motivation. When imposing a deadline, you need to be confident that you have enough negotiating power. An example of a deadline imposed by a negotiator with limited power is when you receive an e-mail informing you that if you do not respond to this notice about a service contract for your vehicle within 24 hours, "Your file will be closed."

Here is an example of how you might use deadlines to gain an advantage in your negotiation when you do have some negotiating power: "If you do not send me the refund that you promised me for my defective phone by September 30, I will cancel my service with your company."

Make a Last-and-Final Offer

In many circumstances, making a final offer will break a deadlock. The same technique has been referred to as a *doorknob price* because it means that the negotiator will leave the room if his or her offer or demand is not met. Having a BATNA facilitates making a last-and-final offer.

A negotiator might frame her message something like this: "All I can possibly pay you for your sushi restaurant is $35,000. You have my number and my e-mail address. Get in touch with me when the restaurant becomes available at that price." Sometimes the tactic will be countered by a last-and-final offer from the other side: "Thanks for your interest. My absolute minimum price for this thriving sushi restaurant is $45,000. Get in touch with me if that offer seems acceptable to you." Either the buyer or the seller will probably give in and accept the other person's last-and-final offer.

Evaluate the Significance of a Last-Minute Demand

It is not unusual for a negotiator to attempt to squeeze out a last-minute concession, even when it appears his or her key demands have been met.[15] At times, the demand might seem harmless. For example, after having agreed on a salary, benefits, and stock options, a newly hired chief executive officer (CEO) might ask, "By the way, how about paying for a trip for my wife and three children to visit the area so that we can look over the area as a family?" Although harmless on the surface, the last-minute demand might suggest that the newly hired CEO is a high-maintenance person who might make frequent demands on top-level management. Perhaps this potential problem should be investigated before actually bringing the CEO on board. The background check ("vetting") of the executive might be reopened.

Allow for Face-Saving

We have saved one of the most constructive negotiating tactics for last. The strategy of negotiating for mutual gains includes the idea that you do not want to diminish or demoralize the other side. You should try to create circumstances that will enable you to continue working with that person if necessary. People prefer to avoid looking weak, foolish, or incompetent during negotiation or when the process is completed. If you do not give the other side an opportunity to save face, you will probably create a long-term enemy. Face-saving might also be considered a part of bargaining in good faith.

Consider this example of how face saving could work: The CEO of a small company winds up paying a higher starting salary for a chief marketing officer (CMO) than she wanted. The representative of the executive placement agency that placed the marketing head says to the CEO, "I know that Patrick cost more than you budgeted, but do not be concerned because you have made an excellent investment. Patrick will increase your market penetration so much that his salary and benefits will be a bargain for you."

The accompanying Negotiation and Conflict Resolution in Action feature illustrates how negotiating can be conducted informally in the sense of not conducting formal negotiation sessions. (A good deal of negotiation takes place through in-person or electronic conversations.)

NEGOTIATION AND CONFLICT RESOLUTION IN ACTION

Virginia Distillery Company Staff Members Negotiate Positive Ways to Cut Costs

The Virginia Distillery Company is an American single-malt whiskey distillery located in the Blue Ridge Mountains region in central Virginia. The Virginia Distillery fuses single-malt whiskey made on-site in Virginia with aged malted whiskey from Scotland. Whiskeys made by the company are sold in many states.

A problem facing the Virginia Distillery, as well as other distilleries located in the state, is high taxes on spirits. Excise taxes on spirits are around $19.93 per gallon, the third-highest rate in the United States. Beer is taxed at 26 cents per gallon, and wine at $1.51. The tax rate for liquor in Virginia is about $2.75 per bottle or liter.

Christine Riggleman, CEO and master distiller at the Silverback Distillery, puts in this way: "Name another business that has to give away more than one-half of the money it makes? I sell a bottle of vodka in my tasting room for $29.89, but after that the ABC takes their cut, and I pay for packaging, material costs, labor and so on. We profit just $2." (The ABC is the Alcoholic Beverage Commission.)

Faced with high taxes and competitive pressures, Virginia Distillery CEO Gareth Moore decided to go through a cost-cutting exercise in the tasting-room operation. Staff members negotiated in good spirits (pun unintended) to bring the tasting-room operation to profitability in a challenging regulatory environment. A major purpose of the informal negotiations was to reduce costs, but firing employees was off the table as an alternative. The goal of holding discussions and negotiations was to use the existing staff in more effective ways.

A starting point was to agree on eliminating an outside cleaning service by replacing it with increased staff hours. The production operation had heavy labor needs for the purposes of labeling and filling bottles. A negotiated solution to this problem was to cover these needs with increased hours from the tasting-room staff. As a result of these two negotiated adjustments, costs were reduced without downsizing the Virginia Distillery Company.

Summary

A negotiation strategy is an overall plan to attain what you want during negotiation. A negotiation tactic is a method of obtaining a more favorable negotiation. Personal-gains bargaining is a situation in which the negotiator's aim is to win as much as possible for his or side at the expense of the other side. Mutual-gains bargaining is a type of negotiation in which both sides attempt to attain mutually beneficial results. In most negotiating situations, it is not entirely clear whether each party is more concerned about personal gains or mutual gains.

Tactics geared toward preparing for the negotiation are as follows: (1) deal with your anxiety about the upcoming negotiation, (2) establish negotiation goals, (3) create a positive negotiation climate, (4) understand the other party's perspective, (5) know your target price and your walkaway terms, and (6) know your best alternative to a negotiated agreement.

Basic tactics to be used during the negotiation session include the following: (1) begin with a plausible demand or offer, yet allow room for negotiation; (2) be ready to compromise; (3) use facts more than threats; (4) make small concessions gradually; (5) impose a deadline; (6) make a last-and-final offer; (7) evaluate the significance of a last-minute demand, and (8) allow for face-saving.

Key Terms and Phrases

BATNA, p. 56
Compromise, p. 57

Mutual-gains bargaining, p. 50
Personal-gains bargaining, p. 50

Discussion Questions and Activities

1. How does a person know whether negotiation is advisable in a given situation?
2. To what extent do you think that personal-gains bargaining is unethical?
3. Visualize a person ready to have a family member buried or cremated. How could mutual-gains bargaining be applied to this situation?
4. It is not unusual for a professional sports agent in fields such as basketball, football, and hockey to demand a player contract of over $10 million per year. What's the possible mutual gain here?
5. You may have heard the term *smash-mouth negotiator.* How does this approach fit the strategy of personal-gains bargaining?
6. Establish two negotiation goals for (a) purchasing a new or used vehicle, and (b) purchasing a home.
7. What might be a BATNA for a person selling a successful restaurant?
8. Establish a plausible demand for a person who wants to work from home as much of the time as possible.
9. Assume that two companies are negotiating about a possible trade-name infringement. How might the side making the accusation implement the tactic of using facts more than threats?
10. Suppose that an employee group has just won an enormous concession about minimum wages from an employer. How might the representative of the employee group engage in face-saving?

Skill-Building Exercise: Negotiating a More Flexible Work Schedule

Jared is a research analyst at the headquarters of an investment bank. His major responsibility is to evaluate the financial situation of companies in the transportation industry. His research focuses on airlines, bus companies, and interstate truckers. Jared has worked for the bank for four years, has high job satisfaction, and has received above-average performance reviews. Jared reports to Cynthia, the director of institutional research.

Jared's standard work schedule is 8:30 a.m. to 4:30 p.m., but he also spends approximately six hours a week working from home on investment research. A major change takes place in Jared's home life. Madison, his wife, gives birth to triplet girls. The bank grants Jared four weeks of paternity leave to help manage the situation of raising triplets. Toward the end of the fourth week, Jared recognizes that his returning to a fixed work schedule would be a hardship for his family of five including three demanding infant girls.

Jared decides to negotiate with Cynthia the idea of him being assigned a flexible work schedule for at least one year. The flexibility would include working from home at least one day a week and flexible work hours for the other four days. In this way, Jared could make more of a contribution to raising the triplets and helping with household tasks and chores. Cynthia is willing to listen, but she thinks that a research analyst needs to spend considerable time in the company office to be a good team player and contribute heavily to the investment bank.

One student plays the role of Jared, who seeks a solution to his problem that will benefit him, his family, and the investment bank. Another student plays the role of Cynthia, who is not eager to grant Jared a flexible work schedule, yet she values his fine job performance. At the same time, Cynthia believes that most aspects of work life have some room for negotiation.

Run the negotiation for about 15 minutes. Observers will provide feedback on how well Jared and Cynthia have attained, or are moving toward, a negotiated solution for mutual gain.

CASE PROBLEM 4A: Katrina Wants Relief from the Open-Office Plan

Katrina has been working as a business development planner at Gold Medal, a telecommunications company, for three years. Gold Medal sells telephone and Internet services to residential and commercial customers. Considering that the telecommunications business is intensely competitive, business development is essential to Gold Medal. Another reason that business development is essential at Gold Medal is that large numbers of customers are dropping their landline telephones and shifting to mobile.

A major part of Katrina's daily work routine is to identify potential customers who do not already have phone and Internet service or who are dissatisfied wither their current provider. In Katrina's words, "I have to do a lot of heavy creative thinking."

Three months ago, top-level management at Gold Medal decided to switch to an open-office plan. Individual managers and workers would no longer be able to work in cubicles or private offices. Instead, everybody would work out in the open, seated closely to one another at long work tables. A few closed-door conference rooms would be available for internal meetings and meetings with commercial customers. A private conference room could also be scheduled for performance reviews, sensitive discussions, and disciplinary meetings.

Katrina took an immediate dislike to the open-office plan. At the top of her concerns was that sitting in close physical proximity to coworkers made concentrating on generating new ideas for business development very difficult. Katrina also thought that the noise from the constant chatter of coworkers was a stressor that interfered with creative thinking.

Katrina scheduled a meeting with Branson, the marketing manager, to see if she could negotiate her way out of being assigned to an open-office plan. A partial transcript of her meeting with Brandon follows:

Katrina: As I said in my e-mail, I can't stand the open-office plan. You can't expect me to do analytical work or think creatively when I feel that I'm working in a subway or on a crowded bus.

Brandon: You sure do feel strongly about the new office plan. But a lot of companies are using open-office space to spark collaboration and creativity among their workers. At Gold Medal, we are buying into an important new movement.

Katrina: I know that management has given a lot of thought to the new office layout. The problem is that it is a disaster for me and a few other workers I have spoken to.

Brandon: Maybe you have to give the new office layout a little more time.

Katrina: I've got a better idea, Brandon. How about authorizing me three days a week to work remotely? When I work from home or some other quiet location, I could do all my analytical and creative work on those days. When I am at Gold Medal headquarters, I can take care of routine work. I know that I can take care of routine work amid noise and distractions.

Brandon: You are asking for too big a change in company policy all at once. Maybe we can talk about this topic again in the near future.

Katrina: Count on me to bug you again.

Case Questions

1. Which negotiating technique or techniques does Katrina appear to be using?
2. How effective is Katrina so far in negotiating for a favorable outcome for herself?

3. To what extent is Brandon looking to find a negotiated solution to Katrina's demands?
4. What suggestions can you offer Brandon to do a better job of negotiating with Katrina?

Associated Role Play

One student plays the role of Katrina, who is intent on negotiating a deal that will exempt her from having to spend all of her time at company headquarters working under an open-office plan. She will present to Brandon at least two alternatives in addition to working remotely, such as from her home. Katrina will attempt to be passionate about her demands.

Another student plays the role of Brandon, who listens to Katrina yet wonders why she thinks she has any negotiating leverage. Brandon is not convinced that an employee asking to be exempt from the open-office plan is a negotiable demand.

Run the role play for approximately 10 minutes. Other students will provide feedback about the effectiveness of the negotiating skills and techniques displayed by the two role players.

CASE PROBLEM 4B: Working Out a Deal for an Empty Detroit Building

Sam and Abigail are a young married couple, with both holding reasonably well-paying positions in Detroit, Michigan. Sam is the sales manager at one location of a discount tire-and-muffler chain. Abigail is the office manager at a large dental practice. Yet the couple has jointly decided they want to take on a more adventuresome occupational role.

Sam and Abigail have been exploring potential opportunities for several months. At this point, they think that opening an uncomplicated restaurant is something they could handle well. After conducting research and thinking hard of alternatives on their own, Sam and Abigail decide that opening a moderate-size soup-and-salad restaurant would constitute a prudent risk. As Abigail said, "We are both pretty good basic cooks, and we could hire my mother to help with meal preparation."

Sam replied, "I agree, but first we have to find a good location for the restaurant." After one week of investigation, Sam and Abigail found a building located on Van Dyke Street in Detroit. The building had seen better days, but it had the charm of an older Detroit building. The building contained 2,034 square feet, sat on a lot of .01 acres, and had an asking price of $30,000. With a stretch, including a small loan from the family, Sam and Abigail decided they could pay cash for the building, but thought they could do better than the asking price. (In 2019, downtown Detroit was making a comeback, yet there were still hundreds of residential and commercial buildings for sale at around $25,000.)

A couple of days later, Sam and Abigail met on a Saturday morning with Carlos, the real estate agent who had listed the property. The building had been vacant for one year and needed considerable renovation to make it suitable for a restaurant.

Carlos spoke first: "Thanks for coming out here. You say you want to convert this nice old building into a restaurant. You are making a smart choice—the location is good for a low-priced restaurant, and the building has solid fundamentals. The owner is letting the building go at $25,000. He is taking a loss but wants to uncomplicate his life."

Abigail responded to Carlos: "The owner could possibly be taking a loss, but so are thousands of other owners of buildings in Detroit. Sam and I both know that most of these buildings cannot be sold and are soon to be demolished under a state and local program. We also know that an old building like this without any parking space has limited appeal."

"You and Sam have done your homework," said Carlos. "But not every old building on the market is headed for demolition. I want you two to get a fair deal, including a promising location for your restaurant."

Abigail and Sam then took a three-minute time-out to confer with each other. Sam then said to Carlos, "We are offering you $21,000 cash that we will pay in 24 hours. Your client won't have to worry about us qualifying for a mortgage."

Carlos, "You are nice people, and I enjoy doing business with you, but my client won't budge on any offer less than $24,500."

"We like doing business with you also. See if your client will change his mind and take a $23,750 cash deal."

Carlos said, "I will get back to my client with your offer of $23,750 later this afternoon. But you run the risk of my client rejecting your offer and a better offer coming along."

Sam replied, "We are prepared to run the risk. We also think that we are making a sensible offer."

Carlos ended the meeting by saying, "We'll be talking or texting later this afternoon. I know that we can reach a good deal for you."

Case Questions

1. Identify at least two negotiating techniques used in this case.
2. What negotiating suggestion might you make to Sam and Abigail?
3. What negotiating suggestion might you make to Carlos?
4. As an aside, what do you see as the chances of a soup-and-salad restaurant prospering in a section of Detroit with such low-priced buildings?

Associated Role Play

Three different students play the roles of Sam, Abigail, and Carlos. The case provides much of the scenario for the role plays. A big difference, however, is that this time, Sam, Abigail, and Carlos end with a deal before they leave. You guessed it: After the deal is complete, the three go out for a soup-and-salad lunch.

Run the role play for approximately 10 minutes. Other students will provide feedback about the effectiveness of the negotiating skills and techniques displayed by the two role players.

Notes

1. Michael E. Roloff, Linda L. Putnam, and Lefki Anastosiou, "Negotiation Skills." In John O. Greene and Brent R. Burleson, editors, *Handbook of Communication and Social Interaction Skills* (Mahwah, NJ: Lawrence Erlbaum Associates, 2003), p. 804.

2. Alison Wood Brooks, "Defusing Anxiety," *Executive Leadership*, September 2014, p. 7.

3. Kimberlyn Leary, Julianna Pillemer, and Michael Wheeler, "Negotiating with Emotion," *Harvard Business Review*, January–February 2013, pp. 96–103.

4. Several major points in this section are based on G. Richard Shell, *Bargaining for Advantage* (New York: Viking/Penguin, 1999), pp. 22–37.

5. Roloff, Putnam, and Anastosiou, "Negotiation Skills" p. 808.

6. Ibid., p. 801.

7. "To Agree or Disagree?" *Chicago Tribute Career Builder*, November 4, 2007, Section 6, p. 1.

8. Alison Wood Brooks, "In Negotiation, Make 'em Laugh!" *Executive Leadership*, January 2018, p. 7. Some of the content for the article was provided by the Program on Negotiation at Harvard Law School.

9. Deepak Malhotra and Max H. Bazerman, "Investigative Negotiation," *Harvard Business Review*, September 2007, pp. 72–78.

10. Paul Ziobro, "Teamsters Tell UPS: No Delivery Drones or Driverless Trucks," *Wall Street Journal*, January 25, 2018, p. B6.

11. Research reported in Kristi Hedges, "Six Surprising Negotiation Tactics That Can Get You the Best Deal," *Forbes* (www.forbes.com), December 5, 2013, pp. 2–3.

12. William Ury, *The Power of a Positive No* (New York: Random House, 2007).

13. Joseph Grenny, "How to Deal with the Irrational Parts of a Negotiation," *Harvard Business Review* (https://hbr.org), June 6, 2016, pp. 1–6.

14. Roloff, Putnam, and Anastosiou, "Negotiation Skills" p. 811.

15. "Fight Last-Minute Negotiation Demands," *Executive Leadership*, March 2015, p. 8. Adapted from Max Bazerman, *The Power of Noticing: What the Best Leaders See* (New York: Simon & Schuster, 2014).

Advanced Negotiation Tactics

CHAPTER 5

Source: comzeal images/Shutterstock

Learning Objectives

After reading and studying this chapter and doing the exercises, you should be able to:

1. Mention a few ideas contained in negotiation theory related to advanced tactics.
2. Describe the steps in the negotiation process.
3. Describe at least five negotiation tactics dealing mostly with facts and information.
4. Describe at least five negotiation tactics dealing mostly with behavior and emotions.

Chapter Outline

A Glance at Negotiation Theory and the Steps in Negotiation

A Few Aspects of Negotiation Theory Related to Advanced Tactics

The Steps in the Negotiation Process

Tactics Dealing Mostly with Facts and Information

Persuasive Arguments

Principled Negotiation

The Min-Max Approach

Sharing Information

Imagining Alternatives

The Stalking Horse

Tactics Dealing Mostly with Behavior and Emotions

Making the First Offer

Asking the Other Side, "What Is It You Want Me to Do?"

Effective Use of Silence

Gaining Leverage

Observing the Other Side's Tone of Voice

Using Ultimatums and the Threat of Walking Out

Dealing with an Impasse

Dozens, if not hundreds, of negotiation tactics have been reported and/or practiced, with new approaches or adaptations of older approaches continuing to appear. Chapter 4 described a handful of well-recognized strategies and tactics. In this chapter we describe tactics that might be considered more advanced, although the distinction between basic and advanced tactics is far from absolute. We also present a concise amount of negotiation theory and a well-established description of the steps in negotiation.

A Glance at Negotiation Theory and the Steps in Negotiation

To provide a conceptual footing for negotiation tactics and strategies, this section introduces some negotiation theory and a process model of negotiation.

A Few Aspects of Negotiation Theory Related to Advanced Tactics

Chapter 1 presented a few useful definitions of negotiation. For a more advanced understanding of negotiation, including advanced tactics, consider this synthesis of the common elements in the definition of negotiation developed by Aldo de Moor and Hans Weigand: In negotiation, there are two or more interdependent participants, each of whom has some individual goals that may be partially incompatible. Following a process, alternatives are investigated, with the purpose of finding one of them acceptable.[1]

Negotiation models differ in whether they are descriptive or prescriptive. *Descriptive models* attempt to carefully describe what actually happens, whereas *prescriptive models* are normative because they prescribe what negotiators should do to attain their goals. Process models agree that there is at least some negotiation preparation, followed by the conduct of negotiation, then implementation of the results. If the results are not as satisfactory as anticipated, renegotiation may be necessary.[2] The negotiation strategies and tactics presented in this chapter are a blend of description and prescription. Our focus is on presenting ideas that result in more effective negotiation results.

According to negotiation theory, a critical reason that negotiators often reach suboptimal agreements is because they fail to bring to bear the appropriate knowledge required for solving the negotiation problem at hand.[3] This perspective justifies the formal study of negotiation.

The Steps in the Negotiation Process

A representative process model of the negotiation process is the one developed by G. Richard Shell,[4] which is described here and outlined in Figure 5.1. The first step is *preparing your strategy*, a cornerstone of negotiation that was included in the section about preparing for the upcoming negotiation presented in Chapter 4. The goal of preparation is to develop a specific plan of action for the situation you face. One situation you might face is a balanced concern between you and the other party. In this situation, you might be prepared for problem solving or reaching a compromise. Another situational variable is how much a relationship is valued by you and the other side, such as a supplier of plumbing supplies wanting to build a long-term relationship with a purchasing manager at Home Depot. To help build the long-term relationship, you would emphasize tactics that facilitate establishing a positive negotiating climate.

The second step is *exchanging information*. The information exchange is designed to accomplish three purposes. One purpose is to foster communication by setting a friendly and personal tone. A second purpose is to determine which specific issues will be negotiated and share perceptions on these matters. A third purpose is to establish how much leverage, or power, each side has. The representative of the plumbing-supplies company

Steps in the Negotiation Process

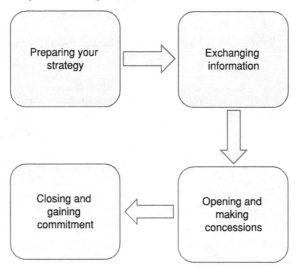

FIGURE 5.1 Steps in the Negotiation Process

Source: The steps in the negotiation process, but not the figure, are from G. Richard Shell, *Bargaining for Advantage: Negotiation Strategies for Reasonable People* (New York: Viking Penguin, 1999), p. 115.

recognizes that his or her company needs Home Depot much more than Home Depot needs the company. Hundreds of plumbing-supplies companies exist, whereas there are only a few customers the size of Home Depot.

The third step in the framework is *opening and making concessions* when the bargaining begins. (More will be said about making the opening bid later in the chapter.) The amount of leverage you have is important, such as the purchasing manager at Home Depot opening the negotiation by stating, "We are asking all our suppliers this season to find a way to reduce their prices by 5 percent. Home renovations have dipped a little lately." The more leverage you have, the less need you have to make concessions. With less leverage, you may need to be more accommodating. Assume that the supplier has a high-demand plumbing fixture that other suppliers are unable to provide. The supplier representative might say, "The only way we could reduce the price by 5 percent is if Home Depot would double the order."

The fourth step in the framework is *closing and gaining commitment.* Closing occurs when the two sides reach an agreement to resolve their problem or differences. A wide variety of tactics might be called upon to arrive at an agreement, including the most basic tactic of all, compromise. Gaining commitment may require substantial follow-up, such as a Home Depot representative getting in touch with the supplier to make sure that deliveries to the stores or a central distribution facility arrive on time. From the supplier standpoint, the company representative might follow up to find out when the actual order will be placed.

Tactics Dealing Mostly with Facts and Information

In this section we deal with negotiation tactics that focus mostly on facts and information, rather than behavior and emotions. Nevertheless, negotiation is a highly subjective process that always involves psychological factors.

Persuasive Arguments

Presenting a persuasive argument for your demands or offer is an obvious negotiating tactic. Yet, developing your argument, including marshaling convincing facts, may take considerable time. In Chapter 3, persuasion skills were presented as a major contributor to effective negotiation. An example of a persuasive argument took place during the week-long Los Angeles teacher strike in 2019. One of the key demands of the teachers' union, United Teachers Los Angeles, was to reduce class sizes. The persuasive argument supporting the union's demands was that when class sizes are too large, less time is available to help individual students, with the quality of education thereby suffering.

Principled Negotiation

A comprehensive negotiating scheme, principled negotiation, was developed by the Harvard Negotiation Project and then made prominent by the classic bestseller *Getting to Yes*, by Robert Fisher and William Ury. **Principled negotiation** is a method of deciding issues on their merit, rather than through a haggling process of what each side says it will and will not do, instead looking for mutual gains.[5] The four components of principled negotiation are presented next.

principled negotiation
A method of deciding issues on their merit, rather than through a haggling process of what each side says it will and will not do, instead looking for mutual gains.

1. *People: Separate the people from the problem.* In negotiation, there is a substantive problem that needs resolution, such as Katrina, a department head, wanting money to update software in the six machines in her department. At the same time, Katrina has to deal with the relationship involved in negotiating this problem with the division president, Malcolm, with whom she wants to maintain a cordial relationship. Fisher and Ury recommend that the negotiator be "soft on people and hard on the problem." Following this advice, Katrina would carefully explain what the existing software cannot do in terms of productivity and what the new software could accomplish to enhance productivity. At the same time, Katrina would not attack Malcolm for being shortsighted or having a limited understanding of technology. Instead, Katrina would position herself as a business partner who wants to improve productivity.

2. *Interests: Focus on interests, not positions.* Rather than clinging to specific negotiating points, keep your overall interests in mind, and try to satisfy them. A key benefit of focusing on interests rather than positions is that it helps you move the emphasis away from winning and toward what you really want to achieve. If you focus on mutual interests, your intent will be to solve a problem rather than to outmaneuver the other side. For example, if a customer makes an unreasonable demand, your best interest is to somehow satisfy that demand without losing money and also to retain the customer.

3. *Options: Invent options for mutual gain.* The essence of integrative bargaining is to find options for mutual gain, the win–win approach. Joint problem solving, including the search for creative alternatives, is usually required to uncover options for mutual gain. In the Los Angeles teacher strike, the decreased class size could be an option for mutual gain. It is conceivable that the students would soon perform better on standardized tests, creating a climate whereby the California legislature would grant the school system more money in future years.

4. *Criteria: Insist on objective criteria.* People can get very emotional when negotiating and may insist that their demand or offer is reasonable. Quite often, the justification for their position is that their intuition, common sense, or sense of justice is the basis for their offer or demand. If both parties agree to use whatever objective criteria, or standards, are available, negotiations can move more quickly. Suppose a potential franchisee is negotiating the required down payment for a fitness center. Because this chain of fitness centers is not well established, room for negotiation exists. Instead of the franchiser and potential franchisee spending many hours negotiating the size of the down payment, they can conduct research about the down payments for comparable fitness centers across the country, perhaps arriving at $75,000 as the average. At a minimum, the negotiation range will now be narrowed, saving both parties considerable time and haggling.

The widely accepted negotiation strategy of the best alternative to a negotiated agreement, or BATNA (discussed in Chapter 4), is another aspect of principled negotiation. A BATNA frees negotiators from thinking that reaching an agreement is an absolute necessity.

The Min-Max Approach

When establishing goals for negotiation, as described in Chapter 4, a negotiator has already thought about the minimum he or she will accept as well as the maximum he or she will give. A min-max specifies the minimum the negotiator will accept as well as the maximum the negotiator will give away. The owner of a lakefront cottage who rents it for part of the summer might conclude, "The minimum I will accept for weekly rentals is $1,000, and the maximum I will ask for is $2,000 per week." Professor Edward G. Wertheim of Northeastern University suggests that to use the min-max approach, you should ask these four planning questions[6]:

1. What is the minimum I can accept to resolve the problem?
2. What is the maximum I can ask for without appearing outrageous?
3. What is the maximum I can give away?
4. What is the least I can ask for without appearing outrageous?

In answering these questions, it is helpful to empathize with the other side so that you can anticipate his or her answers to the same questions. For example, if the cottage owner asked $2,000 for a week-long rental, would the answer be, "Go jump in the lake"?

> **min-max** Specifies the minimum the negotiator will accept as well as the maximum the negotiator will give away.

Sharing Information

As described in Chapter 1, information sharing is a characteristic of an effective negotiating situation and is also an effective negotiating tactic by itself. Sharing information contributes to a positive negotiating climate that is conducive to reaching an agreement.[7] Self-Quiz 5-1 gives you the opportunity to think through your tendencies toward sharing knowledge and information.

Imagining Alternatives

A key challenge during negotiation is to have an alternative in mind in case negotiation does not go your way. The BATNA tactic applies when you really have an alternative. New research suggests that simply imagining an alternative can also bring you some power during negotiation. A series of laboratory studies demonstrated that imagining strong alternatives causes powerless individuals to negotiate more ambitiously. Negotiators reached more profitable agreements when they had a stronger tendency to simulate alternatives or were instructed to simulate an alternative. The researchers point out that the imagined alternative should be a good one and that the technique works best when you make the first offer.[8]

Three examples of potentially effective alternatives are (1) a job hunter imagining that he has already received an attractive job offer elsewhere, (2) a procurement specialist imagining that she has already located another vendor who offers high quality and low price for the product in question, and (3) a small-business owner imagining that he has already located a lower-price garbage hauler when negotiating the price of trash removal.

The Stalking Horse

An advanced and complex negotiation tactic reserved for dealing with bankruptcies of large business enterprises is the *stalking-horse bid*. The term "stalking horse" derives from the 16th century when hunters would hide behind their horse as they moved slowly toward their prey. Companies in financial crisis that are preparing to file for bankruptcy can sometimes accomplish a restructuring of their financial situation with a sale of at least the majority of their assets, if not all. A stalking-horse bid is an initial bid on the debtor's assets. This type of bid implies that sometimes the buyer's offer is hidden from the courts, creditors, and the public. The highest initial bid becomes the bottom price at the auction for the company's assets, and the financially troubled company can then refuse lower bids.

> **stalking-horse bid** An initial bid on the debtor's assets.

When the Sears Holding Company was facing bankruptcy in 2019, its chairman Eddie Lampert was also the owner of the ESL hedge fund. Wearing his hedge-fund hat, Lampert made a stalking-horse bid to buy the remaining assets of the Sears and Kmart stores, thereby keeping over 400 stores open.

My Tendencies Toward Sharing Knowledge and Information

Directions: Indicate whether each of the following statements is mostly true or mostly false as it applies to your own attitudes and behaviors.

Statement about Sharing Knowledge and Information	Mostly True	Mostly False
1. I am very secretive at work or school.		
2. The other side in a negotiation usually cannot be trusted, so reveal as little information as you can.		
3. I post lots of information about myself on social media sites.		
4. During a negotiation, I would be vague about how much I was willing to pay or offer as long as possible.		
5. Only a fool would tell coworkers about a great idea he or she had for a new business.		
6. An effective negotiating trick is to keep the other side guessing about what you really think about his or her offer or demand.		
7. A good path to negotiation success is to be as open and candid as possible.		
8. A good path to negotiation failure is to be as open and candid as possible.		
9. I think that it is important that laws about intellectual property rights be strictly enforced.		
10. During a negotiation, it is essential to be evasive about how well your company is doing financially.		
11. If I were trading in one vehicle for another, I would tell the sales representative the real problems with my trade-in.		
12. I think that the other party in a negotiation should be willing to tell me up front the maximum offer he or she is willing to make.		
13. I think that the other party in a negotiation should be willing to tell me up front the minimum demand he or she is willing to make.		
14. I worry a lot about a manager stealing my ideas, even if he or she appears to be honest.		
15. During the warm-up part of a negotiation, I think that it is a good idea to swap details about the personal lives of all the parties involved.		

Scoring and Interpretation: Give yourself 1 point for having answered Mostly True to the following statements: 3, 7, 8, 11, 12, 13, and 15. Give yourself 1 point for having answered Mostly False to the following statements: 1, 2, 4, 5, 6, 9, 10, and 14.

12 or higher: You have very positive attitudes toward sharing knowledge with others inside or outside of negotiations. However, you might be a little too trusting of people whose intentions you do not know.

5–11: You have about average attitudes toward information sharing.

0–4: You have negative attitudes toward information sharing, and you may need to become a little more open with your knowledge and information to be more effective during a negotiation.

A potential limitation of a stalking-horse bid is that the negotiated bid between the company in debt and the bidder may not be approved by the bankruptcy court or the creditors' committee. Furthermore, a higher bid for the assets might surface during the auction.[9]

The accompanying Negotiation and Conflict Resolution in Action feature illustrates a reliance on facts and information in a negotiation between two of the best-known retailers in the United States.

NEGOTIATION AND CONFLICT RESOLUTION IN ACTION

In early 2019, CVS Health Corp. was in a dispute with Walmart Inc. over the cost of filling prescriptions. As a pharmacy benefits manager (PBM), CVS Caremark reimburses pharmacies when customers with CVS Caremark prescription coverage purchase pharmaceuticals. CVS is a major U.S. pharmacy chain and has close to 10,000 locations. The Caremark division oversees benefits for about 93 million people, including setting up networks of pharmacies where customers can pick up their prescriptions. Walmart is also a major pharmacy operator, with almost 5,000 in-store locations. PBMs like CVS Caremark have been criticized by consumers, lawmakers, and regulators for a lack of transparency about the prices and rebates they negotiate with drug manufacturers.

CVS Health had requested that Walmart continue to fill prescriptions as an in-network participating pharmacy through April 2019.

Caremark said that Walmart wanted an increase in what the retail giant was paid for prescriptions at the company's in-store pharmacies. A negative consequence was that patients would have paid more for their medicine. Another version of the dispute is that Walmart was not asking CVS to increase the amount it paid the retailer when customers filled a prescription. Instead, Walmart demanded CVS to maintain prescription rates at the same level. CVS Health had requested that Walmart continue to fill prescriptions as an in-network participating pharmacy through April 2019.

CVS and Walmart had at first failed to agree on pricing, prompting Walmart to leave the pharmacy network for prescription drug plans that CVS manages for companies, for health insurers, and for the Medicaid program for low-income people.

As negotiations began, CVS noted that it had a large network of 63,000 pharmacies without Walmart. Less than 5 percent of its members enrolled in the plans involved in the dispute relied exclusively on Walmart to fill prescriptions. Walmart decided to stop filling prescriptions for customers who received their pharmacy benefits through the CVS Caremark pharmacy networks. A Walmart spokesperson said that the company was disappointed because "CVS chose not to come to a resolution in a way that is beneficial to their members who are also customers." The spokesperson added that Walmart wanted to pass along savings to its customers rather than to a middleman.

A couple of days after the dispute was made public, CVS and Walmart announced that they had reached a negotiated agreement under which Walmart could continue being a member of the CVS PBM network and Managed Medicaid retail. Owing to the agreement, the CVS pharmacy network will maintain approximately 68,000 outlets.

CVS Caremark CEO Derica Rice commented, "We are very pleased to have reached a mutually agreeable solution with Walmart. As a PBM, our top priority is to help our clients and consumers lower their pharmacy costs." She added that the new agreement accomplished Caremark's top priority and enabled Walmart to continue participating in CVS's commercial and Managed Medicaid pharmacy networks. Additionally, it provided enhanced network stability for the company's clients and the PBM members.

Industry analyst Ross Muken said the speed at which the dispute was resolved demonstrates the negotiating strength of PBMs in contract discussions. Consumers typically have their prescriptions filled where their health insurance is accepted. Walmart would therefore have lost out on an estimated 15 to 20 million prescriptions it receives from customers who are covered by

CVS Caremark. Sean Slovenski, a Walmart senior vice president, said in a press release that the terms of the negotiated settlement were "fair and equitable."

Questions

1. What shared objective might Caremark and Walmart have had that helped attain a speedy negotiated solution to their dispute?
2. What is your opinion about which side held the balance of power in this negotiation?

Source: Original story based on the following sources: "Walmart Exiting CVS Commercial, Managed Medicaid Retail Pharmacy Networks," *Progressive Grocer* (http://progressivegrocer.com), January 15, 2019, pp. 1–2; Anna Wilde Matthews and Sarah Nassauer, "CVS Health and Walmart Could Split over Dispute," *Wall Street Journal*, January 16, 2019, p. B2; Robert Langreth and Matthew Boyle, "Walmart Splits with CVS after a Battle over Prescription Costs," *Bloomberg* (www.bloomberg.com), January 15, 2019, pp. 1–2; "CVS, Walmart Reach Pharmacy Network Agreement," *Breaking the News* (www.breakingthenews.net), January 18, 2019, p. 1; Caroline Humer and Ankur Banerjee, "CVS, Walmart Resolve Pharmacy Contract Impasse," *Reuters* (www.reuters.com), January 18, 2019, pp. 1–2.

Tactics Dealing Mostly with Behavior and Emotions

In this section we describe advanced negotiation tactics that tend to emphasize behavior and emotion rather than facts and information.

Making the First Offer

Plausible arguments have been advanced for making the first offer in negotiations. Business broker Gary Miller notes that conventional negotiating wisdom says it is better to wait. Such advice makes intuitive sense, but it fails to account for the powerful effect that first offers often have on how people think during negotiation. In situations of ambiguity and uncertainty, first offers have an anchoring effect and might exert a strong pull throughout the negotiation. High anchors direct our attention toward a demand or offer's positive attributes. In contrast, low anchors direct attention to the flaws of the demand or offer.

Anchoring research suggests that making the first offer often results in a bargaining advantage for the person or side making the offer. Because numerical values pull judgments toward themselves, they are termed *anchors*. When a seller makes the first offer, the final price tends to be higher than when the buyer makes the first offer.

Despite the advantages of making the first offer, it may not be advantageous when the other side has much more information than you do about the transaction to be negotiated. For example, buyers and sellers represented by investment bankers often have more in-depth knowledge than do unrepresented buyers and sellers.[10]

Christopher Voss was a chief hostage negotiator for the Federal Bureau of Investigation (FBI) and now teaches the art of negotiation as an adjunct professor at two universities. He strongly advocates letting the other side go first, commenting that negotiators typically want to speak first, but they are not listening. Voss says, "You are wasting your time if you go first. In addition, there will be mistakes or omissions in your data." Before committing to a position, it is best to extract as much information as you can from the other side. It is best not to be so certain of what you want at the beginning of a negotiation that you would not take a better offer or demand.[11]

Another relevant observation about the first offer in negotiations is whether to take it seriously. Stephen P. Robbins and Phillip L. Hunsaker recommend paying little attention to initial offers. Instead, treat an initial offer as only a point of departure.[12] Initial offers are frequently unrealistic and fall into the min-max framework, such as a building owner asking $5 million for an office building that has an assessed valuation of $3 million.

Asking the Other Side, "What Is It You Want Me to Do?"

An effective tactic for both negotiation and other forms of conflict resolution is to ask the other side what he or she would like you to do in order to reach an agreement. If you do what the other side wants, you will already have reached an agreement. The underlying psychology is that having suggested the solution, the other side will feel committed. Here is an example:

You and your teammates are dividing up work for a large task. It appears that several of your teammates do not think you are making an equitable contribution. After negotiating your contribution for about 30 minutes, you find that negotiations are stalled. You then ask, "What would you people like me to do?"

Because you are so cooperative, the other team members will probably not make an outrageous demand. Also, they will probably regard your contribution as equitable because they formulated it.

Effective Use of Silence

Silence is frequently an effective negotiation tactic. If you are silent, the other party is likely to think about what you just offered or demanded, thereby reinforcing what you just stated. The use of silence, however, must be executed strategically. You first make your offer or demand, then wait for your counterpart's reaction instead of elaborating more on what you just said. The silence creates a void that the other party might feel obliged to fill with words, and these words might work in your favor.[13] An investor in accounts receivable might say to a city official, "I see some value in that bucket of long-overdue taxes. I will give you 25 cents on the dollar for your entire portfolio of unpaid taxes." The investor then says nothing, and the city official says, "Twenty-five cents on the dollar is better than what we have now. I will get back to you after I talk with the debt committee members."

Silence is frequently an effective negotiating tactic.

Gaining Leverage

In negotiation, the person who has leverage holds a perceived advantage that can give him or her an edge in attaining his or her goal. Leverage is the power that one side of a negotiation has to influence the other side to accept his or her position. Having leverage means about the same thing as having psychological power, and it is based on one side's ability to award benefits and impose costs on the other side.

leverage The power that one side of a negotiation has to influence the other side to accept his or her position.

A current example of negotiators with exceptional leverage is the sales representatives from Aardvark, the leading manufacturer of paper straws. The leverage stems from the fact that many municipalities are banning or planning to ban plastic drinking straws. From 2017 to 2018, the demand for the high-quality paper straws increased by 50 times the previous period (5,000 percent). A high-quality paper straw holds up for more than one hour when immersed in a drink. Aardvark is currently producing more than 1 million straws per day and cannot keep up with demand.[14] A sales representative for Aardvark would therefore have considerable leverage in selling straws to McDonald's or Burger King.

Professional negotiator Derek Gaunt suggests that an effective way of gaining leverage is to *identify a black swan*, or something that has a major impact on the negotiation. The black swan is usually a valuable piece of information that can change the direction of the conversation and, by extension, the outcome of the conversation.[15] An Aardvark representative, for example, might inform a customer representative about pending legislation banning plastic straws.

An Aardvark representative, for example, might inform a customer representative about pending legislation banning plastic straws.

Observing the Other Side's Tone of Voice

According to Voss, the most reliable nonverbal indicator of a change in demand by the other party is a change in voice tone. A former general manager of the L.A. Dodgers told Voss that in a two-hour negotiation, there will be 90 seconds of solid gold, and that is the key to the entire deal.[16] The "solid gold" might be a lowered tone of voice, such as a union representative saying to her counterpart softly, "We still think the absence of time-recording devices is important." Earlier in the negotiation, she might have spoken in a loud tone about the demand for getting rid of time-recording devices for indicating when employees check in and out of work.

Using Ultimatums and the Threat of Walking Out

When faced with an apparent impasse during negotiations, some people become emotionally upset and/or issue ultimatums. For example, "If you can't find any money in your budget, why should I bother talking to you?" Or the negotiator might leave the negotiation temporarily or permanently, quickly dooming any potential deal under consideration. Walking away from a negotiation that is going poorly is included in both the BATNA and min-max tactics.

Negotiating specialist and business professor Stuart Diamond suggests, "Keep your emotions in check or you'll be checking out of your negotiation." Diamond writes that as a headhunter (executive search specialist), he has heard hardline reactions from both job candidates and hiring managers. When hearing Diamond relay the offer from a hiring manager, a candidate might say, "There is no way I am even going to consider such a ridiculous salary." And when Diamond returns to the hiring manager with a counteroffer from the candidate, a hiring manager might say, "This is all we are going to offer for the position, and the candidate can take it or leave it." When both parties take such irrevocable positions, the negotiation outcome is lose-lose.[17]

Dealing with an Impasse

impasse A situation that takes place when the two sides attempting to resolve a problem are unable to reach an agreement and become deadlocked.

The threat of walking out of negotiations, followed by an actual walking out, leads to a breakdown in negotiation. An impasse takes place when the two sides attempting to resolve a problem are unable to reach an agreement and become deadlocked. The consequences of an impasse can be severe, such as government services being shut down, a labor union going on strike, or an employer locking out workers. The Program on Negotiation at Harvard Law School recommends four techniques that professional negotiators can use to build trust and overcome an impasse when the bargaining becomes adversarial[18]:

1. *Adopt a gain frame.* Negotiations dealing with costs and losses, such as a mortgage foreclosure or a budget shortfall, are generally more competitive and challenging than those involving benefits and assets, such as a home purchase or budget surplus. A rigid attitude can be self-defeating when negotiating over losses. Attempt to identify any benefits that accompany the difficulties you anticipate, and encourage your counterpart to do the same. For example, if you receive a much smaller budget than anticipated, develop greater fiscal restraint, such as searching for a lower-cost supplier.

2. *Think multiple steps ahead.* When you are faced with an unappealing demand or offer, think multiple steps ahead before refusing to negotiate or compromise unless the other party submits to meeting your conditions. Rigid positions and outright rejections can trigger a protracted impasse.

A rigid attitude can be self-defeating when negotiating over losses.

It can work to advise the other party about what aspects of your offer are the most palatable and what the other party might ask for in return for concessions. For example, "If we renovate your storm-damaged building at a price higher than your other bids, you will know that an excellent job will be accomplished on time. Maybe you would want us to throw in renovating an older office that was not storm damaged."

3. *Keep talking.* Refusal to negotiate on an issue of major importance can have dysfunctional consequences. Individuals and organizations sometimes refuse to negotiate, thinking that the counterpart will back down as the costs inflicted by an impasse mount. A problem often overlooked in the negative emotions involved in the negotiation is that the impasse imposes substantial damages on both sides. As time passes, the two sides often become more unyielding. If the two parties do agree to restart negotiations, the ill will that accumulates during the impasse will make the talks more tension-filled and challenging. An example would be a schoolteacher strike that lasts for three months, leaving both sides bitter, as well as students and parents suffering the consequences.

4. *Attempt to build trust and goodwill.* Negotiation is usually a more hopeful means of resolving a conflict and ending an impasse than refusing to negotiate. When talks have reached an impasse, try building trust and goodwill by proposing that relatively minor issues be negotiated first. However bitter the negotiations, a display of empathy can help build trust and goodwill. For example, in an impasse between management and the labor union, a management representative might say to a union leader, "I recognize that it is a living nightmare for your workers to be going without pay. They are probably missing mortgage, rent, and car payments. We have to find a solution to this negation breakdown together."

Summary

Negotiation models differ in whether they are descriptive or prescriptive. Process models agree that there is at least some negotiation preparation, followed by the conduct of negotiation, then implementation of the results. If the results are not as satisfactory as anticipated, renegotiation may be necessary. Negotiations often fail because the negotiators do not bring to bear appropriate knowledge.

According to a representative model, the steps in the negotiation process are as follows: preparing your strategy, exchanging information, closing and gaining commitment, and opening and making concessions.

Tactics dealing mostly with facts and information include the following: (1) persuasive arguments, (2) principled negotiation, (3) the min-max approach, (4) sharing information, (5) imagining alternatives, (6) the stalking horse.

Tactics dealing mostly with behavior and emotion include the following: (1) making the first offer; (2) asking the other side, "What is it you want me to do?"; (3) effective use of silence; (4) gaining leverage; (5) observing the other side's tone of voice; (6) using ultimatums and the threat of walking out; and (7) dealing with an impasse. Four recommendations for dealing with an impasse are (1) adopt a gain frame, (2) think multiple steps ahead, (3) keep talking, and (4) attempt to build trust and goodwill.

Key Terms and Phrases

Impasse, p. 74
Leverage, p. 73
Min-max, p. 69

Principled negotiation, p. 68
Stalking-horse bid, p. 69

Discussion Questions and Activities

1. If you were going to negotiate a starting salary for yourself, what kind of preparation should you make?
2. Many employee groups are demanding a minimum wage of at least $15 per hour for entry-level workers even for service industries such as restaurants. What concessions could these employee groups make to management in order to attain their demands?
3. What persuasive argument could a supplier of wood for the furniture industry use to negotiate a price increase of 25 percent?
4. Assume that you are negotiating to purchase a distressed property in order to renovate the property and then sell it at a profit ("flipping" the house). Give an example of how you could be "soft on the people but hard on the problem."
5. As a team leader in a manufacturing company, you are negotiating for funds to outfit your team of 12 people in team T-shirts and caps. Where could you find "objective criteria" to use in your negotiation?
6. Why might leadership in a company that was going bankrupt be willing to listen to a stalking-horse bid?
7. A hostage negotiator mentioned in the chapter strongly advocates letting the other side go first in a negotiation. What kind of first offer could a hostage-taker make who has five people trapped in a bank?
8. What is your opinion of the potential effectiveness of the tactic of asking the other side, "What do you want me to do?"
9. Imagine a sales representative for paper straws working for Aardvark, negotiating prices with customers and potential customers. Considering all his or her leverage, why should the sales rep worry about building a positive negotiating climate?
10. Imagine that you have just paid $3,000 more than you anticipated for the vehicle of your choice. What type of "gain frame" can you possibly adopt?

Skill-Building Exercise: Imagining Alternatives in Negotiation

Research cited in this chapter suggests that in many negotiating situations, having imaginary or simulated alternatives leads to an effective outcome for the negotiator. A caveat, however, is that the imagined alternative should be of high quality. For each of the five following scenarios, develop a sensible alternative to the stated negotiating offer or demand. The alternative might also be regarded as a backup possibility in case the demand or offer is not met.

Scenario 1: You have five years of work experience in your field, and you are job hunting to advance your career. Develop an imaginary alternative you have to staying in your present position to give you more strength in your job hunt.

Scenario 2: A couple living in Toronto, Ontario, wants to relocate to the West Coast, so they place their three-bedroom condominium on the market for $750,000. Give this affluent couple an imaginary alternative as they review offers from potential buyers.

Scenario 3: A nonprofit social agency provides help, including memory training, to people experiencing Alzheimer's disease. Fantasia, the agency head, is going to ask the state to provide her agency $1 million to help keep it running for the upcoming fiscal year. Fantasia knows this is a lot of money to demand, but she is passionate about her agency's purpose and the services it provides. Develop an imaginary alternative to not receiving $1 million in funding from the state.

Scenario 4: Rondo, the owner of a small software development company, has developed a computerized camera and sensing device that detects unsafe exhaust systems as vehicles pass through a highway toll booth. The owners of the vehicles are then sent a request to replace or repair the defective exhaust system. Rondo thinks that because of the interest in climate change, a device that can help reduce noxious emissions from vehicles is very valuable. A major high-tech firm offers to acquire Rondo's firm for $25 million. Develop an imaginary alternative offer for Rondo's firm as he negotiates with the high-tech firm.

Scenario 5: Your retired parents are relatively young and in good health, but they are bored. They decide they would like to own and operate a small boutique, perhaps four days a week, to give more purpose to their lives. On the Internet, you find a dog- and cat-grooming business, Heavenly Groomers, for sale that you think would be ideal for your parents. Using your parents' funds, you will offer a maximum of $35,000 for Heavenly Groomers. Develop an alternative to purchasing this business to give you strength in your negotiation.

Abigail is a branch manager at Property Appraisals LLC, a regional company whose primary business is appraising the value of residential properties. The appraisals serve a couple of important purposes. Sellers sometimes use the appraisals to provide guidelines for setting the price of a property placed on the market. A more extensive use of the appraisals, however, is by mortgage lenders, such as banks, that want an accurate value of a house before issuing a mortgage. Abigail has a staff of four property appraisers plus an administrative assistant.

Branch revenue has shown a decline for nine consecutive quarters even though residential sales in Abigail's city have shown a slight increase over the same period. Gwenn, the CEO of Property Appraisals, has been upset with the declining number of appraisals conducted at Abigail's branch. During a face-to-face meeting with Abigail at her branch, Gwenn asked, "Will you please explain why you cannot stop the decline in business?"

Abigail responded, "As you well know, the property appraisal field is suffering from automation, and particularly algorithms. A lot of potential customers are simply visiting Zillow.com to figure out how much their home is worth. The Zestimate provided is absolutely free. Stan Humphries, the chief analyst at Zillow, boasts that the company values about 100 million homes every night, with an error rate of 4.3 percent. That's pretty tough competition."

Gwenn then countered, "Okay, I can see that if somebody wants a quick estimate of the value of a house, they might use Zillow. But what about when a person wants an appraisal that is not simply plucked off the Internet?"

Abigail said with a pained expression, "You must be aware that people are getting estimates supplied by firms in India for about $25. The Indian firm never gets near the property. They assess information from the Internet, including Google photos, and make their estimates using software. Again, that type of competition is hard to beat when we charge about $375 for an appraisal."

Gwenn said, "I am aware of the problems the home appraisal industry is facing, but I still think that your office can do better. There is still demand for customized, professionally prepared appraisals of residential properties. Stop blaming automation, and look at what you could be doing to enhance revenue in your branch."

Abigail responded, "Maybe we could work together on deciding how much of a revenue enhancement would please you."

Case Questions

1. How justified do you think Abigail is in blaming low-priced Internet appraisals for the decline in revenue at her branch?

2. Why should Gwenn bother to negotiate with Abigail about revenue-enhancement targets?

3. What approach to negotiation should Abigail take to arrive at a reasonable target for revenue enhancement for her branch?

Source: A few of the facts in this case are from the following sources: "Why Automation Is Killing the Property Appraisal Business," *Knowledge@Wharton*, August 21, 2017, pp. 1–4; Joe Light, "Mama, Don't Let Your Babies Grow Up to Be Appraisers," *Bloomberg Businessweek*, July 17, 2017, pp. 29–30.

Associated Role Play

Abigail and Gwen agree to have a discussion about negotiating a revenue-enhancement goal for Abigail's branch. One student plays the role of Abigail, who plans to open negotiations with a goal of a 2 percent revenue increase. Another student plays the role of Gwen, who opens the negotiation session with a goal of a 10 percent increase in revenues. The role players can choose any basic (Chapter 4) or advanced (Chapter 5) negotiation techniques they think will work well in this scenario. Run the role play for about 10 minutes. Observers might provide feedback on the negotiation skills of the role players.

Apple Corp. and chipmaker Qualcomm have been embroiled in an ugly legal battle for several years. Both sides have made bitter accusations against each other and filed lawsuits against each other in several countries in addition to the United States. Apple has accused Qualcomm of unfair licensing practices, and Qualcomm has countered by accusing Apple of patent infringement. Qualcomm is the major supplier of modem chips that enable smartphones to communicate over cellular networks. More than one-half of the company's profits derive from patent license fees paid by smartphone manufacturers.

Apple filed a lawsuit against Qualcomm in January 2017 that accused the company of monopolistic practices that harm Apple and the entire industry. The Federal Trade Commission filed similar charges against Qualcomm at about the same time. Qualcomm continues to insist that its business practices are legal.

Apple has disputed Qualcomm's legal right to charge very high royalties for the use of its technology. Also at issue is the Qualcomm requirement that Apple pay a percentage of the iPhone's revenue in return for the use of Qualcomm patents.

During a television interview, the Apple CEO said, "The issue we have with Qualcomm is that they have a policy of no license, no chips. This, in our view is illegal. The have an obligation to offer their patent portfolio on a fair, reasonable, and non-discriminatory basis and they don't do that. They charge exorbitant prices."

Qualcomm CEO Steven Mollenkopf and other company executives have said several times that the company expects to settle the dispute with Apple outside of court. Reports from Apple deny the possibility of such a settlement.

A key development in the controversy was that in December 2018, Apple faced trouble in China with respect to the sale of iPhones. Qualcomm won a ruling on patent infringement that banned the sale of some older iPhone models, with recent models not being affected. China is a key market for Apple, generating about one-fifth of the company's revenues. Despite the ruling, Apple continued to sell the older models through its many Apple stores in China. Apple spokesman Josh Rosenstock said, "Qualcomm's effort to ban our products is another desperate move by a company whose illegal practices are under investigation by regulators around the world." In turn, Qualcomm's general counsel Don Rostenberg said, "Apple continues to benefit from our intellectual property while refusing to compensate us."

A major development in the dispute is that Qualcomm has accused Apple of stealing valuable trade secrets and then giving them to Intel as a way of boosting the performance of Intel's chips on iPhones. Apple has been reducing its reliance on Qualcomm and instead purchases more modem chips from Intel to install in its latest iPhones.

A smaller development in the controversy between the two tech giants was that the Manheim District Court in Germany dismissed a patent lawsuit from Qualcomm against Apple. The suit was filed by Qualcomm based on Apple's use of the former's chips in Apple smartphones. The court decided that Qualcomm's lawsuit against Apple was without merit. The patent centered on the use of constant voltage in the smartphone. Because the Apple smartphones in question did not have a constant voltage, the smartphones were ruled to not violate the patent.

Qualcomm conducted an aggressive public-relations campaign against Apple. The chipmaker hired the firm Definers Public Affairs to publish negative articles about Apple on a conservative website. Another tactic was to start a false campaign to draft Tim Cook as a candidate for the president of the United States in the 2020 election. The campaign announcement might have annoyed President Trump.

Attorneys representing the U.S. International Trade Commission (ITC) have issued statements that essentially support Qualcomm's claims with respect to Apple's alleged patent infringement. A negative development for Qualcomm is that the company is facing a $1.2 billion fine from antitrust regulators in Europe after it was revealed that Qualcomm had been paying Apple to use its chips instead of chips made by competitors. The regulators contended that Qualcomm paid Apple billions of dollars to shut out competitors between 2011 and 2016. If Apple stopped using a Qualcomm chip in a device, the payments would end, and Apple would have to return a percentage of the payments made.

Qualcomm president Derek Aberle said, "If you peel apart all the arguments Apple is making, we believe firmly they are all without merit. At the end of the day, they essentially want to pay less for the technology they are using. It's pretty simple."

Case Questions

1. What hope do you see that the differences between Apple and Qualcomm are negotiable?
2. Assuming that company representatives from both sides decide to negotiate a solution to their problems, how should they begin after all the bitterness on both sides?

3. Suggest a primary offer for both Apple and Qualcomm in this complicated case.

4. How was this case settled as revealed by news sources?

Source: Original cased based on facts and alternatives in the following sources: Don Clark and Jack Nicas, "Chinese Court Says Apple Infringed on Qualcomm Patents," *New York Times* (nytime .com), December 10, 2018, pp. 1–3; "In Brief," *Bloomberg Businessweek*, December 17, 2018, p. 9; "Germany Court Dismisses Qualcomm Patent Lawsuit Against Apple," *Jurist* (www .jurist.org/news), January 15, 2019, pp. 1–4; Sara Salinas, "Apple CEO Tim Cook Rips into Qualcomm. Leaves Little Chance of Settlement in Patent Dispute," *CNBC* (www.cnbc.com), January 8, 2019, pp. 1–2; Mark Jansen, "Apple vs. Qualcomm; Everything You Need to Know," *TechMadness*, December 16, 2018, pp. 1–10.

Associated Role Play

Three role players are representatives of Apple, and three other role players are representatives of Qualcomm. The six people are engaged in a preliminary negotiation to see if the two sides can find some common ground to find a solution to their problem. Attempt to see what can be done to reduce some of the animosity between the two sides in order to attain a constructive outcome from this preliminary negotiation. Observers might provide feedback about whether this 15-minute session is productive.

Notes

1. Aldo de Moor and Hans Weigand, "Business Negotiation Support: Theory and Practice," *International Negotiation*, January 2004, p. 32.

2. Ibid.

3. Laurie R. Weingart, Elaine B. Hyder, and Michael J. Prietula, "Knowledge Matters: The Effect of Tactical Descriptions on Negotiation Behavior and Outcomes," *Journal of Personality and Social Psychology*, No. 6, 1996, pp. 1205–1217.

4. G. Richard Shell, *Bargaining for Advantage: Negotiation Strategies for Reasonable People* (New York: Viking Penguin, 1999), pp. 115–200.

5. Robert Fisher and William Ury, *Getting to Yes: Negotiating Agreement without Giving In* (New York: Penguin Books, 1983), p. xii.

6. Edward G. Wertheim, "Negotiations and Resolving Conflicts: An Overview," *EUROPARC* (https://www.europarc .org/communication-skills/pdf/Negotiation%20Skills.pdf), 2019, p. 6.

7. Kristi Hedges, "Six Surprising Negotiation Tactics That Get You the Best Deal," *Forbes* (www.forbes.com), December 5, 2013, p. 2.

8. Michael Schaerer, Martin Schweinsberg, and Roderick I. Swaab, "Imaginary Alternatives: The Effects of Mental Simulation on Powerless Negotiators," *Journal of Personality and Social Psychology*, January 2018, pp. 96–117; Schaerer, Schweinsberg, and Swaab, "Research: When You Don't Have an Alternative in a Negotiation, Try Imagining One," *Harvard Business Review*, April 19, 2018, pp. 1–6.

9. Chad Van Horn, "How Does a Stalking Horse Bid Work?" and "Stalking Horse Bid," *Investopedia* (www.investopedia .com), updated April 3, 2018, pp. 1–3; Jaason Racki, "Sears Bankruptcy and the Need for Transparency," *Fox Business* (www.foxbusiness.com), January 14, 2019, pp. 1–3.

10. Gary Miller, "Gary Miller: When to Make the First Offer in Negotiations," *The Denver Post* (www.denverpost.com), July 17, 2016, pp. 1–4.

11. Kathryn Tyler (Interviewer), "It's Negotiable: How to Get What You Want When the Going Gets Tough," *HR Magazine*, October 2015, p. 28.

12. Stephen P. Robbins and Phillip L. Hunsaker, *Training in Interpersonal Skills: Tips for Managing People at Work*, 2nd edition (Upper Saddle River, NJ: Prentice Hall, 1996), p. 245.

13. Francis Cyriac, "10 Sales Negotiation Skills Every Sales Rep Must Master," *Inside Sales Box* (www.insidesalesbox .com), 2018, p. 3.

14. Kate Krader, "Manufacturing the Good Straw," *Bloomberg Businessweek*, October 8, 2019, p. 47.

15. Derek Gaunt, "How to Gain Leverage During a Negotiation," *The Black Swan Group* (https://blog.blackswanltd .com), July 17, 2018, pp. 1–7.

16. Tyler, "It's Negotiable," p. 26.

17. "4 Ways to Win Workplace Negotiations," posted by Personal Branding Blog, *Glassdoor* (www.glassdoor.com/ blog) January 4, 2013, pp. 3–4.

18. Katie Shonk, "Will You Avoid a Negotiation Impasse?" *PON—Program on Negotiation at Harvard Law School* (www.pon.harvard.edu), December 8, 2018, pp. 1–2.

International and Cross-Cultural Negotiation

Source: UfaBizPhoto/Shutterstock.

Learning Objectives

**After reading and studying this chapter and doing the exercises,
you should be able to:**

1. Understand how cultural factors influence negotiating style.
2. Describe the influence of at least six cultural values on negotiating style.
3. Summarize face-negotiation theory.
4. Explain how cultural sensitivity is important for negotiating effectively.
5. Identify at least six international differences in negotiating style.

Most phases of business and the world economy have been profoundly affected by globalization. For the past several decades, we have moved away from a world in which individual business firms and national economies have been relatively isolated from each other by trade barriers, distance and time zones, and language. As observed by Australian professor of negotiations John Saee over a decade ago, we now live in interdependent global economic systems.[1]

An obvious implication for negotiators of globalization is that many negotiations take place with counterparts from another culture, including negotiations over the telephone, by electronic messaging, or in person. Much of the global trade involves face-to-face negotiations among corporate representatives and entrepreneurs of firms making business deals. A negotiation becomes cross-cultural when the negotiators belong to different cultures and therefore might not share the same ways of thinking, feeling, and behaving.[2]

Most of what we have already described about negotiation applies to negotiation with people from another culture. For example, establishing a positive negotiating climate is an effective universal negotiating strategy. Negotiating with people from other cultures, however, requires a layer of knowledge beyond the basics of negotiation. In this chapter we discuss cultural influences on negotiation and negotiating tactics specifically geared toward bargaining with people from other cultures.

How Cultural Factors Influence Negotiation

Cultural factors influence cross-cultural negotiations in many ways.

Cultural factors influence cross-cultural negotiations in many ways. In this section we describe how specific cultural values impact negotiation, as well as the face theory of negotiation, which helps explain cultural differences in negotiating style.

The Influence of Cultural Values on Negotiating Style

Negotiating style and effectiveness are closely related to negotiating skill and personal attributes such as cognitive ability and personality traits. Cultural values, such as a belief in sharing rewards, also influence how people go about negotiating, or their negotiating style. Here we focus on dimensions of cultural values most likely to have an impact on negotiating style. Our discussion therefore does not include all the most frequently identified dimensions of cultural values.[3] Cultural values are broad stereotypes that might apply to a typical individual from a specific culture.

individualism A mental set in which people see themselves first as individuals and believe that their own interests take priority.

collectivism A feeling that the group and society receive high priority.

1. *Individualism versus collectivism.* The dimension of cultural values most frequently linked to negotiating style is individualism versus collectivism. At one end of the continuum is individualism, a mental set in which people see themselves first as individuals and believe that their own interests take priority. Collectivism, at the other end of the continuum, is a feeling that the group and society receive high priority. Members of a society that values individualism are more concerned with their careers than with the good of the firm. Members of a society that value collectivism, in contrast, are typically more concerned with the organization than themselves. Two examples of individualistic societies are the United States and Canada. Japan and Hong Kong are among the countries that strongly value collectivism.

   Negotiators who value individualism are more likely to search for outcomes that provide them the maximum benefit, or distributed outcomes. Collectivistic negotiators are more likely to look for outcomes that benefit both sides, or integrative solutions.

2. *Egalitarianism versus hierarchy.* In some cultures, egalitarianism among workers is preferred, whereas in other cultures, hierarchy is more accepted. The extent to which employees accept the idea that members of an organization have different levels of power is also referred to as power distance. Employees, as well as people in general, who believe in power distance have a fundamental acceptance of hierarchy. They believe that people who are more experienced, older, and have more formal power should be respected.

power distance The extent to which employees accept the idea that members of an organization have different levels of power.

In a hierarchical, or high-power-distance, culture, the boss makes many decisions simply because he or she is the boss. Group members readily comply because they have a positive orientation toward authority. In a low-power-distance culture, employees do not readily recognize a power hierarchy. They accept directions only when they think the boss is right or when they feel threatened. Two examples of high-power-distance cultures are India and France, with two examples of low-power-distance cultures being the United States and Sweden.

A negotiator who strongly accepts authority and believes in hierarchy will tend to defer to a negotiator who has higher rank and more experience. The person who accepts authority will be more willing to make concessions to the person with more formal authority and will also be more willing to compromise.

3. *Long-term orientation versus short-term orientation.* Workers from a culture with a long-term orientation maintain a long-range perspective and thus are thrifty and do not demand quick returns on their investments. A short-term orientation is characterized by a demand for immediate results and a propensity not to save. Pacific Rim countries are noted for their long-term orientation. In contrast, the cultures of the United States and Canada are characterized by a more short-term orientation.

long-term orientation Workers that maintain a long-range perspective and thus are thrifty and do not demand quick returns on their investments.

short-term orientation Characterized by a demand for immediate results and propensity not to save.

The short-term versus long-term perspective has a substantial impact on negotiation behavior. If Jud, a sales representative for a microchip manufacturer, has a long-range perspective, he will be predisposed to accepting a smaller profit margin on the first sale to a toy manufacturer in order to develop a long-term, mutually beneficial relationship with the toy maker. Relationship building during negotiation is also important to a person who holds the cultural value of a long-term orientation.

4. *Formality versus informality.* A culture that values formality attaches considerable importance to tradition, ceremony, social rules, and rank. At the other end of the continuum, informality refers to a casual attitude toward tradition, ceremony, social rules, and rank. Workers in Latin American countries highly value formality, such as lavish receptions and processions. Americans, Canadians, and Scandinavians are much more informal. The workplace across the world has become much more informal, with workers at all levels making less use of titles and last names. The informality of communication via the Internet has fostered informality.

formality Attaches considerable importance to tradition, ceremony, social rules, and rank.

informality Refers to a casual attitude toward tradition, ceremony, social rules, and rank.

A negotiator who adheres to the value of informality is likely to approach negotiations in an informal manner in ways such as making frequent jokes, not being conscious of rank, and breezing over facts and figures. A potential problem for the informal negotiator is being inappropriately informal and offending a highly formal counterpart. Imagine that Daisy, an American negotiator, is in Japan negotiating a key deal. One of the people seated at the negotiating table is Harry Osaka, the 75-year-old CEO. At the start of the negotiations, Daisy says with a smile, "How are you doing, Harry? Know any good sushi restaurants?" Negotiations are off to a poor start with the formal Mr. Osaka.

5. *Urgent time orientation versus casual time orientation.* Individuals and nations have different views on the importance of time. People with an urgent time orientation perceive time as a scarce resource and tend to be impatient. People with a casual time orientation view time as an unlimited and

The workplace across the world has become much more informal, with workers at all levels making less use of titles and last names.

unending resource and tend to be patient. Americans are noted for their urgent time orientation. They frequently impose deadlines and are eager to get started doing business during negotiations. Asians and Middle Easterners, in contrast, are patient negotiators. Although rarely reported, time orientation also shows some variation with respect to the size of the city. People from large metropolitan areas tend to have a more urgent time orientation than people from smaller locations.

6. *High context versus low context.* A high-context culture is one in which societies or groups have close connections over an extended period of time. Members of the high-context culture know what type of thinking and behavior is expected based on years of interaction with each other. Nonverbal behavior, such as smiling and nodding, is used frequently during negotiation. A family business in which people have worked together for a long period of time would most likely have a high-context culture. People from high-context cultures are more formal and perceive aggression and confrontation as uncomfortable. South Korea and India are two examples of countries with high-context cultures.

A low-context culture refers to societies where people have many short-term connections. In these societies and groups, cultural behaviors and beliefs may need to be spelled out explicitly. As a result, newcomers to an organization know what types of behavior are expected. People from low-context cultures are focused more on tasks than building relationships. In low-context cultures, written contracts and legal documents are given considerable weight. Two examples of countries with low-context cultures are the United States and Germany.[4]

A negotiator from a high-context culture would prefer to build long-term connections with his or her counterparts, similar to a person with a long-term orientation. In contrast, a negotiator from a low-context culture would feel comfortable in making one-term deals with his or her counterparts. When dealing with negotiators from a high-context culture, it is important to build harmony and avoid bluntness.

A meta-analysis of gender differences in negotiation performance revealed that males outperformed females in low-context cultures. Conversely, in high-context cultures, women performed better than men. A plausible explanation for these gender differences is that women are more skilled at building relations during negotiation.[5]

7. *Risk tendency.* Cultural differences influence negotiators' willingness to assume risk. The bureaucratic systems in some cultures prefer to make decisions only when sufficient information is available. A Japanese negotiating principle is to reduce risk as much as possible and avoid face-to-face conflict. The underlying reason is that the Japanese prefer to avoid being held personally responsible for the consequences of a decision. Japanese employees therefore seldom make decisions independently to avoid being blamed for making the wrong decisions. In more entrepreneurial cultures, such as the United States and Canada, practicality and efficiency are valued. Inside or outside of negotiations, people in such cultures are willing to make decisions even if they lack some potentially useful information.

8. *The nature of agreements.* An "agreement" does not necessarily mean the same thing across cultures. For Chinese negotiators, an agreement is often used to indicate the formalness of a relationship. American negotiators often believe that an agreement is reached through a logical framework and is official and legally binding. In some countries, such as Nigeria, a contract has no associated sanctions. Negotiators in these countries believe that it is impractical to expect the other party to fulfill obligations when two parties cannot trust each other.

9. *Negotiation rituals linked to culture.* Although rituals are not cultural values, they are usually based on values and other cultural differences. For example, Americans tend not to place a strong emphasis on the counterpart's gender or job title. In contrast, Europeans are more likely to make note of the other party's job title and give light emphasis to gender. Europeans prefer that negotiators have comparable job titles or positions. Another ritual of significance is that in Southeast Asian nations, such as China

or Japan, paper business cards are formally used when parties introduce themselves to each other. A negotiator who neglects to bring a business card or writes on the other person's business card is considered to be deliberately ignoring his or her counterpart.[6]

10. *Tightness versus looseness.* An attribute of cultural values is how strong a hold they have on members of the culture. A relatively tight culture is one in which the norms for social behavior in a variety of situations are clearly defined, pervasive, and consistently imposed through sanctioning. In a tight culture, people adjust their behavior to the norms and sanctions of a given situation. A relatively loose culture is one in which norms are less pervasive and behavior is less controlled because systems for social monitoring are weakly developed. Cultural looseness essentially means that people can exercise more options in their behavior. A tight culture is more likely to be found in a more homogeneous culture such as Japan or Denmark than in a more heterogeneous culture such as the United States or Canada.

Because individual behavior is influenced by context, people living in tight cultures become accustomed to basing their behavior on the strong norms and sanctioning systems that surround them in many situations. People living in loose cultures, in contrast, become accustomed to choosing their own behavior from a range of reasonably acceptable options.[7] An example of a tight culture in action during negotiation would be when a young Japanese business analyst present at the negotiation does not correct an older Japanese executive who has made an error. A public correction of this type would result in the young analyst being scorned by the group. Correcting an elder when he or she seems way off base would be more acceptable in the United States, provided the young person was a little tactful.

11. *Holistic versus analytical mind-set.* Some of the differences in how people from different cultures communicate have been attributed to cognitive differences in processing information. A mind-set is a system of thought that directs attention and reasoning. People with a holistic mind-set tend to emphasize the context of an idea, taking into account the situation as a whole. Conversely, people with an analytical mind-set focus more on content and tend to use linear reasoning. When an analytical thinker faces a contradiction, he or she prefers to choose one perspective over another.

People in Eastern cultures tend to be holistic, and people in Western cultures tend to be analytical. Negotiators from cultures with a holistic mind-set might be able to generate higher levels of insight into each other's interests and priorities. They would also be more likely to attain more joint gains from distributive bargaining than would more analytical people. In contrast, negotiators from cultures with an analytical mind-set may generate higher levels of insight and joint gains from integrative bargaining than would holistic people.[8] (Note that this is speculative theorizing and may not be influential in developing an effective negotiating strategy.)

People in Eastern cultures tend to be holistic, and people in Western cultures tend to be analytic.

Source: Stephen Coburn/Shutterstock.

Cultural specialist Jeanne M. Brett has synthesized considerable research about the differences in negotiators from Western and Eastern cultures. She concludes that there is a major cultural divide between the East and West. People from Western cultures tend to be individualistic and egalitarian and tend to use low-context communication. (In a high-context culture, limited information is in the message itself, but it must be inferred. In a low-context culture, the transmission of information is more direct.) The Eastern cultural profile emphasizes collectivism, hierarchy, and high-context communication. A caution about these broad-brush stereotypes about values is that they grossly oversimplify more fine-grained cultural differences in cultural norms. Within each region, there are many differences in negotiating norms.

Just because negotiators are from different cultures does not mean that their negotiation strategies will inevitably clash and that they will fail to reach optimal agreements. At times, negotiators representing different cultural groups may appreciate each other's cultural differences and attain high-quality results. Three factors help people negotiate successfully with representatives from different cultural groups. The first is a desire to share information. The second is having a good method to search for information, such as good interviewing techniques. Third is the motivation to search for information while negotiating.[9] The Negotiation and Conflict Resolution feature presented later in the chapter illustrates how negotiation across cultures can be successful.

Face-Negotiation Theory to Help Explain Cross-Cultural Differences in Negotiating Style

Americans and Asians have broad differences in managing conflict, including negotiations, that are due to their social upbringing. Based on their membership in collectivistic cultures, they tend to think of their whole group before making a decision when resolving a dispute. For Asians, it is more important to protect their image than it is to Americans. (See Figure 6.1.)

face-negotiation theory The theory stating that differences in handling conflict are part of maintaining face in society.

In **face-negotiation theory**, as formulated by Stella Ting-Toomey of California State University, differences in handling conflicts are part of maintaining face in society. *Face* in this context refers to the identity and personality we let others see, or our public image. The face represents oneself in society.[10] You will recall from Chapter 4 the basic negotiation skill of allowing for face-saving. Although this tactic is not based on face-negotiation theory, it contains the idea that people prefer not to be embarrassed a result of the outcome of the negotiation.

In more technical terms, face is an individual's claimed sense of favorable image in the context of social and relational networks. The process of negotiation can be considered both a social and relational network. *Facework* refers to the behavior that people use to implement a self-face and to challenge another version of their perceived face or image.

Although face-negotiation theory emphasizes cultural factors, later versions of the theory also take into account individual and situational influences on facework and conflict behavior. People from all cultures and in all situations prefer to save face when

FIGURE 6.1 Face-Negotiation Theory

dealing with conflict. The fundamental assumption of face theory is that people in all cultures attempt to maintain and negotiate face in communication. Conflict is essentially a face-negotiation process that is influenced by cultural as well as individual factors.

Face-negotiation theory continues to expand in terms of its details and propositions, but one key proposition is particularly relevant to negotiation. Members of a collectivistic culture or individuals who are interdependent in terms of defining themselves tend to be more mutual-face oriented, avoiding, obliging, compromising, and integrating. In contrast, members of individualistic cultures or individuals who are independent of others in their self-definition tend to be more self-face oriented and competing. The cultural stereotype here is that a negotiator from Japan, China, or Taiwan, would be more eager to bargain his or her way to an integrated solution than would an American.

A practical implication of face-negotiation theory is that individualistic people attempt to resolve conflicts in a competing and aggressive way. Collectivistic people, on the other hand, attempt to resolve conflicts in a compromising and accommodating way. Collective behavior is more likely to be present in people who are more worried about their image in society. Ting-Toomey points out that people from a collectivistic culture try to save face for others also. For example, if a coworker were late for work, the collectivistic individual might mention to the boss that the main highway getting to the office was clogged that morning.

Face-negotiation theory, as with any other approach to formulating cultural stereotypes, has its limitations. Within every culture, there are individual differences in how people prefer to negotiate conflict. Also, cultural values shift over time. In the United States, for example, there is so much emphasis on teamwork in the workplace, in sports, and in the community that there might be less emphasis on individualism today than there was in the past.

Cross-Cultural and International Negotiation Tactics

Negotiation is one of the single most important skills for the international manager or specialist. A challenge facing the international worker is how to negotiate successfully with people from other cultures. Part of the challenge is that there are many other differences in negotiating styles and techniques across cultures. We approach this challenge with a discussion of three key topics: developing cultural sensitivity, adapting to differences in negotiation style, and preparing for possible cross-cultural barriers.

Developing Cultural Sensitivity

A major requirement for becoming a multicultural worker as well as a multicultural negotiator is to develop cultural sensitivity, an awareness of and a willingness to investigate the reasons why people of another culture act as they do.[11] People with cultural sensitivity will recognize certain nuances in customs that will help build better relations with people from different backgrounds than their own. A positive example is that for an executive to conduct business and negotiate successfully in China, he or she must build a *guanxi*, a network of relationships or connections among parties. The *guanxi* must be built internally with subordinates, peers, and superiors, as well as externally with clients, suppliers, and government officials. Relationship building of this type takes time, but it is a cultural imperative in China.[12]

cultural sensitivity An awareness of and a willingness to investigate the reasons why people of another culture act as they do.

Developing cultural sensitivity is helpful in figuring out what would be an effective negotiating tactic in a given situation. The specific tactics described in this chapter are helpful, but they are based on cultural stereotypes that are a starting point in knowing how to behave in a given negotiation. The culturally sensitive negotiator will observe how the counterpart acts and reacts, thereby learning what the best course of action is. A negotiator who is typically impatient might observe that the other negotiators in a cross-cultural setting permit other people to finish their sentences before they jump in with a comment. Being culturally sensitive, she now controls her impatience and does not speak to a counterpart until the latter has finished his or her sentence. A more superficial example of cultural sensitivity follows:

> A negotiator from Chicago was visiting Rome, Italy, for a major potential deal. While attending a dinner the night before the negotiation, he was the only man present who was not wearing a tie. At the company headquarters in Chicago, male executives almost never wore ties, but in Rome, executives typically wear expensive ties. Early the next morning before the negotiation, the Chicago executive purchased a tie in the hotel lobby and wore it to the negotiation. He felt much more comfortable during the negotiation.

Another challenge related to cultural sensitivity facing the cross-cultural negotiator is whether a translator is necessary or desirable. In recent years, the need for a foreign-language translator has diminished considerably. English has become the language of international business, replacing French many years ago. Today, most people at the managerial and professional level not only speak and understand English but also welcome the opportunity to speak English with people whose native language is English.

Nevertheless, if you are able to speak the language of your counterpart from another culture, it will help you establish rapport. Perhaps outside of the negotiating sessions you will have the opportunity to converse in the language spoken by your counterpart. Yet during negotiation, particularly with several people present, the negotiation will most likely be conducted in English.

Adapting to International Differences in Negotiating Style

By sizing up what constitutes an effective negotiating style, the negotiator stands a reasonable chance of achieving a collaborative solution. Considerable study and practice are therefore required to negotiate effectively in another culture, combined with cultural sensitivity. Following is a group of specific suggestions to adapt more effectively to differences in negotiating styles in other cultures.

Decide Whether Integrative versus Distributed Outcomes Are Preferred

A starting point in cross-cultural negotiations is whether members of the culture tend to seek integrative or distributed outcomes. A synthesis of many studies suggests that negotiators for Western nations (e.g., the United States, Germany, Israel, Norway, Sweden) are more likely to use an integrative bargaining approach. In contrast, East Asian nations (e.g., China, Hong Kong, Japan, and Thailand) are more likely to favor distributive bargaining. Negotiators from Middle Eastern/South Asian nations (e.g., India and Qatar) are more likely to favor distributive bargaining.[13]

Obtain Advance Knowledge of the Other Culture's Negotiation Style

Source: Blue Planet Studio/Shutterstock.

Americans tend to believe that a relationship develops after a contract is signed, whereas Chinese believe that a good relationship precedes signing a contract.

Part of doing your homework for negotiating in another culture involves having an awareness of negotiation stereotypes for the other culture. A few possibilities: Japanese prefer an exchange of information to confrontation; Russians love combat; Spanish negotiators are individualistic; Koreans are team players; Asians are high in context. So, you have to watch for the body language and what is *not* said.[14] These stereotypes serve as guidelines as to what negotiating style you will most probably encounter.

Emphasize Relationship Building

Professor Lieh-Ching Chang from the Hsuan Chuang University reminds us that the biggest difference between American negotiators and those of other countries is that Americans are preoccupied with the articles in a negotiation. Negotiators in other countries tend to focus on the relationship between themselves and their counterparts. Americans tend to believe that a relationship develops after a contract is signed, whereas Chinese believe that a good relationship precedes signing a contract. A blind spot of many Americans is that they believe people throughout the world want to be similar to Americans. Even when negotiating with people from other countries on their own turf, they want to do it their way. The preference of Americans for quick results in negotiation will often interfere with relationship building.[15]

Build Cognitive Trust and Affective Trust

Being trusted by the other party is a winning tactic in most negotiations and is particularly important in dealing with people from another culture. Trust includes both the cognitive and affective domains. Cognitive trust is based on the confidence one party has in another person's accomplishments, skills, knowledge, and reliability. It is trust based on logical reasoning and is task based. Affective-based trust stems from feelings of emotional closeness, empathy, or friendship. Affective trust is relationship based and arises from feelings of closeness that develop gradually, such as through dining together several times.[16]

Use a Team Approach

Many American managers are convinced they can handle any negotiation by themselves, whereas other countries rely on negotiation teams. Bringing several Americans to the negotiating table may convey seriousness of purpose and commitment. The bigger the deal and the more complex the negotiations, the more important the emphasis on a team approach.

Avoid Being Too Frank

Frank L. Acuff explains that Americans often have a no-nonsense approach to negotiation. A key attitude underlying the U.S. approach to negotiation is "Tell it like it is." A problem with this type of frankness and seeming impatience is that people from other cultures may interpret such behavior as rudeness. The adverse interpretation, in turn, may lead to a failed negotiation. Acuff gives an example: "It is unlikely in Mexico or Japan that the other side is going to answer 'yes' or 'no' to any question. You will have to discern answers to questions through the context of what is being said rather than from the more obvious direct cues that U.S. negotiators use."[17]

Related to the point just made, many Americans believe that "laying one's cards on the table" is a valuable negotiating tactic. As a consequence, they expect honest information and are frustrated when it is not forthcoming. Because many foreign negotiators routinely practice small deceptions at the negotiating table, less than full disclosure must be tolerated.

Be Patient

A striking difference between American negotiations and those in foreign cultures concerns time. Japanese, Chinese, and Arab negotiators, for example, are willing to spend many days negotiating a deal. Much of their negotiating activity seems to be ceremonial (including elaborate dining) and unrelated to the task. This often frustrates the "strictly business" American.

Use Silence as Part of Negotiation

Unlike Asian negotiators, Americans often become uncomfortable when more than 10 seconds elapses without somebody making a task-related comment. It is sometimes fruitful to remain silent and wait for the other side to make an offer or reveal the nature of his or her thinking.

Avoiding Yes-or-No Questions

A confusing aspect of international negotiations is that in some cultures, the word "yes" may be used when the true answer is "no." In other cultures, "no" is a reflex response but could mean "Let's discuss this further." A specific example is that in Indonesian culture, it is considered rude to look directly at someone whom you respect and like and say no to a request. An Indonesian manager said, "Instead we try to show 'no' with our body language or voice tone."[18]

Related to avoiding yes-or-no questions is a willingness to accept "no" when it seems appropriate. Americans tend to be highly competitive during negotiations and take each loss personally. Foreign customers and suppliers, in contrast, are often willing to lose one negotiation session to build a solid, long-term relationship with people and firms.

Know Whether to Put the Final Deal in Writing

According to cross-cultural specialist Erin Meyer, in the United States and Northern Europe, summarizing the agreement is standard practice. Yet this seemingly efficient practice can backfire in Africa or in Asia. A spoken agreement is preferable in African and Asian countries, where relationships are more important than written contracts. A Nigerian manager explained, "If the moment we come to an agreement, you pull out a contract, I start to worry. Do you think I won't follow through? Are you trying to trap me?"[19]

Deal with Trusting versus Distrusting the Other Side

It may prove helpful to vary your negotiation approach according to whether you trust or distrust the other side. Trust is often an issue in cross-cultural negotiations, such as one side fearing that the other side will steal the company's technology. Trust building is essential for establishing a positive negotiating relationship in most cultures. Three illustrative tactics to use when you trust the other side are as follows: (1) get to know your counterpart's personality, (2) engage in reciprocal questions and answers, and (3) keep agreements tentative until the end. Three illustrative tactics to use when your distrust the other side are as follows: (1) look for hidden patterns and clues in your counterpart's offers and responses; (2) make reciprocal concessions; and (3) express sympathy, apologize, or compliment your counterpart.[20]

Know the Decision-Making Authority of Your Counterpart

An effective negotiating tactic is to investigate the extent of decision-making authority held by the other party. In Chinese culture, for example, higher-level officials seldom participate in the negotiation process. When negotiating with a Chinese person, it is therefore important to identify how much authority he or she has to make negotiating decisions.[21]

A useful perspective on these suggestions is that a person is rarely on a level playing field when negotiating in another culture. Adapting to the other side's negotiating tactics may help to place negotiations on an equal footing. However, Americans should not necessarily be the only group adapting their negotiating tactics to fit different cultures. Businesspeople from around the world may have to develop a cross-cultural negotiating style that incorporates many of the elements described in the previous 10 suggestions.

Preparing for Possible Cultural Barriers

The Harvard University Program on Negotiation offers advice on how to prepare for possible cultural barriers while negotiating in another culture.[22] The reference here is to barriers directly affecting negotiation, not to barriers to cross-cultural communication in general. The first step is to research your counterpart's background and experience. If that individual is a member of LinkedIn, you can quickly obtain information about his or her résumé. One potential challenge is that when your counterpart has considerable international negotiating experience, he or she might engage in cultural stereotyping, such as thinking that an American will be impatient to complete a deal.

A second recommendation is to enlist an advisor from your counterpart's culture, particularly if the counterpart has little or no international or cross-cultural experience. Plan out signals before the actual negotiations to indicate when you should take a break to process additional advice. Your "cultural guide" can help you size up the situation, coach you if necessary, and even advise you if you have made a serious error or misinterpretation.

Third, pay close attention to the communication process during the negotiation. If you are dissatisfied with the answers from your counterpart, reframe your questions and try again. Paraphrase the other side's key responses to make sure that you are interpreting the comments correctly. As in all negotiations, the counterpart from another culture may interpret what you say differently than was your intention. For example, if an American says he would like to put an offer "on the table," he means he plans to take the offer seriously. A counterpart from the United Kingdom might think he means to "table the offer," indicating that the offer is taken out of consideration.

The accompanying Negotiation and Conflict Resolution feature illustrates how cross-cultural negotiation over major issues can be achieved.

NEGOTIATION AND CONFLICT RESOLUTION IN ACTION

Disneyland Negotiates Its Way to a Successful International Expansion

Disneyland is a worldwide success, with theme parks in the United States, Hong Kong, China, Japan, and Paris. The overseas theme parks combine beloved Disney characters with local stories and traditions, all carefully negotiated to satisfy the demands of American interests and those of the operators in the other country. Disneyland began its international theme park operations after company leadership observed how many Japanese tourists visited the two Disney parks in the United States. Tokyo Disneyland has been doing well since the 1980s, and its success prompted the company to open three more theme parks outside the United States.

Over 135 million people visit Disney's six resorts around the world each year. The guests who have visited Disney parks in more than one country do not notice any major difference between the fairytale-themed parks in each country. A major reason for the similarity is that Disney combines original Disney characters with national traditions and tastes. These small differences are carefully negotiated. For example, Japanese customs profoundly affected the Japanese design of Disney's log-flume ride called Splash Mountain. The seating arrangement in California has guests straddling the seats in a line, much like a hobby horse. A problem was that sitting in close proximity to others is not part of the Japanese culture. Imagineers therefore had to redesign the log to enable guests to sit side by side.

Cultural differences are so powerful that they can affect the content of the themed lands or even the total appearance of the park. What is feasible has to be negotiated, with Disney executives typically finding a workable compromise. At Disneyland Paris, there is a major Alice in Wonderland presence because the Imagineers knew that a multitude of British guests would visit. (The story of Alice in Wonderland was written by an English author.) More visitors to Disneyland Paris are from England than any other country except France. The French preferences are catered to with an area themed to the cartoon version of Paris appearing in the movie *Ratatouille*. Similarly, the science-themed Discovery Land in Paris was inspired by a novel of the French writer Jules Verne and presents a Victorian vision of the future.

Negotiations to build Disneyland Paris were contentious back in the early 1990s. In France, where practically no meal is complete without a glass of wine, Disney was not willing to lift its worldwide ban on alcoholic drinks in its parks. To soften its stance, Disney executives argued that Euro Disneyland (the original name in France) was of higher quality than other parks. In a show of confidence, Paris chefs were invited to taste the food being served at Euro Disneyland.

To appease the French who feared cultural colonialism, Disney negotiators made a point of emphasizing that many Disney characters, from Peter Pan to Cinderella, were based on European fables. The Disney CEO at the time, Michael Eisner, said the park had "European folklore with a Kansas twist."

Questions

1. With American culture being so well known throughout the world, why should Disneyland executives worry about negotiating culture-specific themes in its overseas parks?
2. What do you think of the merits of Disney leadership insisting that its ban on alcoholic beverages was nonnegotiable at the time? (In 2019, the ban was lifted in California for Oga's Cantina in the Star Wars: The Galaxy's Edge themed area.)

Source: Original story based on facts and observations in the following sources: Robin Raven, "Disney Theme Parks around the World," *USA Today Travel Tips* (https://traveltips.usatoday.com), March 8, 2018, pp. 1–6; Alan Riding "Only the French Elite Scorn Mickey's Debut," *New York Times*, April 13, 1992, pp. 1–4; Christian Slyt, "The Secrets behind the International Expansion of Disneyland," *Forbes* (www.forbes.com), November 19, 2015, pp. 1–3; "Business in Brief: Walt Disney Lifts Ban on Alcohol," *GoErie.com* (www.goerie.com), September 13, 2018, p. 1.

Summary

Cultural factors influence cross-cultural negotiations in many ways. The dimensions of cultural values most likely to have an impact on negotiation style are as follows: (1) individualism versus collectivism, (2) egalitarianism versus hierarchy, (3) long-term orientation versus short-term orientation, (4) formality versus informality, (5) urgent time orientation versus casual time orientation, (6) high context versus low context, (7) risk tendency, (8) the nature of agreements, (9) negotiation rituals linked to culture, (10) tightness versus looseness, and (11) holistic versus analytical mind-set.

Americans and Asians have broad differences in managing conflict, including negotiations, that are due to their social upbringing. According to face-negotiation theory, differences in handling conflict are part of maintaining face in society. The "face" is a public image that represents oneself in society. The fundamental assumption of face theory is that people in all cultures attempt to maintain and negotiate face in communication. A practical implication of face-negotiation theory is that individualistic people attempt to resolve conflicts in a competing and aggressive way. In contrast, collectivistic people attempt to resolve conflicts in a compromising and accommodating way.

A major requirement for becoming a multicultural worker as well as a multicultural negotiator is to develop cultural sensitivity. People with cultural sensitivity will recognize certain nuances in customs that will help build better relations with people with backgrounds different from their own. Developing cultural sensitivity is helpful in figuring out what would be an effective negotiation tactic in a given situation.

Specific suggestions to adapt more effectively to differences in negotiating styles in other cultures include the following: (1) decide whether integrative versus distributed outcomes are preferred, (2) obtain advance knowledge of the other culture's negotiation style, (3) emphasize relationship building, (4) build cognitive trust and affective trust, (5) use a team approach, (6) avoid being too frank, (7) be patient, (8) use silence as part of negotiation, (9) avoid yes-or-no questions, (10) know whether to put the final deal in writing, (11) deal with trusting versus distrusting the other side, and (12) know the decision-making authority of your counterpart.

To deal with possible cultural barriers to negotiation, research your counterpart's background and experience. Enlist an advisor from your counterpart's culture, and pay close attention to the communication process during the negotiation.

Key Terms and Phrases

Casual time orientation, p. 84
Collectivism, p. 82
Cultural sensitivity, p. 87
Face-negotiation theory, p. 86
Formality, p. 83
High-context culture, p. 84
Individualism, p. 82

Informality, p. 83
Long-term orientation, p. 83
Low-context culture, p. 84
Power distance, p. 83
Short-term orientation, p.83
Urgent time orientation, p. 84

Discussion Questions and Activities

1. If you work for a powerful and wealthy multinational company such as Apple or Caterpillar, why should you worry about pleasing negotiators in other countries? Shouldn't they be trying to please you?

2. Assume that an American negotiator is meeting with the CEO of an Indian company that is quite hierarchical. How might the American show respect for the CEO?

3. Under what circumstances do you think it would be satisfactory to conduct a business negotiation at a McDonald's or Starbucks in a country outside of the United States?

4. If you were conducting negotiations online with a counterpart from another country, how would you demonstrate to that person that you had an urgent time orientation?

5. Why do people from a collectivistic culture want to please the other side during negotiation?

6. Give an extreme example of cultural insensitivity during an international negotiation.

7. How cool do you think it would be to use your smartphone as a translator during negotiations with a counterpart or counterparts for whom your language was not their native language?

8. How about complimenting your counterpart's physical appearance to help build a relationship during international negotiation?

9. Assume that your company expects you to bring back a signed contract from your negotiation in another country, but your counterpart is uncomfortable with a signed contract. Now what do you do?

10. Explain what would be, or is, the most enjoyable part of conducting cross-cultural negotiations for you.

The idea of this skill-building exercise is to practice using two contrasting styles to negotiate the terms of a major contract, using exaggerated stereotypes of cultural differences. One negotiating team involves three representatives from a clothing manufacturer in Brooklyn, New York. This team tends to be impatient, aggressive, and impulsive. The team wants to move quickly in negotiating with its potential subcontractor. The other negotiating team involves three representatives from Tokyo, Japan, who tend to be patient and polite and emphasize relationship building—yet they still want to negotiate a favorable contract for themselves.

The potential deal in play is for the Japanese company to manufacture about 500,000 sweaters, yoga pants, jeans, and hoodies per year for the American firm. The meeting takes place in the Tokyo headquarters of the Japanese firm. The team from Brooklyn was willing to visit Tokyo because they wanted a firsthand look at the manufacturing facilities.

The two teams will spend about 15 minutes in the negotiation, using their contrasting negotiating styles. Both teams are eager to be partners with the other side, but making a decent profit from the relationship receives a high priority.

CASE PROBLEM 6A: Quinn Struggles with Making a Big Sale in Mexico City

Quinn is a key sales representative at her company that manufactures, sells, and installs large-scale heating and air-conditioning systems in new buildings as well as those undergoing renovation. The company is located in San Antonio, Texas. Quinn often makes an initial visit to a potential customer. If preliminary negotiations go well, she is then backed up by a sales engineer as well as several technicians. Quinn was sent to Mexico City to meet with the executive team that was converting an elegant old church into condominium units.

Quinn knew that the sale and service on this potential contract were worth about 3 million U.S. dollars (or about 57 million Mexican pesos). She met with the executive team at the construction company on Friday morning for an all-day discussion of her company's product and services. All was going well, and Quinn could picture a big commission and loads of exciting work coming her way. When Quinn mentioned a price tag of about 57 million pesos for the sale and service, a couple of the construction company executives said the price was close to the maximum they were willing to pay. The executive team then invited Quinn to stay over on Saturday and Sunday, attend a big soccer game, dine at a couple of restaurants, and tour the city.

Quinn thought that the invitation was excessive in terms of her personal time, so she attempted to tactfully decline the invitation. The representative of the team seemed taken back, but he said he understood that she had a busy schedule.

When Quinn returned to her office in San Antonio on Monday morning, she found an e-mail message from the lead executive on the condominium development team. He said that he liked what her company had to offer, and the price was in their negotiating range. Yet, they would need much more time to study her proposal. The

executive also pointed out that in Mexico, developing a good relationship comes first—before signing a contract.

Quinn was horrified and wondered what she did wrong. She was also trying to figure out what to do next to nail down this giant contract.

Case Questions

1. What might the executive have been referring to in terms of "developing a good relationship before signing a contract"?
2. What significance might the weekend stay offered to Quinn have had for the condominium development team?
3. What attempts should Quinn have made to negotiate the weekend stay?
4. What advice can you offer to Quinn from the standpoint of cross-cultural values to salvage this sizable contract?

Associated Role Play

One student plays the role of Quinn, who pleads on the phone with the condominium representative to have another chance to win the contract for her firm. She decides that she wants to demonstrate how important building a relationship before negotiating a deal is to her and her firm. Another person plays the role of Carlos, the lead executive on the condominium project. He dislikes the American negotiating attitude of getting down to business so quickly, but he has some sympathy for Quinn's sincerity.

Observers might look for any signs that Quinn is making progress toward having another opportunity to engage in a sales negotiation with Carlos and his team. Look also for signs that Carlos has empathy for Quinn's mistakes.

Negotiations have entered their third day between representatives of a major hotel and resort chained based in the United States and their counterparts from a leading manufacturer of computer hardware based in Taiwan (the Republic of China). The Taiwanese company has many offices in the United States but relies on home-country representatives for major sales. Negotiations are taking place in a company hotel in Tampa, Florida. The negotiating team from the hotel chain consists of Buzz, Karen, and Calvin. Their counterparts are two men, Kuan-yu and Chun-hung, and one woman, Shu-fen.

The major issue being negotiated is a price for the sale and service of 3,500 all-in-one desktop computers and laptops for use throughout the hotel chain. At this point, the Americans are seeking an average price of $550 dollars that would include a one-year service contract. The Taiwanese think that a generous average price per unit would be $650. A partial transcript of the negotiations follows:

Buzz: I just can't understand why you folks don't jump on our bid of $550. You know as well as I do that the PC and tablet markets are shrinking worldwide. Just think of the hundreds of thousands of guests from all over the world who would see your computers on display in our lobbies. That would be great publicity for your company.

Karen: Buzz is right on target. Why isn't at least one of you responding right away to Buzz?

Chun-hung: We are not saying that your offer is completely unfair, but maybe we should get to know your team a little better.

Calvin: Get to know us better? This is our third day of negotiation, and we have already had lunch together twice. Should we go on a week's vacation together before closing the deal?

Shu-fen: I hope that we did not hurt your feelings. But becoming business partners with people we know quite well is important to us.

Kuan-yu: We need a little time to think about your final offer. Profit is important to us also.

Kuan-yu: We have studied the numbers carefully, and we think that $650 is a fair price. Do not forget that we are world leaders in providing follow-up technical support for our hardware. But take as much time as you would like to reach a decision.

Karen: If we make you a final offer this afternoon that you think is right, do you have the authority to accept our offer?

Chun-hung: That could very well be, but our honorable executive team in Taiwan likes to be included in major decisions.

Shu-fen: We want to reach a final deal. But we want to make sure that the computers we are offering you will be just what you need and add to the productivity of your hotels. We think you would be a valuable partner for our company.

Karen: I enjoy talking about how we are going to become long-time business partners. But my clock is ticking on this deal. I say $575 average cost per unit. Let us know in 15 minutes, or we will be in touch with one of your competitors tomorrow morning.

Case Questions

1. What do the Americans seem to be doing right in this negotiation?
2. What errors in cross-cultural negotiations do the Americans seem to be making?
3. What do the Taiwanese seem to be doing right in this negotiation?
4. What errors in cross-cultural negotiations do the Taiwanese seem to be making?

Associated Role Play

Six role players are needed for this exercise, one for each of the people. Focus on the final offer made by Karen and the response of the negotiating team from the computer manufacturer. Attempt to illustrate the most likely negotiating styles of the American and Taiwanese teams. Observers might provide feedback on the realism of the negotiation and the negotiating skills of the players involved.

Notes

1. John Saee, "Best Practice in Global Negotiation Strategies for Leaders and Managers in the 21st Century," *Journal of Business Economics and Management*, 9(4), 2008, p. 309.
2. Ibid.
3. Geert Hofstede, *Culture's Consequences: International Differences in Work-Related Values* (Beverly Hills, CA: Sage, 1980); updated and expanded in "A Conversation with Geert Hofstede," *Organizational Dynamics*, Spring 1993, pp. 53–61; Jim Kennedy and Anna Everest, "Put Diversity in Context," *Personnel Journal*, September 1991, pp. 50–54; Asuman Akgunes and Robert Culpepper, "Negotiations between Chinese and Americans: Examining the Cultural Context and Salient Factors," *Journal of International Management Studies*, No. 1, April 2012, pp. 191–199; Robert J. House et al., *Culture, Leadership,*

and Organizations: The GLOBE Study of 62 Societies (Thousand Oaks, CA: Sage, 2004).

4. "Communicating across Cultures," *Culture at Work* (www.culture-at-work.com), 2019, p. 1.

5. Wen Shan, "Culture as a Moderator of Gender Differences in Negotiation Performance: A Meta-Analysis," *Academy of Management Proceedings*, No. 1, 2014, p. 1.

6. Lieh-Ching Chan, "Differences in Business Negotiations between Different Cultures," *Journal of Human Resource and Adult Learning*, November 2006, p. 136.

7. Jeanne M. Brett, Brian Gunia, and Brosh M. Teucher, "Culture and Negotiation Strategy: A Framework for Future Research," *Academy of Management Perspectives*, November 2017, p. 293.

8. Ibid., pp. 291–292.

9. Jeanne M. Brett, "Culture and Negotiation," *International Journal of Psychology*, No. 2, 2000, p. 103.

10. Qin Zhang, Stella Ting-Toomey, and John G. Oetzel, "Linking Emotion to the Conflict Face-Negotiation Theory: A U.S.-China Investigation of the Mediating Effects of Anger, Compassion, and Guilt in Interpersonal Conflict," *Human Communication Research*, 40, 2014, pp. 373–395; "Face-Negotiation Theory," *Communication Theory* (www.communicationtheory.org), 2019, pp. 1–3; "Face Negotiation Theory," *Businesstopia*, Copyright © 2018, pp. 1–4; "Intercultural Negotiation," *International Management at Wiki* (www.interculturalmanagement.wikia.com/wiki), 2019.

11. Arvand V. Phatak, *International Dimensions of Management* (Boston: Kent, 1983), p. 167.

12. Juan Antonio Fernandez and Laurie Underwood, "Succeeding in China: The Voices of Experience," *Organizational Dynamics*, No. 4, 2005, p. 404.

13. Brett, Gunia, and Teucher, "Culture and Negotiation Strategy," pp. 291–292.

14. Marc Diener, "Culture Shock," *Entrepreneur*, July 2003, p. 77.

15. Lieh-Ching Chan, "Differences in Business Negotiations between Different Cultures," *Journal of Human Resource and Adult Learning*, November 2006, p. 139.

16. "Overcoming Cultural Differences in Negotiations," Thunderbird School of Global Management (https://thunderbird.asu.edu), January 28, 2018, p. 2.

17. Frank Acuff, *The World Class Negotiator: An Indispensable Guide for Anyone Doing Business with Those from a Foreign Culture* (New York: AMACOM, 1992).

18. Erin Meyer, "Getting to *Si, Ja, Oui, Hai,* and *Da,*" *Harvard Business Review*, December 2015, p. 79.

19. Ibid, pp. 74–75.

20. Brian Gunia, Jeanne Brett, and Amit Nandkeolyar, "In Global Negotiations, It's All about Trust," *Harvard Business Review*, December 2012, p. 26.

21. Asuman Akgunes and Robert Culpepper, "Negotiations between Chinese and Americans: Examining the Cultural Context and Salient Factors," *Journal of International Management Studies*, No. 1, April 2012, pp. 191–199.

22. "International Negotiations: Cross-Cultural Communication Skills for International Business Executives," *PON—Program on Negotiation at Harvard Law School* (www.pon.harvard.edu), pp. 3–4.

Ethics in Negotiation

Source: EtiAmmos/Shutterstock.

Learning Objectives

After reading and studying this chapter and doing the exercises, you should be able to:

1. Summarize the pressures toward unethical negotiation behavior in organizations.
2. Describe the guide to ethical decision making during negotiations.
3. Identify several clearly unethical negotiating tactics.
4. Identify several borderline unethical negotiating tactics.
5. Pinpoint and be ready to implement several suggestions for being an ethical negotiator.

Ethical issues enter into almost all aspects of organizational life, even in areas that would appear to be devoid of ethical considerations, such as the food served in the company cafeteria. For example, is it ethical to serve food high in cholesterol that might trigger cardiac problems among some employees? Or is it ethical to serve food that runs counter to the religious and cultural values of some employees? Ethical issues enter into almost every negotiation because of the many opportunities to lie, deceive, trick, manipulate, and not honor agreements.

ethics   The set of moral choices a person makes.

Ethics is the set of moral choices a person makes. An individual's beliefs about what is right and wrong, good and bad, are the basis for his or her ethics. Ethics can also be regarded as the vehicle that converts values into action. You might value everybody's right to make a decent living, so you would not offer a ridiculously low price to a street vendor for his or her piece of jewelry. Ethics and legality are not the same thing. It would be legal to offer the street vendor a pitifully low price for the jewelry, but it would be unethical. A big-business example of a legal but unethical act is when a private-equity firm purchases a company with the intent of saddling the company with so much debt it goes bankrupt. The private-equity firm then profits from the company by settling its debt and selling what is left of the purchased company. No illegal act has been committed, but many people would judge the private equity firm to have behaved unethically.

Source: garagestock/Shutterstock.

Ethics is the set of moral choices a person makes.

A general perspective on negotiation ethics developed by Roy J. Lewicki, David M. Saunders, and Bruce Barry provides helpful guidelines on the subject. Some minor forms of untruth, such as misrepresentation of one's true position to the counterparts, bluffing, and emotional faking, may be seen as ethically acceptable and within the rules to the majority of people. In contrast, outright deception and false claims are generally seen as going beyond the rules.[1]

Our approach to the ethics of negotiation is to describe pressures toward being unethical and provide a brief guide to ethical decision making. We then describe a variety of unethical negotiating tactics, followed by suggestions for becoming an ethical negotiator.

Pressures toward Unethical Negotiation Behavior

Many factors prompt people to negotiate unethically. Major contributors to unethical behavior are *an individual's greed and gluttony*, or the desire to maximize self-gain at the expense of others. If carried to an extreme, distributive bargaining maximizes self-gain. A related factor that results in unethical negotiation is *low moral character*, or a weak conscience. In a model developed by professors Lily Morse and Taya R. Cohen, it is proposed that a negotiator's moral character influences his or her attitudes, motives, and behaviors throughout all stages of negotiation. For example, two negotiators with low standing in moral character will adopt a distributive, competitive frame toward the negotiation. The dyad will also engage in mutually reinforcing acts of dishonesty and competition during the negotiation process.[2]

Another major contributor to unethical negotiation behavior is *an organizational atmosphere that condones such behavior.* If the leaders at the top of the organization take imprudent, quasi-legal risks, other workers throughout the firm might be prompted to behave similarly. For example, a negotiator for a supermarket chain might demand excessive "stocking fees" from a packaged food supplier. This means that the supplier has to pay a big fee just to get the company's products on the supermarket shelves. As a result, the supplier makes a very slim profit on the sale. The risk involved is that the supermarket will develop a negative reputation in dealing with food producers and manufacturers.

Unethical negotiation behavior is often triggered by *pressure from higher management to achieve goals*, such as attaining overseas sales even if bribes are necessary. Research conducted by the Harvard Business School suggests that unrealistic goal setting can encourage workers to make compromising choices in order to reach targets. The unrealistic goals invite managers and other workers to cheat in two ways. They will cut corners to achieve a goal, such as using low-quality components to attain cost-cutting goals. Or, workers might lie when reporting how much of a goal they have actually attained.[3]

Sometimes negotiators stretch the truth unintentionally, getting enticed into *bounded ethicality* by engaging in unethical behavior without realizing what they are doing. This happens because *ethical fading* occurs, meaning that people are unable to perceive the ethical implications of their actions because of their strong urge to win.[4] In a desperate attempt to close a big sale, an industrial sales representative might sway to the purchasing manager, "If we close this deal by this afternoon, I will make it very worth your while."

A final cause of unethical negotiation behavior mentioned here is *unconscious biases* that lead to unfair judgments and discriminatory practices. Suppose a manager believes that men are much better at coding than women, and the manager is not aware of his bias. He might begin starting-salary negotiations at a lower point for a woman than a man with comparable skill, experience, and education. (This behavior might border on being both unethical and illegal.) It is difficult to overcome an unconscious bias, yet progress can be made by remembering to broaden one's options when negotiating in the workplace.[5]

The accompanying Self-Quiz 7-1 provides you an opportunity to think through your level of tendencies toward ethical negotiating.

A Guide to Ethical Decision Making during Negotiation

Several guides to ethical decision making have been developed by scholars. William R. Wieringa developed a brief guide to ethical decision making with respect to organizational politics that can be readily adapted to the ethics of negotiation. A negotiating strategy or tactic is ethical if it satisfies three moral principles[6]:

1. *If the negotiating tactic provides the greatest good for the greatest number of people, it is ethical.* In contrast, if the negotiating tactic mainly benefits the individual or harms others, the negotiating tactic is unethical. An example here would be a chief financial officer negotiating with the head of human resources about the use of

My Tendencies toward Ethical Negotiations

Indicate whether you mostly agree or mostly disagree with the following statements as they apply to your beliefs about and attitudes toward negotiation.

Statement about Negotiation	Mostly Agree	Mostly Disagree
1. I would purposely scratch an expensive piece of furniture in a store in order to get a discount for damaged merchandise.		
2. To help close a deal, it is a good idea to make up a false fact, such as "Twenty percent of Fortune 500 companies are already using our service."		
3. In order to win a concession during negotiation, I like the idea of faking sadness, perhaps even shedding false tears.		
4. I think it is okay to use an under-the-table bribe to close a big deal.		
5. During negotiation, fake a "flinch" if you must to get what you want. (To flinch is to involuntarily act with surprise or pain.)		
6. A worthwhile negotiating technique is the "good-person, bad-person routine." (One negotiator on the team acts mean and unreasonable, and the other acts kind in order to win a concession.)		
7. After an agreement is reached or a deal is signed, introduce additional costs that you had forgotten to explain during the negotiation.		
8. It is a good idea to keep challenging the facts and opinions offered by the other side to lower his or her self-confidence.		
9. If I changed my mind a few days after I agreed to a deal or signed a contract, I would cancel the deal.		
10. After it appears that a negotiation has ended, I see no problem with asking for one or two more small concessions.		
11. After a lengthy negotiation is completed, it would be enjoyable to poke fun at the other side and say that you would have done the deal for less.		
12. Lying is an acceptable policy during negotiation.		
13. I like the idea of not submitting to a request by saying, "I think what you are asking for is reasonable, but my boss refuses to go along with the offer."		
14. For every concession I would make in a negotiation, I would raise my initial offer or demand by an equivalent amount.		
15. Whether or not the other party would lose money by accepting my offer is his or her problem, not mine.		

Scoring and Interpretation: The greater the number of statements you marked "Mostly Agree," the stronger is your tendency to negotiate unethically. If such a pattern continued among some of the same counterparts, you would develop a reputation as an unethical negotiator. As a result, some people might refuse to negotiate with you.

performance evaluations to assist in downsizing. If a deal is reached to conduct the evaluations as objectively as possible, and the employees with the lowest evaluation scores are downsized, then the agreement on using the appraisals would be considered ethical. However, if the deal reached is to purposely assign low evaluation scores to the people that top-level management would like to get rid of because they are disliked, then negotiations have been conducted in an unethical manner.

2. *If the negotiating tactic does not violate anyone else's legal or moral right, it is ethical.* However, if the negotiating tactic threatens another person's privacy, due process, free speech, or other right, then it is inappropriate and unethical even if it benefits the larger group. Assume that Mia, the vice president of finance, is accused of sexual harassment by an entry-level worker in the finance department. The woman who accused Mia presents no supporting evidence. Nevertheless, the CEO negotiates with Mia a way to deal with the accusations. He basically imposes on Mia the choice between resigning or being demoted. The CEO negotiates unethically because Mia has been denied due process. (The CEO has behaved so unethically, and perhaps illegally, that he might soon be hearing from an attorney hired by Mia.)

3. *If the negotiating tactic treats all parties fairly, it is ethical.* However, if the tactic benefits those who are better off at the expense of people who are already well off, it is inappropriate behavior and therefore unethical. Assume that Sean, the director of operations, is losing popularity, so he negotiates for larger bonuses for influential people in his chain of command. Sean funds the larger bonuses by giving very small bonuses to less influential (and less well-paid) employees because his overall budget for bonuses is fixed. Sean's negotiated deal would be unethical by this third moral principle. In contrast, if he had negotiated for the same size (or same percentage) bonus for all deserving workers in the operations group just to build goodwill, he would be acting ethically.

You might apply the moral principles test to negotiating strategies and tactics you are contemplating that are not obviously ethical or unethical. It would also be useful to apply broader ethical screens that you may have learned in your study of ethics.

A Variety of Unethical Negotiation Tactics

Numerous studies have shown that unethical behavior in negotiations takes place frequently. Studies suggest that 28 percent of negotiators habitually misrepresent the facts, 25 percent of retailers do not fully communicate information about their products, and more than 60 percent of entrepreneurs rely on building false images of their company.[7] Whether or not a given negotiation strategy or tactic is ethical can be partially determined by the guide to ethical decision making just presented. The negotiator's values also help decide the ethics of a given strategy or tactic. For example, a person might believe that lying is a natural part of negotiation and would therefore regard lying and deceiving to be ethical.

In this section we describe a variety of unethical negotiation tactics, but we divide them into *clearly unethical* and *borderline unethical*, as outlined in Figure 7.1.

Unethical behavior in negotiations takes place frequently. Studies suggest that 28 percent of negotiators habitually misrepresent the facts.

Source: fizkes/Shutterstock.

Clearly Unethical	Borderline Unethical
1. Lying about facts and promises	1. Ignoring the bargaining zone
2. Something for nothing	2. Bluffing
3. The missing-person maneuver	3. Haggling over price
4. Selective disclosure or misrepresentation to constituencies	4. Exaggerated or fake flinching
5. Machiavellianism	5. Feigning anger
6. Being obnoxious on purpose	6. Gloating after the deal has been attained
7. Escalating demands	7. Nibbling
8. Lowballing	

FIGURE 7.1 A Variety of Unethical Negotiation Tactics

Clearly Unethical Tactics

The negotiation strategies and tactics described in this section would most likely be described as unequivocally unethical by businesspeople and scholars.

1. *Lying about facts and promises.* The general purpose of lying is to make oneself look better or protect one's self-esteem. A negotiator might lie about facts or make false promises about the follow-up to the negotiation in order to close a deal. For example, a negotiator might say that her business firm's profit margin on the price offered by the buyer would be only 2 percent, when the true margin would be 9 percent. Or the negotiator might say, "We will be available 24/7 to answer your questions or make emergency repairs," when customer-care and technical support is really quite limited.

   The recently developed Deception Consequences Model challenges the idea that lying in negotiation is universally harmful. Instead, the model suggests that deception or lying is a complicated construct with outcomes that range along a continuum from harmful to helpful. Some forms of deception are therefore not only moral but also desirable.[8] Take the case of business owner Liu, who, along with his team of four workers, restores distressed properties for investors who flip houses. (A "flipper" buys a distressed property, makes renovations quickly, and then sells the property for a profit.) Liu has the opportunity to bid on a contract to restore a restaurant that burned down. In his eagerness to get the contract, Liu says that he and his team have experience in restoring burned-down properties, which is not true. Liu gets the contract, does an outstanding job of restoring the restaurant, and keeps his team of contractors working, satisfied, and well paid.

   As recommended by the Harvard University Program on Negotiation, a potentially effective way to reduce the likelihood that you will face deceptive tactics is to begin negotiations with a discussion of ethics. Tell the other party that you intend to behave as fairly and truthfully as possible and that you expect him or her to do the same.[9] When an apparent lie does surface during the negotiation, discuss the matter directly in a nonhostile manner, such as "How serious are you that you could provide tech support for this machinery 24/7?"

2. *Something for nothing.* The tired cliché that something is "too good to be true" applies here. An offer that sounds too attractive usually has a built-in problem, such as purchasing a new vehicle with a no-interest, five-year loan. In reality, the premium price you pay for the vehicle compensates for the loss of interest to the dealer, who receives a portion of the profits on the loan issued by a lender. A potentially effective counter to an offer of *something for nothing,* is "Please explain to me how you could possibly offer me this deal and still make money."

Source: fizkes/Shutterstock.

When an offer is "too good to be true," the offer usually has a built-in problem that hasn't been disclosed.

3. *The missing-person maneuver.* During negotiation, it is falsely announced that the person with final authority to make a decision is missing. One purpose of the missing-person maneuver is to stall the final agreement in order to lower the aspiration level of the other party. Another purpose is to make a better deal with another party using the deal struck in the current negotiation. Often the party left waiting may prefer to lower the price or increase the offer, or make other concessions, when the missing person finally appears. To deal with the missing- person maneuver, it is helpful to clarify the other party's decision-making authority before the negotiation begins. A countermeasure to the tactic is to place a time limit on your offer or to consider walking away from the deal.[10]

4. *Selective disclosure or misrepresentation to constituencies.* The negotiator may misrepresent the other party's expectations, demand, or offer to his or her constituencies or client in order to justify his or her choices and decisions.[11] To look good to the person or persons the negotiator is representing, the negotiator fakes what the other party says. Suppose a business owner wants to sell his business for $3 million, and the broker who represents him finds a potential buyer. The agent thinks the business is worth only $2 million and wants to sell the business quickly to earn her commission. She then tells the owner that the prospect will only go as high as $2 million, even though the prospect has not yet made an offer. If the agent can now sell the business for $2 million, she gets her commission quickly, and the seller will be satisfied.

5. *Machiavellianism.* Machiavellianism refers to a personality trait that compels someone to ruthlessly manipulate others, often for his or her personal advantage. A Machiavellian-style negotiator would be highly aggressive and attempt to manipulate the emotions of the other party.[12] During a negotiation with a counterpart who appears to be strongly in need of a deal, the Machiavellian might say, "It looks to me that you are in a financial mess as well as being ill-informed, so here is I what I am offering you."

   Machiavellians will also sometimes mock and sneer at their opposition's proposals to upset the other side into something that will be regretted later. For example, "If my offer is really that bad, I will accept 20 percent less." The later regret is that it is difficult during negotiation to later ask for more than you said you would accept or offer earlier in the negotiation.

   Personal attacks also fit into a Machiavellian style of negotiation. The attacking negotiator might make such comments as, "It looks like you were up all night" or "Are you having health issues?" Your status might be attacked by making you wait or responding to a phone call or text message during negotiation.[13]

   A counter-strategy to being the recipient of any form of aggressive or demeaning behavior is to bring to the behavior to the aggressor's attention, such as, "I dislike you making negative comments about my physical appearance," or "I think that our negotiation is important enough for you not to respond to text messages while we are working on a solution."

> **Machiavelliamism** Refers to a personality trait that compels someone to ruthlessly manipulate others, often for his or her personal advantage.

6. *Being obnoxious on purpose.* Closely related to Machiavellian tactics, negotiators will sometimes be obnoxious on purpose just to wear down their counterpart or counterparts. Obnoxious negotiation behaviors include shouting, swearing, faked yawing, twirling a pen or pencil, and frequent looking at the watch or smartphone. Following the principle of *negative reinforcement*, the counterpart might be willing to grant what the obnoxious person wants just to flee the aversive situation. According to a series of three laboratory experiments, being purposely obnoxious and other displays of negative emotion proved to be ineffective negotiating tactics.[14] The recommended counterpunch is to state calmly to the obnoxious negotiator, "I choose to exit the negotiations until you treat me in a more civil manner."

7. *Escalating demands.* A negotiator will sometimes elevate one of his or her demands for every concession he or she makes on another. Issues that appear to have been settled might be reopened. Faced with escalating demands, the other side might want to agree quickly before any other demands are increased.[15] A supplier of the valuable metal cobalt might be negotiating with representatives of a company that manufactures and sells lithium batteries. Knowing that cobalt is vital to the production of batteries, yet the supplies are limited, the negotiator grants one small concession, but then increases another demand: "Okay, we will shorten the delivery time by 10 days, but you will have to pay for a higher percentage of our shipping costs."

8. *Lowballing.* In the widely used tactic of lowballing, the other side gets you committed to the deal before revealing the actual total cost to you.[16] Lowballing is widely used in sales, as in this example: A new SUV is offered at a price well below the manufacturer's suggested retail (MSR) price. After agreeing to buy at

> **lowballing** Widely used tactic where the other side gets you committed to the deal before revealing the actual total cost to you.

that price, the buyer is informed of two conditions. One, the buyer must finance at least half the value of the vehicle through the financial institution chosen by the dealer. Two, the low purchase price is contingent upon purchasing a two-year warranty plan. With these two contingencies, the lowball price is not really so attractive.

Lowballing also takes place outside the realm of sales, such as not receiving a complete job description or explanation of the conditions of employment before accepting a job offer. McKinsey accepts a position as a customer-care technician at a call center that performs outsourcing work for multiple business enterprises. One week into the job, McKinsey is informed that she will have to take her turn working from midnight until 7 a.m. every 10 days.

Borderline Unethical Tactics

1. *Going outside the bargaining zone.* In distributive bargaining, each side has a target point that he or she would like to achieve. Each side also has a resistance point that indicates the lowest acceptable outcome, or the point at which each side would walk away from the negotiation. In the past, this was referred to as the "doorknob price," indicating the point at which a person would walk out the door of the negotiating room. The area between the target points and the resistance point is the settlement zone, as shown in Figure 7.2. As long as there is a little space where the aspiration ranges overlap, a settlement can be reached. If you are aware of the settlement range and the other party's resistance point, it borders on being unethical to ignore the range and the point. You might be forcing the opposition into a hardship situation, and you are not bargaining in good faith.

   A minor ethical issue is that if a negotiator ignores the bargaining zone, he or she may not accomplish the job that he or she was sent to do. Imagine that a purchasing specialist was authorized to purchase a used corporate jet. During negotiation, he senses that the seller's resistance point is $3 million, yet his maximum bid is $2,000,500. As a result, the purchasing manager does not acquire the jet that the CEO wanted. The purchasing manager must now restart his search for a corporate jet—and disappoint the CEO for now.

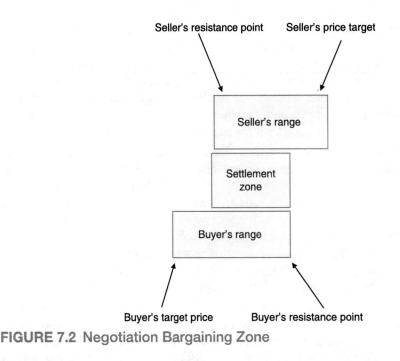

FIGURE 7.2 Negotiation Bargaining Zone

2. *Bluffing.* A bluffer does not tell an outright lie but hints at a course of action to achieve a desired reaction from the other party. A union representative might say, "If we do not get a 5 percent salary increase for all our members, I could see us calling a 30-day strike." In truth, the union representative would not call for a 30-day strike because of the damage it would do the finances of union members. Notice that the phrase "could see" does not mean "we will."

3. *Haggling over price.* To haggle is to bargain over the price of something, or to *dicker.* For many people, their first memorable negotiating experience was haggling over the price of a vehicle. For example, the used-car sales representative says, "I have checked with my manager, and he says the rock-bottom price we can let this vehicle go for is $5,100." The potential buyer responds, "Okay, I will give you $5,050." Annoyed, but wanting to close the sale, the sales rep agrees, and she will have to explain the lowered price to her boss. The ethics of haggling might be challenged because the seller will have usually invested considerable time in negotiating and may be close to the seller's resistance point. In the used-car situation, the extra $50 discount might be taken from the sale representative's commission.

> haggle   To bargain over the price of something, or to *dicker.*

4. *Exaggerated or fake flinching.* As mentioned in the self-assessment quiz, to flinch is to involuntarily act with surprise or pain. Examples of fake flinching include screaming in anger, or saying, "You must be out of your mind." The idea is that the person encountering the flinch will feel that he or she must relieve the concern of the flincher by justifying his or her position or granting a concession. An experienced negotiator says that the key to responding to the flinch is to take the opportunity to explain your position more fully.[17]

5. *Feigning anger.* Laboratory experiments suggest that feigning anger can be an effective negotiating tactic. The ethical issue, however, is that faked anger is dishonest and a method of manipulating the other party. Current research points to another problem with feigning anger: it jeopardizes implementation of the deal reached during negotiation and the subsequent exchange of information. A finding from four experimental studies with working adults and college students found that false representation of anger produced considerable and strategic disadvantage. The disadvantage surfaced because of a "blowback" effect. Faked anger by the negotiator creates and action–reaction cycle that triggers true anger and diminishes trust in both the negotiator and the counterpart.[18]

6. *Gloating after the deal has been attained.* After a deal is reached and you have attained a clear win, doing a victory dance is in poor taste and of questionable ethics. The gloater smiles and says that he or she would have done the deal for much less, such as, "We were really ready to offer you $650,000 for that warehouse, so we are thrilled that you sold it to us for $500,000." The gloat will often make the other side feel foolish and is the opposite of helping the other side save face.[19]

7. *Nibbling.* Another standard negotiating technique of borderline ethics is the nibble. Just before closing an agreement, or immediately after, one or two parties adds a small demand that would not be perceived as a deal changer. Imagine that a teachers' union and a school district are ready to sign a contract after 10 months of negotiation. At the last minute, a negotiator for the teachers' union states, "One more small thing. We would like a contingency fund of $100 per teacher per year to cover what they pay for school supplies on their own." The school district representatives go along with the nibble rather than going through the aggravation of reopening negotiations. A useful way to combat a nibbler is to say something to the effect of, "Sorry I cannot accommodate you, but the terms of our deal have already been concluded."

> nibble   Just before closing an agreement, or immediately after, one or two negotiating parties adds a small demand that would not be perceived as a deal changer.

The accompanying Negotiation and Conflict Resolution in Action feature illustrates how big-business negotiations can be viewed from an ethical perspective.

Walmart Inc. Drives a Hard Bargain with Suppliers

Walmart Inc., the mega-retailer best known for its Walmart and Sam's Club chains, generates approximately $500 billion in annual sales. With that huge sales volume and 16,000 stores worldwide, Walmart has considerable clout when negotiating with suppliers about price and supply-chain demands. A few years ago, Walmart held a summit close to its headquarters in Bentonville, Arkansas, with key product suppliers, including Johnson & Johnson, Unilever, and Kraft Heinz. Walmart demanded a 15 percent reduction in the prices they charge the retailer. During the presentation, Walmart representatives said that they wanted suppliers to help them beat the competition on store prices 80 percent of the time.

To meet the demands of Walmart, the suppliers said they would have to negotiate with their own suppliers to cut wholesale prices or make other cost adjustments to make the 15 percent target. A Walmart representative justified the demand for a price reduction from suppliers with the statement, "We continuously look for ways to deliver savings to our customers—it's part of our DNA."

During the summit, Walmart also announced that it wanted suppliers to make logistics improvements that would help the company attain $1 billion more in sales by working harder on shipping orders in full and on time. These maneuvers would trim delivery costs, reduce reorders, and reduce out-of-stock problems. Jason Goldberg, the head of a digital agency that works with major brands and retailers, said that the brands that agreed to the negotiating terms at Walmart could expect better distribution and more strategic help. Not going along with these demands could result in limited distribution. Furthermore, every few years, Walmart tells suppliers to take the money they are spending on marketing initiatives and invest it in lower prices. "They sweep all the chips off the table and drill you down on price," said Goldberg.

Back in 2015, when Walmart Inc. experienced an earnings dip, the company negotiated extra hard for lower prices from suppliers. Vendors were worried about having their brands removed from Walmart's shelves because of a dispute over pricing. That year, the squeeze on suppliers was evident to those selling to Sam's Club warehouse outlets. Buyers from Sam's Club summoned major vendors to meetings and told them that a "cost-gap analysis" indicated that they should be delivering at lower prices and demanded millions of dollars in discounts. Unlike previous summits, vendors were told they could not ask questions at the meetings. Queries, however, could be handled later via e-mail.

During the same period, Walmart stores were told of sweeping changes to supplier agreements that sought to extend payment terms in some cases. New fees were introduced to warehouse goods and place products in stores. Suppliers who had their goods manufactured in China were told that they should share with Walmart any benefit gained from the decline in the value of the Chinese yuan.

Walmart spokeswoman Deisha Barnett emphasized that the company sees its relationship with suppliers as essential to the company's success. "We will work with every supplier to ensure that terms and agreements are mutually agreed upon," she said.

Despite some resistance to Walmart's continuing negotiations to lower prices from vendors, one consumer-goods supplier reckoned that most will eventually submit to Walmart's market power, although not without a fight. Sarah Talley, who at one time negotiated with Walmart about prices for Frey Farms, offers this advice: "Don't spend time griping. Be problem solvers instead. Approach Walmart by saying, 'Let's work together and drive costs down and produce it so much cheaper so you don't have to replace me, because if you work *with* me, I could do it better.'"

Another part of Walmart's strategy to lower costs from vendors is to negotiate directly with them and avoid dealing with middlemen when possible. Walmart looks to remove the markup of any firms between the company and direct suppliers and providers.

Questions

1. What best alternative to a negotiated agreement (BATNA) could a supplier have in negotiating prices with Walmart Inc.?
2. How would you rate the ethics of Walmart in negotiating prices for Walmart and Sam's Club?

Source: Original story based on facts and observations in the following sources: "Negotiating with Walmart Buyers," *Negotiation Experts* (www.negotiations.com), July 14, 2017, pp. 1–4; Sa-San Sit, "Wal-Mart Squeezes Suppliers in Price War," *Supply Management* (www.clips.org), March 31, 2017, pp. 1–5; "Wal-Mart's Push to Negotiate with Suppliers—Continuing the Power Play to Control Every Supply Chain It Touches?" *LTD Management* (www.ltdmgt/com), 2019, pp. 1–3; Nathan Layne, "Wal-Mart Puts the Squeeze on Suppliers to Share Its Pain as Earnings Sag," *Reuters* (www.reuters.com), October 19, 2015, pp. 1–6.

Suggestions for Being an Ethical Negotiator

A key positive consequence of being an ethical negotiator is that you are more likely to develop a positive reputation. In turn, it is much easier to achieve win-win outcomes when you have a reputation for being fair, honest, and wanting to do the right thing.[20] Using the guide to ethical decision making presented earlier in the chapter would be an effective tactic for being an ethical negotiator. If the decisions you make in relation to negotiation pass this type of ethical screen, you would be an ethical decision maker. Here we look at a few other suggestions for being an ethical negotiator.

A robust way of being an ethical negotiator is to *treat others with dignity and respect.* As Michael Kaplan notes, although it is essential to project strength and confidence during the process, successful negotiators avoid being rude or condescending. Even when the counterpart becomes stressed and combative, treating him or her with dignity and respect will frequently motivate others to respond in kind.[21] To promote positive ethics during negotiation, negotiators should *slow down and deliberate on important decisions.*[22] Deliberating helps allow time for thinking through the ethics of the decision, such as, "Should I really ask for additional money in my budget when we are squandering some of the money we already have?"

Focusing on being honest is an obvious, but often overlooked, method of ethical negotiation.[23] If the counterpart says he or she will close the deal if you can deliver the needed components in 10 days and you know the deadline cannot be reached, an ethical response would be, "I want to sign the deal today, but it will take us 20 days." This type of honesty will help build a long-term relationship with the customer." You have behaved ethically by saying "No" to a request you cannot meet.

Being honest also involves *avoiding willful misrepresentation.* It might be ethical not to reveal certain information, but misrepresentation is unethical. Assume that Nick operates a landscaping business and is negotiating a contract to be the sole landscaper for an office building complex. It might be okay for Nick not to reveal that he would have to hire a few new landscapers to manage the contract. In contrast, it would be a misrepresentation to say, "My staff is big enough right now to easily handle this great contract."

Another way of negotiating ethically is to *insist on fair procedures,* such as in the age-old way to divide a piece of cake between two children: one child cuts the cake, and the other chooses.[24] At times, the fairest procedure is to have a third-party arbitrator decide which side wins. For example, two division heads might be negotiating with the executive team about which division will have responsibility for a newly acquired company. Each division head presents his or her best proposal. A small committee composed of members from outside the two divisions and the office of the CEO then decides which division has the best plan for being responsible for the new acquisition.

Lying about facts and promises is a negotiation tactic that is clearly unethical.

Source: Twinsterphoto/Shutterstock.

Summary

Ethical issues enter into almost every negotiation because of the many opportunities to lie, deceive, trick, manipulate, and not honor agreements. A negotiating tactic can be unethical but still legal. Among the contributors to unethical behavior are an individual's greed and gluttony, an organizational atmosphere condoning such behavior, pressure from higher management to achieve goals, bounded ethicality, ethical fading, and unconscious biases. Bounded ethicality is about not knowing what you are doing; ethical fading is about not recognizing the ethical implications of an act out of a desire to win.

A negotiating strategy or tactic is ethical if it satisfies three moral principles: (1) provides the greatest good to the greatest number of people, (2) does not violate anyone else's legal or moral rights, and (3) treats all parties fairly.

Negotiation strategies and tactics classified here as being clearly unethical are as follows: (1) lying about facts and promises, (2) something for nothing, (3) the missing-person maneuver, (4) selective disclosure or misrepresentation to constituencies, (5) Machiavellianism, (6) being obnoxious on purpose, (7) escalating demands, and (8) lowballing.

Negotiation strategies and tactics classified here as borderline unethical are as follows: (1) going outside the bargaining zone, (2) bluffing, (3) haggling over price, (4) exaggerated or fake flinching, (5) feigning anger, (6) gloating after the deal has been attained, and (7) nibbling.

Being an ethical negotiator enhances one's reputation and leads to more win-win outcomes. Suggestions for being an ethical negotiator include the following: (1) treat others with dignity and respect, (2) slow down and deliberate on important decisions, (3) focus on being honest, (4) avoid willful misrepresentation, and (5) insist on fair procedures.

Key Terms and Phrases

Ethics, p. 98
Haggle, p. 105
Lowballing, p. 103

Machiavellianism, p. 103
Nibble, p. 105

Discussion Questions and Activities

1. Among the unethical strategies and tactics described in this chapter, which one or two do you think are the most widely used in business?
2. Identify an unethical negotiation strategy or tactic that has been used against you, and explain how it was used.
3. How ethical is it for Amazon.com to negotiate with a business enterprise to lower the price of the products the company sells on Amazon?
4. What do you think of the ethics of a contractor offering to give a $25,000 gift to a government official in order to attain a construction contract?
5. Give an example of a type of negotiation in which *ethical fading* might take place.
6. What is your opinion about the belief that negotiation is inherently unethical?
7. Suppose a person admits to and is convicted of manslaughter based on drunk driving. How ethical would it be for the person's lawyer to negotiate for a shorter-than-usual prison sentence for the convicted person?
8. At an Apple store, a person purchases $5,000 worth of computer equipment and software. At the checkout counter, he or she says, "Throw in a thumb drive at no cost, or I will cancel my order." How ethical a negotiator is this person?
9. How should the person working at the counter at the Apple store respond to the person who demanded the thumb drive at no cost?
10. Ask any person with business experience in your network what he or she thinks is an example of an unethical negotiating tactic. How well does the tactic you uncover fit any of the tactics described in this chapter?

Skill-Building Exercise: Negotiating with a Dirty Trickster

In the three scenarios presented here, one student plays the role of a negotiator who is attempting to be deliberately unethical or play a dirty trick. Another role player attempts to counteract the dirty trickster. Run each role play for about 10 minutes.

Scenario 1

One person is attempting to sell a line of decorative carrying cases for men and women to the operator of an online fashion store. The store owner will purchase the cases when she receives an online order. She demands a wholesale price that would give the producer of the cases a profit margin of 2 percent. The store owner says, "I may be one online store, but my network of other potential purchasers of your cases is enormous. If you accept the price for your cases that I am willing to pay, you will soon receive some awesome referrals." The producer of cases attempts to deal with this apparent exaggeration, if not outright lie.

Scenario 2

One student plays the role of the head of a nonprofit agency that provides physical exercise and activities, such as punching-bag boxing, for developmentally disabled children. The agency head is negotiating a lease for empty space in a shopping mall. Another student plays the role of a real estate agent who represents the shopping mall and who wants to spend considerable time negotiating a lease. The agency head begins to think that the agent lacks the authority to come to an agreement on the final terms of the lease. He or she decides to authenticate whether the agent really has the authority to reach a deal on the lease.

Scenario 3

One student plays the role of a person who wants to purchase a food truck restaurant that is fully equipped to sell Greek food, such as gyros, and has a permit to occupy a street location in a busy downtown district. The owner of the truck has physical health problems, forcing him or her to retire. Another person plays the role of the owner, who intentionally becomes insulting and demeaning toward the buyer in hopes of intimidating him or her and therefore obtaining a high price for the food truck. The potential purchaser wants to combat the insults but at the same time feels that he or she needs to make a deal because the Greek food truck would be ideal.

CASE PROBLEM 7A: Denver Public School Teachers Return to Work

In February 2019, Denver public school teachers went on strike to demand higher, more stable salaries because the public school district used unpredictable bonuses to compensate for low base pay. Another goal of the strike was to attain high enough wages to keep more educators from leaving Colorado, where the cost of living had surged in recent years. Lindsey Rutledge, a high school psychologist, said, "The rent has skyrocketed over the past few years. After we pay our rent, our student loan bill, our car payments, we have nothing left over. Most people who work in schools have to have second and third jobs."

The strike had short-term costs for the teachers. Each day of the strike cost them hundreds of dollars in missing salary, further worsening their financial situation. Costs for the school district were also substantial. Approximately 1,400 central staff members and 400 substitute teachers had to fill in for more than 2,600 striking teachers. A spokeswoman concluded that each day cost the district more than $400,000, partly because substitute teachers were offered double pay.

As the January 18 expiration date of the ProComp (the incentive plan) approached, bargaining sessions between the representatives of Denver Public Schools (DPS) and the Denver Classroom Teachers Association became more intense. A few of the sessions ended in tears and squabbles, with representatives of both sides exhausted and frustrated. The union voted on January 22 to authorize a strike after negotiations with DPS failed to produce the desired outcome of a new contract governing teacher compensation through the ProComp system. The two sides were about $8 million apart in their compensation proposals.

An 11th bargaining session held on a Monday became contentious. The issue was that union representatives rejected a new DPS proposal that would eliminate 150 central office positions in an effort to free up $23 million for additional teacher pay. But the proposal did increase incentives for teachers working in high-poverty schools, a key point for the union.

Representatives for the district and the union returned to the bargaining table on Tuesday following a day of picketing and student walkouts in support of teachers. The two sides negotiated for 12 hours, including overnight, at the Denver Central Library, exchanging proposals and meeting in private to study them. Representatives issued a joint statement saying the two sides had worked in good faith to find common ground. When negotiations resumed on Wednesday morning, DPS revealed its proposal, which was met with immediate acceptance by teachers in the audience, who clapped, cheered, and snapped their fingers in approval. The union representatives expressed their approval of the proposal indirectly by saying they had no questions. Just after 6 a.m., Rob Gould, the lead union negotiator, said, "We are recommending to our members that we officially end the strike."

The highlights of the negotiated deal, according to union and district officials, included the following:

- An average 11.7 percent increase in base salary for the following year
- A "transparent" 20-step salary schedule that starts at $45,800 and maxes out at $100,000 for teachers with 20 years of experience and a doctorate
- Full cost-of-living increases in the second and third year of the agreement
- An end to bonuses for senior DPS district administrators
- An additional $23.1 million to fund teacher compensation
- $2,000 in incentives for hard-to-staff positions
- $3,000 in incentives for educators in the 30 highest-priority schools

"The agreement is a win, plain and simple, for our students, for our educators, and for our communities," said union president Henry Roman. He also said, "We are thankful that both sides were able to come together after 15 months of bargaining to ensure our educators have a transparent salary schedule with a professional base salary scale and less reliance on unpredictable bonuses that disrupt our school."

Superintendent Susana Cordova said, "This is strong investment in our teachers—in both their base salary and the equity incentives. I am very pleased we were able to reach a deal and in the collaborative way we worked together." Cordova also noted that the two sides shared many areas of agreement. "We worked hard to listen and find common ground on the few areas where we had different perspectives."

After the strike was concluded, Governor Jared Polis said that Denver's kids were the biggest winners in the agreement. He emphasized that students and teachers would be in school working together to build a brighter future for themselves and the community.

Case Questions

1. What appeared to be the key reason, or reasons, that the teachers' union and the public school district were able to negotiate a successful resolution to their differences within three days?
2. How ethical was the proposal to eliminate 150 central office positions in order to fund the extra $23.1 million in teacher compensation?
3. Identify two negotiating tactics that were used in this case.

Source: Original cased based on the following sources: Kelly Ragan, "Denver Public Schools Teacher Strike Ends after Three Days," *Fort Collins Coloradoan* (www.colorodan.com), February 14, 2019, pp. 1–4; Dakin Andone, Holly Yan, and Sara Weisfeldt, "This Is What Denver Teachers Got after 3 Days on Strike," *CNN.com*, February 14, 2019, pp. 1–3; R. J. Sangosti, "Denver Public Schools, Union Reach Tentative Agreement to End City's First Teacher Strike in 25 Years," *The Denver Post* (www.denverpost.com), February 14, 2019, pp. 1–8.

Associated Role Play

Two students play the role of representatives of the Denver Classroom Teachers Association, and two other students play the role of representatives of the DPS administrators. The goal of the negotiating session is to find common ground to end the strike. Run the role play for about 10 minutes. Observers might provide feedback on the authenticity of the common ground that the two sides find.

CASE PROBLEM 7B: Alicia's Tainted Salary-Increase Negotiation

Alicia, a digital marketing specialist, and her husband, Todd, a department manager in a supermarket, are in tough financial shape. Among their fixed expenses are about $2,000 per month in loan principal and interest payments, vehicle payments of $800 per month, rent of $2,300 per month, before-and-after work childcare of $750 per month, and $250 for smartphones. Despite their combined income of $135,000 per year, they have a monthly shortfall of $350.

Alicia and Todd have been working diligently to cut expenses, such as Alicia styling her own hair instead of visiting a salon and Todd purchasing low-price beer instead of imports or fancy craft beers. The couple decides that they must generate more revenue to supplement their cost savings in order to break even financially each month. One night after their daughter, 5-year-old Melody, is asleep, the couple brainstorms ideas for earning more money.

Alicia says, "I think I have a good idea. I am up for a salary review next week. The average salary increase is about 3 percent, but I will make a case for getting 6 percent, based somewhat on our financial pickle." Todd likes the idea and says, "Lay it on thick. I know you can do it."

During her salary review with her boss, marketing manager Dion, Alicia makes these points: "I'm asking for a 6 percent salary bump for the upcoming year. I know this is high, but I've got some good reasons. At the top of the list, I have a few fantastic new ideas for digital marketing that will increase our digital sales by about 20 percent next year.

"On the personal side, I need more money. My husband and I are facing financial difficulties. Our daughter Melody is a special needs child who will require a lot of private tutoring in order to learn how to read when she gets to kindergarten and the first grade. I've also run up some unanticipated family expenses. My mother has developed pancreatic cancer, and I have to help pay for some of her extra care and medicine."

With a sympathetic expression, Dion responds, "First of all, I would like to learn more about this digital marketing breakthrough you have planned. Second of all, we do not grant extra-large salary increases based on personal need. But I would like to see some documentation about your daughter and mother's situations."

With a frown, Alicia says to Dion, "I guarantee you that my marketing idea will be a winner, but the idea needs a little more polishing before I submit it to you. I must say, I am a little disappointed that you want me to document the misfortune in my family."

Case Questions

1. How convincing is Alicia in her attempt to negotiate a 6 percent raise?
2. How effective is Dion in dealing with his skepticism of the rationale Alicia presents for a salary increase that is about twice the going rate in the company?
3. Assuming that the company could afford it, how ethical is Alicia in presenting presumably false reasons for needing a high salary increase?

Associated Role Play

One student plays the role of Alicia, who is becoming alarmed that Dion does not seem to be swallowing the reasons she is offering for an exceptional raise. Alicia then decides to argue her case with more passion and force. Another student plays the role of Dion, who is about ready to challenge the truthfulness and ethics of Alicia's claims and tactics.

Notes

1. Roy J. Lewicki, David M. Saunders, and Bruce Barry, *Negotiation*, 7th ed. (New York: McGraw-Hill Education, 2015), p. 163.

2. Lily Morse and Taya R. Cohen, "Moral Character in Negotiation," *Academy of Management Perspective*, February 2019, pp. 12–25.

3. Ron Carucci, "Why Ethical People Make Unethical Choices," *Harvard Business Review*, December 16, 2016, p. 3.

4. McKenzie Rees, Ann Tenbrunsel, and Max Bazerman, "Bounded Ethicality and Ethical Fading in Negotiations," *The Academy of Management Perspectives*, February 2019, pp. 26–42.

5. Mahzarin R. Banaji, Maz H. Bazerman, and Dolly Chugh, "How (Un)ethical Are You?" *Harvard Business Review*, December 2003, pp. 56–64.

6. William R. Wieringa, "Office Politics," *Fair Practices LLCI* (www.fairpractices.com), 2004, pp. 1–2.

7. Elzbieta Kowalczyk and Pawel Kieka, "Selected Determinants of Interpersonal Communication—between Openness and Manipulation," *Social Sciences*, 2, 2015, p. 11.

8. Cited in "Tag Archive: Unethical Negotiation," *KARRASS* (www.karrass.com), 2019, p. 4.

9. Joseph P. Gasppar, Redona Methansi, and Maurcie Schweitzer, "Fifty Shades of Deception: Characteristics and Consequences of Lying in Negotiations," *Academy of Management Perspectives*, February 2019, pp. 62–81.

10. "Tag Archive," p. 6.

11. Kowalczyk and Kieka, "Selected Determinants of Interpersonal Communication," p. 11.

12. Tomas Chamorro-Premuzic, "The Personality Traits of Good Negotiators," *Harvard Business Review*, August 7, 2017, p. 4.

13. Robert Fisher and William Ury, *Getting to Yes: Negotiating Agreement without Giving In* (New York: Penguin Books, 1983), p. 141.

14. Shirli Kopleman, Ashley Shelby Rosette, and Leigh Thompson, "The Three Faces of Eve: Strategic Displays of Positive, Negative, and Neutral Emotions in Negotiation," *Organizational Behavior and Human Decision Processes*, 99, 2006, p. 98.

15. Fisher and Ury, *Getting to Yes*, p. 145.

16. G. Richard Shell, *Bargaining for Advantage: Negotiation Strategies for Reasonable People* (New York: Viking Penguin, 1999), p. 238.

17. "Tag Archive," p. 2.

18. Rachel L. Campagna, Alexandra A. Mislin, Dejun Tony Kong, and William P. Bottom, "Strategic Consequences of Emotional Misrepresentation in Negotiation: The Blowback Effect," *Journal of Applied Psychology*, May 2016, pp. 605–624.

19. Barbara Buell, "Negotiation Strategy: Seven Common Pitfalls to Avoid," *Stanford Business*, January 15, 2007, p. 2.

20. Peter B. Stark and Jane Flaherty, "Ethical Negotiations: 10 Tips to Ensure Win-Win Outcomes," *The Negotiator Magazine* (http://negotiatormagazine.com), © 2003, pp. 1–3.

21. Michael Kaplan, "Do You Have These 11 Successful Negotiation Traits," *Veteran Talent* (www.workofhonor.com), October 10, 2016, pp. 1–2.

22. Dina Gerdeman, "Why Ethical People become Unethical Negotiators," *HBS Working Knowledge* (forbes.com/hbsworkingknowledge), July 30, 2018, p. 3.

23. William Taylor, "The Importance of Ethical Negotiations," *The Gap Partnership* (www.thegappartnership.com), 2019, p. 1.

24. Fisher and Ury, *Getting to Yes*, p. 89.

Major Sources and Types of Conflict

Source: sirtravelalot/Shutterstock.

Learning Objectives

After reading and studying this chapter and doing the exercises, you should be able to:

1. Describe the evolution of conflict theory.
2. Identify several positive and negative consequences of conflict.
3. Identify and summarize five frequent sources of workplace conflicts.

A frequent observation is that managers spend approximately 20 percent of their time resolving conflicts. This 20 percent includes the time managers spend in dealing with their own conflicts with others and also the time spent helping group members resolve their conflicts. The study of conflict and its resolution is therefore of substantial practical value for managers, as well as many other workers whose position involves interaction with people.

conflict Refers to the opposition of persons or forces, giving rise to some tension, or to a disagreement between two or more parties that are interdependent.

Conflict refers to the opposition of persons or forces, giving rise to some tension, or to a disagreement between two or more parties that are interdependent.[1] A conflict occurs when two or more parties pursue mutually exclusive goals, values, or events. Almost all conflict occurs because resources are limited: all individuals and groups cannot get what they want. Each side believes that what it wants is incompatible with what the other wants, such as two groups wanting the same conference room at the same time. Conflict can also take place at the individual level when a person has to decide between two incompatible choices. For example, a person might have to choose between accepting a job transfer and remaining in town with family and friends. Refusing to transfer could mean a job loss, whereas accepting the transfer would mean less contact with family and friends.

Source: mamagio/Shutterstock.

Conflict can take place at the individual level when a person has to decide between two incompatible choices.

In this chapter we examine the evolution of conflict theory, the positive and negative consequences of conflict, as well as a few sources and types of conflict. The following two chapters describe conflict-resolution methods. The negotiation strategies and tactics described previously are also aimed at resolving conflicts.

A potentially fruitful starting point in studying conflict is to take Self-Quiz 8-1 that provides you an opportunity to think about your own tendencies for entering into conflict with others.

My Tendencies toward Conflict-Proneness

Indicate the extent to which each of the following statements describes your attitude or behavior by circling one number. The numbers refer to very inaccurate (VI), moderately inaccurate (MI), neither accurate nor inaccurate (N), moderately accurate (MA), and very accurate (VA). Consider enlisting the help of someone who knows your behaviors and attitudes well to help you respond accurately to the statements.

Statement Related to Conflict Proneness	VI	MI	N	MA	VA
1. I like a good fight on the job.	1	2	3	4	5
2. I prefer that coworkers be candid with me if they disagree with something I have said or written.	1	2	3	4	5
3. I rarely (or would rarely) criticize another person on the job.	5	4	3	2	1
4. Competing against coworkers is enjoyable if I do well.	1	2	3	4	5
5. If somebody at work insulted me, I most likely would not respond.	5	4	3	2	1
6. I enjoy criticizing others when the criticism is even a little bit justified.	1	2	3	4	5
7. It seems to me that some departments in a large organization are just a waste of time and money.	1	2	3	4	5
8. It is almost never justified for an employee to devote time to work outside of his or her regular working hours.	1	2	3	4	5
9. I have gotten along well with almost everyone I have worked with.	5	4	3	2	1
10. I enjoy (or would enjoy) working with people who have different work specialties than I do.	5	4	3	2	1
11. Business is war.	1	2	3	4	5
12. I like the idea of different departments in the same organization competing for their share of the overall budget.	1	2	3	4	5
13. If I noticed a spelling error in somebody else's PowerPoint presentation, I would poke fun at the presenter.	1	2	3	4	5
14. I believe strongly in the old saying, "Let sleeping dogs lie."	5	4	3	2	1
15. If a company thinks that one of their patents is being infringed upon, they should sue the other company immediately.	1	2	3	4	5
16. I think that "turf wars" are (or would) be a lot fun on the job.	1	3	3	4	5
17. I prefer to walk away from conflict.	5	4	3	2	1
18. Conflict with people is a natural part of work.	1	2	3	4	5
19. Conflict with other people gets me discouraged and lowers my productivity.	5	4	3	2	1
20. Conflict with other people is exciting and boosts my productivity.	1	2	3	4	5
21. The less conflict I face in a job, the better off I am emotionally.	5	4	3	2	1
22. I worry (or would worry) about my job interfering with personal life.	5	4	3	2	1
23. I worry (or would worry) about my personal life interfering with my work.	5	4	3	2	1
24. I enjoy (or would enjoy) the excitement of dealing with a workplace bully.	1	2	3	4	5
25. If another person at work treats me rudely, I would retaliate with rudeness of my own.	1	2	3	4	5

Scoring and Interpretation: Calculate your score by adding up the numbers circled.

65–75: You are highly prone toward entering into conflict with others in the workplace. Be on guard against entering into needless conflict with others and developing the reputation of a troublemaker.

41–64: You have an average tendency toward conflict-proneness in the workplace. You most likely do not look to enter into conflict, but you are willing to deal constructively with conflict when it surfaces.

25–40: You are prone to avoid conflict as much as possible in the workplace and to minimize the stress that stems from conflict. Because so much conflict exists on the job, it might prove helpful to you to deal with rather than avoid conflict.

The Evolution of Conflict Theory

During the last 100 years, three different perspectives on conflict have developed. First is the *traditional view* that was widely accepted in the 20th century. The key proposition of the traditional view is that conflict has destructive consequences for the group and should therefore be avoided. According to the traditional perspective, conflict stems from dysfunctional managerial behavior, and it is therefore essential to stop conflict at its source. If the manager were replaced, the conflict would be stopped.

Second is the *human relations view* that was the predominant perspective from about 1940 to 1970. According to this view, conflict is the natural and unavoidable result of people interacting in groups. Instead of conflict necessarily being harmful or destructive, it can be a creative, positive, and constructive force that contributes to group functioning. At times, conflict can be dysfunctional, and it can be functional at other times, but conflict is ever present.

Third is the *interactionist view* contending that conflict is both inevitable and, at the same time, produces a level of tension that can be helpful in keeping the group energized and creative. (The interaction suggested by the term *interactionist* refers to interaction and understanding between two people or two systems.) According to this perspective, conflict is a positive force for change within interpersonal relationships, groups, and the total organization. The managerial challenge is to find constructive ways of managing conflict while still allowing for some differences that energize a group toward ongoing discussion and creative thinking.[2]

The Consequences of Conflict in Organizations

Conflict results in both positive and negative consequences. The right amount of conflict may enhance job performance, but too much or too little conflict lowers performance. If the manager observes that job performance is suffering because of too much conflict, he or she should reduce the amount. If performance is low because the workers are too placid, the manager might profitably increase conflict. For example, the manager might establish a prize for top performance in the group.

Positive Consequences of Conflict

Many managers and scholars believe that job conflict can have positive consequences. When the optimum amount of conflict is present in the workplace, one or more of the consequences described in the following paragraphs can be anticipated.

1. *Higher group performance.* Conflict about the task, or the work itself, often leads to higher group performance. Task conflict concentrates on the resolution of problems caused by differences in viewpoints, ideas, and opinions. The enhanced performance often stems from increased effort. People become so motivated to win the conflict that they may surprise themselves and their superiors with their work output. (An example of task conflict would be strong disagreements about the best way to collect data about customer preferences.) A study was conducted with 145 work teams in 63 Korean organizations in various industries, including telecommunications, heavy equipment, and banking. The results indicated that task conflict showed a slightly positive relationship with group performance. In contrast, interpersonal conflict, such as a personality clash, was negatively related to group performance.[3]

2. *More reflective communication that facilitates task performance.* When conflict is moderate, group task performance tends to increase. A study was conducted with both teams of college students and groups within a financial organization. It was found that when a majority of group members perceive low levels of task conflict within the group, whereas a minority perceived high levels of conflict, group performance was higher. The researchers reasoned that moderate conflict prompted group members to engage in reflective communication, the process of openly sharing ideas and reflecting on these ideas and opinions. In turn, more in-depth thought was given to problem solving.[4]

3. *Increased creativity.* Talents and ability surface in response to conflict. People become inventive when they are placed in intense competition with others. The anger that stems from conflict can lead to imaginative problem solving, such as being so angry about being passed over for a promotion that the individual finds a way of becoming more promotable. A surprising finding is that anger helps people calm down and get ready to address a problem and not run from it.[5]

4. *Increased diagnostic information.* Conflict can provide valuable information about problem areas in the department or total organization. When leaders learn of conflict, they may conduct investigations that will lead to the prevention of similar problems. For example, a CEO might be apprised of age discrimination complaints in one department and might then investigate whether age discrimination is a problem throughout the organization.

5. *Increased cohesiveness within the group.* When a group competes intensely with another group to the point that the competition becomes an intergroup conflict, the group tends to become more cohesive. Group members pull together to outperform the competing group, partially because they perceive themselves to be facing a common enemy. Imagine that a product development team within a beverage company is competing with a similar team from another beverage company. The goal of both teams is to develop a healthy energy drink aimed at young adults. Group cohesion is likely to increase in both groups as they pull together to produce a more appealing drink than the competition.

6. *Opportunity for learning and growth.* Almost every conflict holds some opportunity for learning and growth. Managers and team leaders might ask themselves, "What larger lessons can be learned from this conflict?" and "How can we use those lessons to prevent future conflicts?" By asking the right questions, managers and team leaders can create internal innovation and improve the workplace.[6] If several employees become upset and sue the employer after being fired, managers working with human resources professionals might look for ways to make the firing process less conflict-prone. Perhaps the fired workers need to be shown more documentation about why they were fired and be treated more compassionately.

Negative Consequences of Conflict

When the wrong amount or type of conflict exists, job performance may suffer. Some types of conflict have worse consequences than others. A particularly bad form of conflict is the one that forces a person to choose between two undesirable alternatives, such as a business owner choosing between declaring bankruptcy or liquidating the business. The negative consequences of conflict are described in the following paragraphs.

1. *Poor mental and physical health.* Intense conflict is a source of stress. A person under prolonged and intense conflict may suffer stress-related disorders. Workplace harassment, defined as interpersonal behavior aimed at intentionally harming other employees, is an example of an intense conflict that triggers stress. A meta-analysis of studies of workplace harassment showed that it damaged the well-being of victims. The aspects of well-being negatively affected include anxiety, depression, burnout, frustration, and physical symptoms such as headaches or chest pains.[7]

2. *Wasted resources.* Employees and groups in conflict frequently waste time, money, and other resources while fighting their battles. An example would be the head of one division being unwilling to share ideas about money-saving technology with another division because the two division presidents are bitter rivals. The resource wasted is the technology from one division that could have helped the other division.

3. *Poor performance and side-tracked goals.* When emotional conflict is too strong, team performance may suffer because not enough attention is paid to the task. Emotions may run so high that group members may be unable to discuss their differences in a

Emotions may run so high that group members may be unable to discuss their differences in a rational way.

rational way. This problem has been found to be prevalent in multicultural groups.[8] As members of different cultures have become the usual way of life in organizations, this type of conflict is most likely decreasing.

4. *Heightened self-interest.* Conflict within the group often results in extreme demonstrations at the expense of the group and the larger organization. Individuals or groups place their personal interests over those of the rest of the company or customers. One common result of this type of self-interest is hogging resources (a form of wasted resources). A team member might attempt to convince the team leader to place him on an important customer-troubleshooting assignment even though he knows that his rival is better qualified.

5. *Workplace aggression.* Interpersonal conflict is positively related to interpersonal aggression and organizational aggression. An example of interpersonal aggression is yelling or swearing at a work associate, and an example of organizational aggression is damaging workplace equipment. A meta-analysis of 59 different samples found that interpersonal conflict and the personality trait of anger had relatively strong links to interpersonal aggression. Interpersonal conflict along with job dissatisfaction also showed a positive relationship to organizational aggression.[9] These findings reinforce the reality that conflict with others can be upsetting enough for people to take it out on coworkers or equipment.

6. *Workplace violence.* A disastrous consequence of intense workplace conflict is that it may result in workplace violence. Employees who are angry with their supervisor, or who think they may be terminated, or who argue intensely with coworkers may be so enraged that they go on a shooting rampage. One terrifying example is that in 2019, five employees at the Henry Pratt Company in Aurora, Illinois, were shot to death by an employee in the process of being fired. The killer had previous problems that involved assaulting other people.[10]

Major Sources and Types of Workplace Conflict

The sources, types, and antecedents, or outright causes, of conflict are numerous, and the list is dynamic. At any given time, a new and potent source of conflict might emerge, such as the management of a brokerage firm deciding to use artificial intelligence (AI) to replace many finance professionals who were managing investment portfolios. Here we describe five major sources of workplace conflict, as outlined in Figure 8.1. In Chapter 11 we focus on the workplace conflicts created by incivility, bullies, and difficult people.

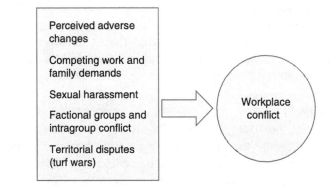

FIGURE 8.1 Major Sources and Types of Conflict

Perceived Adverse Changes

A high-impact source of conflict is a change in work methods, conditions of work, or employment opportunities that the people involved perceive negatively. Downsizing, the laying off of workers to reduce costs and increase efficiency, is one such change. (Downsizing also refers to reducing physical assets, such as selling one part of a business or consolidating a few offices.) An aspect of downsizing that continues to gain momentum is the automation of jobs, such as replacing rapid-service restaurant workers with kiosks and table computers that customers can use to order food. As mentioned previously, AI is a form of automation that can sometimes replace professional-level workers. People who want the jobs are in conflict, as are the people who see their coworkers dismissed.

> **downsizing** The laying off of workers or reducing physical assets to reduce costs and increase efficiency.

Continuous downsizing even when business conditions improve can precipitate labor-versus-management conflict. Management wants to eliminate as many jobs as possible, whereas the labor union values job security for its members. In 2019, the United Auto Workers Union (UAW) sued General Motors in federal court to stop plant closings in Michigan, Ohio, and Maryland. The union claimed that the company was forbidden from idling plants under the contract at the time.[11] Despite these conditions, all parties do not perceive downsizing as an adverse change. Company executives may believe that downsizing is rightsizing, leading to an efficient, competitive firm that will attract investors.

Competing Work and Family Demands

Balancing the demands of career and family is a major challenge facing today's workforce. The challenge is particularly intense for employees who are part of a two-wage-earning family. Work–family conflict occurs when the individual has to perform multiple roles: worker, spouse, and often parent or guardian of a dependent parent. (Work–family conflict is usually referred to as *work–life* conflict, but that term overlooks the reality that work is a big part of life. The term *work/personal life* would be more precise.)

> **work–family conflict** Occurs when the individual has to perform multiple roles: worker, spouse, and often parent or guardian of a dependent parent.

Work–family conflict is frequent because the multiple roles are often incompatible. Imagine having planned to attend your child's championship basketball game and then being informed at the last minute that a late-afternoon meeting has been scheduled. Both men and women experience considerable work–family conflict because of the desire to be successful at work and also spend a lot of time engaged in family activities, including being a good parent.[12]

Work–family conflict works in two directions. Work can interfere with the family, and the family can interfere with work. Work interfering with family life and family life interfering with work can both produce strain on the individual, according to a synthesis of 33 studies.[13] An example of the latter would be when a person's partner says, "If you don't work fewer hours and spend more time at home, I'm going to leave you."

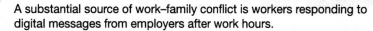

A substantial source of work–family conflict is workers responding to digital messages from employers after work hours.

A substantial source of work–family conflict is workers responding to digital messages from employers while participating in family activities, even during dinners and children's sporting events. A survey conducted by the American Psychological Association

Men as well as women experience considerable work–family conflict because of the desire to be successful at work and also spend a lot of time engaged in family activities, including being a good parent.

Center for Organizational Excellence found that more than 50 percent of employed adults check work messages at least once a day over the weekend, before or after work, and while home sick. Furthermore, it was found that 44 percent of workers responded to e-mails and text messages from work during vacation.[14]

Impact on Individual

Work–family conflict is significant for the individual. A survey of 513 employees in a *Fortune 500* company supports the plausible finding that working long hours interferes with family life. The long hours, in turn, lead to depression for some individuals and stress-related health problems, such as ulcers.[15] Work–family conflict is also a problem for employers because stressed-out workers are often less productive due to reduced ability to concentrate on work. Furthermore, a study revealed that dual-earner couples who experienced work–family conflict were more likely to experience family interruptions at work, tardiness, and absenteeism.[16]

Reducing Work–Family Conflict

The general resolution to work–family conflict is to have workplaces where employees have a choice of when, where, and how they do their work. Of course, this is not always easy for an employer to accomplish. Organizational programs to help reduce work–family conflict include flexible working hours, work-at-home programs, dependent-care centers, and parental leave programs. Time off to take care of urgent family demands, including parent–teacher conferences, is another approach to alleviating work–family conflict.

A note of caution for career-minded people is that a conflict-free balance between work and home life may be difficult to attain because significant career accomplishments require so much commitment. Few people can have a successful management, leadership, or professional career if they are willing to work only 40 hours per week.

A Theory of Four Basic Action Strategies to Attain Work and Family Goals

Research on the interface between work and personal life continues to increase at a rapid rate. In an attempt to integrate this wide-ranging research, theories of how people deal with the balance between work and personal life have emerged. The most relevant theory in terms of resolving conflict is an action-regulation model developed by management professors Andreas Hirschi, Kristen Shockley, and Hannes Zacher.[17]

The core of the model or theory is that humans are self-regulating agents who do more than passively react to demands imposed on them by work and family roles. Instead, they also actively shape their environment and development by establishing, pursuing, adapting, and/or abandoning family goals. They accomplish this through the use of different action strategies. Based on both action-regulation theory and research on multiple goals, the researchers propose that people use four basic action strategies to attain work and family goals. As a result, they ultimately attain work–family balance. The four action strategies are described next, with the first two being related to engagement and the second two being related to disengagement.

The first strategy is *allocating*, defined as the intentional activation and allocation of existing resources to achieve work and family goals. The aim of the strategy is to find ways to simultaneously attain work and family goals. An example would be to take advantage of existing policies that support goal attaining, such as the opportunity to work at home one day per week.

The second strategy is *changing*, the intentional increase of resources and/or reduction of barriers related to work and family goals. The aim of this strategy is to increase resources that enable the attaining work and family goals at the same time and to reduce barriers that prevent this from happening. One example of increasing resources would be to acquire new skills such as time-management skills, that would free up more time for work and family life. A way of reducing barriers would be to lessen exhaustion through meditation.

The third strategy is *sequencing*, the intentional prioritizing of some work or family goals in the short term so that other goals can be achieved in the long run. The aim is the same as the definition of the strategy—attain some work or family goals first in order to attain other family or work goals in the future. One example of the sequencing strategy would be to postpone having a family until attaining a promotion. Another would be to complete a key project first before spending more time with the family later.

The fourth strategy is *revising*, the intentional revision of present work or family goals and replacing them with new goals. The aim of the strategy is to disengage from work and family goals by changing demands. Another part of the aim is to select new work and family goals that can be attained simultaneously considering the resources and barriers that presently exist. One example of this strategy would be to reduce one's performance expectations for goals. Or, the person might establish new goals that are attainable with existing resources.

Few people who use these action strategies are aware that they are conforming to the theory. Yet, their intuition drives them to take a sensible course to reduce the conflict between work and family. An overburdened corporate professional might find a way to work at home five days per month and use the decrease in commuting time to take care of family chores.

The accompanying Negotiation and Conflict Resolution in Action feature describes how a well-known online travel agency helps employees deal with work–family conflicts.

NEGOTIATION AND CONFLICT RESOLUTION IN ACTION

Expedia Focuses on Balance between Work and Personal Life

The online travel company Expedia has been rated the best employer for work–life balance in the United Kingdom (UK). Expedia also rates highly in the United States for helping employees attain a good balance between the demands of work and personal life. At the company's two huge offices near a tube (subway) station in London, there are indoor Formula One simulators, a huge roof terrace for staff parties, various free bars, and chill-out zones. The boundaries between work and personal life are blurred in a positive way. Liz Estaugh, the director of technology, said, "What we try to encourage here at Expedia is to make it feel like we're big kids in a big kid's sandbox."

Ryan Johne, the reporting and analysis manager of the Expedia Group in Bellevue, Washington, posted this comment about the company: "Most other companies offer an open talent market as well, but together with the work/life balance and the Rockstar benefits at Expedia Group, being able to try new roles and/or teams is butter-cream frosting on an already delicious baked good."

Becky Waller, a program manager in Bellevue, posted that a work–life balance is not only valued, it's encouraged. She writes that people dedicate a portion of their days to the company, but they also take time off and have flexible work schedules. They do not have a manager pressuring them to give up part of their weekend to complete a project before Monday. Expedia Group recognizes that most employees have families and hobbies and that they need a good night's sleep.

Waller comments that leadership at the Expedia Group is extremely friendly to mothers who value their time with their families. "When I come home in the evening," she writes, "I'm not bone tired. I have energy to spend time with my children and my husband. I'm happy to dedicate a portion of my life to a company who allows me to dedicate so much of my life to my world outside of work."

The career-advice firm Fairygodboss conducted a survey of women about the work–life balance at the Expedia Group. Seventy-seven percent of women responded that the company has work–life-friendly policies, versus the industry average of 51 percent. Sixty-nine percent responded that the company has a work–life-friendly culture, versus an industry average of 59 percent. On a scale of 1 to 5, women employees rated the Expedia Group an average of 4.1 on work–life balance and whether the company offers remote jobs, part-time jobs, or is a flexible place to work.

Sexual Harassment

sexual harassment Unwanted sexually oriented behavior in the workplace that results in discomfort and/or interference with the job.

Many employees experience conflict because of sexual harassment by a manager, co-worker, customer, or vendor. Sexual harassment is unwanted sexually oriented behavior in the workplace that results in discomfort and/or interference with the job. Such harassment creates conflict because the goals of the harasser and the harassed are incompatible. The sexual harasser intends to have an exciting sexual experience or exert power, whereas the victim wants a peaceful work environment. High-profile cases of sexual harassment regularly receive extensive formal media and social media attention in many fields, including traditional business, show business, politics, civil service, the military, labor unions, and professional and amateur sports. Even religion professionals have been accused of and charged with sexual harassment.

Types and Frequency

Sexual harassment is divided into two types. In *quid pro quo* harassment, the employee's submission to or rejection of unwelcome sexual advances is used as the basis for a tangible employment action against or for the employee. An example of a tangible employment action is hiring, firing, or failing to promote a person. The demands of the harasser can be explicit or implied. Sexual harassment is considered illegal when it takes place so frequently or is so severe that it adversely affects the person's job or creates a hostile work environment.

Hostile work environment harassment occurs when someone in the workplace creates an intimidating, hostile, or offensive work environment. A tangible employment advantage or adverse economic consequence does not have to exist. The hostile-environment type of harassment is subject to considerable variation in perception and interpretation. A marketing executive might be developing a strategy to penetrate the rural African market. As part of his PowerPoint presentation, he shows a few photos of an African village that has images of topless women, naked young children, and adult males wearing loincloths. Some people would find these photos to be offensive and intimidating. Other workers present might compliment the executive for presenting realistic images of life in rural Africa.

Sexual harassment in the workplace was first recognized as men creating conflict for women. Over the years, many accusations have been made by males against females, males against males, and females against females. Complaints of transgender sexual harassment have surfaced in recent years. Estimates about the frequency of sexual harassment vary widely, with women being harassed much more frequently than men. A representative finding is that about 51 percent of women and 12 percent of men say they have been the direct victim of sexual harassment at work.[18]

Source: SpeedKingz/Shutterstock.

Sexual harassment in the workplace was first recognized as men creating conflict for women. Over the years, many accusations have been made by males against females, males against males, and females against females.

One problem in interpreting statistics about the frequency of harassment is that many employees may be hesitant to file a claim because of possible retaliation. More than two-thirds of workers who filed sexual harassment charges with the Equal Employment Opportunity Commission (EEOC) say that they suffered some form of retaliation, including job transfer, shift changes, and getting fired. The findings were based on an analysis of 45,000 complaints filed with the EEOC during a three-year period.[19]

Another type of sexual harassment that might go unreported is the harassment of women industrial sales representatives by a member or members of a major account. If the woman does report the incident, a frequent management action is to allow her to be taken off the account, rather than confronting the harasser. The sales rep then might suffer financially from losing a major account.[20]

Sexual harassment has substantial consequences. Multiple studies indicate that experiencing harassment prompts women to leave their jobs, taking their ideas, work relationships, and potential away with them. Costs are incurred when new employees have to be recruited and trained to fill the roles vacated. Harassment can also damage group cohesiveness and functioning, leading to lowered productivity and increased employee turnover.[21]

Eliminating and Decreasing Harassment

A company policy that emphasizes the illegality of sexual harassment is helpful in minimizing its presence. The policy should be supported by an organizational culture that promotes the just treatment of employees by managers and coworkers. A highly effective preventive measure is for individual workers to assert their rights at the first instance or hint of harassment. An example would be a woman explaining to a supervisor who hugged her suggestively that she will not tolerate such behavior and that she will file a report to upper management should the incident be repeated. The policy is an important first step, but a U.S. federal court ruling specified that proof merely of the existence of an antiharassment policy is insufficient. The court wants to see that the policy was effective in practice in reasonably preventing and correcting any harassing behavior.[22]

A major problem in controlling sexual harassment, according to the research of Vanessa K. Bohns and Lauren DeVincent, is that people who make romantic advances generally underestimate the discomfort their overtures create for their targets of affection. The pursuers believe that the intended recipients of their affection feel more comfortable and willing to reject their advances than is actually true. The studies also found that when women were pursuing a romantic relationship, they also inaccurately judged the comfort level of their targets.[23]

Many recommendations to managers have been advanced to prevent sexual harassment in the workplace and therefore reduce this major source of conflict. A particularly useful one is offered by attorney Jonathan A. Segal, who suggests that managers detail what constitutes prohibited contact. Managers should make three key points:

- Offensive conduct can occur not only in the workplace but also at company-sponsored business and social events and can even include pursuing a romantic relationship with a coworker by calling or texting him or her during nonworking hours.

- Harassing behavior beyond that of other employees can be reported, including the behavior of customers, vendors, and suppliers.

- Harassment taking place through social media, e-mail, and text messages is within the scope of prohibited conduct.[24]

The combination of federal, state, provincial, and local government guidelines and company policies against harassment helps reduce conflict over sexual harassment because the source of the conflict is reduced or eliminated. For example, not feeling forced to listen to the lewd comments of a supervisor, coworker, or customer makes for a less conflictual and more peaceful work environment.

Despite all the efforts to prevent and control sexual harassment, complaints about and formal charges of sexual harassment continue to surge. One possible reason for the surge is that people who have been sexually harassed feel freer to report the incidents. For example, the #MeToo movement has encouraged thousands of women and men to report on incidents of being sexually harassed. Another possibility is that the publicity about such behavior entices many people to harass others, much like a "copycat crime."

One of the reasons that sexual harassment is difficult to prevent and decrease is that it is about power as well as sex. James Campbell, a professor of leadership and management at the University of Texas at Arlington, says that sexual harassment is about power, aggression, and manipulation and is an abuse of power.[25]

Katherine Klein, a management professor at the Wharton School of the University of Pennsylvania, focuses on the role of organizational culture in preventing sexual harassment. She says that in order to prevent sexual harassment in the workplace, "You need a culture that makes it clear that sexual harassment won't be tolerated. And at the same time, you need a culture that makes it psychologically safe for employees to express concerns, complaints, and suggestions."[26] Fostering a workplace culture of tolerance, acceptance, and civility is more effective in preventing harassment than conducting an occasional antiharassment training program.[27]

Management must carefully evaluate all accusations and not assume that the accused person is guilty. A person accused of sexual harassment deserves to present his or her side of the story and should receive due process from the organization.

Factional Groups and Intragroup Conflict

Interpersonal conflict often takes place because there are different factions (subgroups) within groups with differing points of view and different loyalties. Factions may occur as a result of a merger, for example, when groups are formed to balance the representatives from the two merged companies, such as two merged telecommunications firms. Factional groups may also arise when a joint venture takes place, such as two companies working together to produce top-of-the-line home-entertainment centers. Each of the two parent companies assigns a few of its own managers to be on the new, joint venture's management team.

Often the factional groups consist of two subgroups, each with several representatives, such as a cost-cutting task force consisting of three representatives each from marketing, operations, and finance. The potential for conflict within factional groups increases when the subgroups differ substantially in demographic characteristics, such as age, gender, and educational level.

Factional group conflict is often referred to as *intragroup conflict* because the problems exist inside the group among its members. Intragroup conflict can arise from various sources, such as diverse opinions and perspectives, and generational conflict. Incivility and bullying also contribute to intragroup conflict.

Territorial Disputes (Turf Wars)

territorial disputes Disputes that involve protecting and hoarding resources that give one power, such as information, relationships, and decision-making authority.

Also referred to as turf wars, territorial disputes involve protecting and hoarding resources that give one power, such as information, relationships, and decision-making authority. The purpose of territorial disputes is to vie for three kinds of *territory* in the modern corporate survival game: information, relationships, or authority. A relationship is hoarded through such tactics as discouraging others from visiting a key customer or blocking a high performer from getting a promotion or transfer.[28] For example, a manager might tell others that her outstanding performer is mediocre to prevent the person from being considered for a valuable promotion possibility. The dispute comes about when the person's mediocre evaluation is challenged.

Territorial disputes also arise when two different team leaders or department heads disagree over who has responsibility for a project. As organizations evolve and change, people sometimes wind up duplicating the work of other groups, such two different groups working on the development of a new app to attract customers. Conflict arises because neither group wants to give up the project. Brian Uzzi, professor of leadership and organizational change at the Kellogg School of Management at Northwestern University, says, "Research shows that taking something away from someone is experienced as far more harmful than putting an additional burden on him or her."[29]

Source: fizkes/Shutterstock.

Territorial disputes arise when two different team leaders or department heads disagree over who has responsibility for a project.

Summary

A conflict occurs when two or more parties pursue mutually exclusive goals. During the last 100 years, three different perspectives on conflict have developed: the traditional view, the human relations view, and the interactionist view.

Conflict results in both positive and negative consequences. Among the positive consequences are (1) higher group performance, (2) reflective communication that facilitates task performance, (3) increased creativity, (4) increased diagnostic information, (5) increased group cohesiveness, and (6) opportunity for learning and growth.

Among the negative consequences of conflict are (1) poor physical and mental health, (2) wasted resources, (3) poor performance and sidetracked goals, (4) heightened self-interest, (5) workplace aggression, and (6) workplace violence.

The sources, types, and antecedents of conflict are numerous and include the following: (1) perceived adverse changes, (2) competing work and family demands, (3) sexual harassment, (4) factional groups and intragroup conflict, and (5) territorial disputes or turf wars.

Our study of competing work and family demands includes the impact on the individual, reducing work–family conflict, and a theory of four basic action strategies to attain work and family goals. Our study of sexual harassment includes types and frequency and methods of eliminating and decreasing harassment.

Key Terms and Phrases

Conflict, p. 114
Downsizing, p. 119
Sexual harassment, p. 122

Territorial disputes, p. 124
Work–family conflict, p. 119

Discussion Questions and Activities

1. What would it be like working for someone who scored 75 on this chapter's self-quiz, "My Tendencies toward Conflict-Proneness"?
2. Provide an example from your work or personal life in which conflict led to higher group performance.
3. What factor or factors do you think tend to make athletic teams so cohesive?
4. What should a worker do if he or she thinks that a coworker might become violent based on that worker's Facebook posts?
5. Provide an example you have observed, or can imagine, in which family life interfered with work. How might the conflict have been resolved?
6. What practical uses do you see for the action-regulation model (four basic strategies to attain work and family goals)?
7. Several high-tech companies provide free dinners to staff members who work late. In what way do these "free dinners" contribute to work–family conflict?

8. What compels people to sexually harass work associates when they probably know that many other people have suffered major negative consequences from being charged with harassment?
9. Some women corporate professionals think that receiving a compliment about their appearance is a mild form of sexual harassment. Explain your position on this issue.
10. What kind of territorial dispute might exist at a college or university?

Skill-Building Exercise: Field Information about Sources of Workplace Conflict

The purpose of this exercise is to collect fresh information about sources of workplace conflict. Organize into teams of about five people. Each person asks three people he or she knows to identify the one or two major sources of, or reasons for, conflict in his or her place of work. Each student can include him- or herself in the three respondents. Use the most appropriate medium of communication, whether it be digital or an in-person conversation.

After all the responses have been collected by all group members, make a frequency distribution of the sources of conflict identified. Which sources of conflict are the most frequent among all the responses received? How do these sources of conflict you have uncovered compare to the sources of conflict mentioned in this chapter?

CASE PROBLEM 8A: The Concerned Sales Trainee

Emma was thrilled about the position she just landed as a sales representative for a company that provides data backup and storage for small organizations throughout the country. She was assigned a sales territory in San Diego, California, where she lived with her husband and two preschool-aged children. Before working her territory, Emma was required to attend 10 days of training and onboarding at company headquarters in Cleveland, Ohio.

One of the key trainers in the program was Wesley, an energetic and successful man in his early fifties. During a beverage-and-food break on the first morning of the training and onboarding program, Wesley approached Emma and complimented her on her "great California tan," and "knockout appearance." Emma was not particularly comfortable with the comments, but she let them pass.

Before the dinner meeting on the second night of the program, Wesley approached Emma and engaged her in a conversation about how she was enjoying the sales training and onboarding. He then handed her a business card and said, "I thought perhaps that you might be a little lonely being away from home for 10 days, so here is my business card. Please get in touch with me if you would like to hang out with me a little."

Emma thought that Wesley was stepping over the line of good business judgment, but she smiled politely and said, "Thanks anyway, but I am so overwhelmed with all this important information I am receiving that I have no spare time. I'm not too lonely because I use Skype to stay in touch with my husband and children."

The following morning, Emma received a text message from Wesley that said, "You are totally charming and beautiful. Get back to me."

Emma later phoned her best friend Crystal and said, "Wesley is influential because he is the national sales manager. But I think that his behavior toward me might constitute sexual harassment. Yet, five days into my job, I guess I shouldn't attempt to lodge a complaint about a company executive."

Crystal replied, "You have got to do something. The national sales manager is a predator."

Questions

1. To what extent is Wesley sexually harassing Emma?
2. If Wesley is guilty, what type of sexual harassment is he committing?
3. What steps should Emma take so that she can stop Wesley's advances yet still maintain a good working relationship with him?
4. What would be the advantages and disadvantages of Emma filing a complaint about Wesley with the company?

Associated Role Play

One student plays the role of Emma, who wants to succeed at the company and recognizes that it is important for her not to have an antagonistic reputation with the national sales manager, Wesley. At the same time, she does not want to submit to any of his advances. Another student plays the role of Wesley, who makes another advance toward Emma, with the role player choosing the nature of the advance. Both Emma and Wesley are determined to attain their goals. Run the role play for about 10 minutes. Observers might provide feedback on how well Emma fends off the advances of Wesley while not jeopardizing her chances of getting off to a good start with the company.

Amanda is the vice president of administrative services and human resources at Belmont Travel, a national travel agency serving corporations and large government agencies. Although the Internet has replaced most travel agencies, Belmont has found a niche in organizing travel for business meetings and controlling travel costs. Amanda is facing a bothersome problem related to internal conferences.

"Like so many of our clients," says Amanda, "we have a small amount of office space for our number of employees, particularly with respect to the availability of conference rooms. Our people love to meet in person and thrash out problems and plan our next moves. We do conduct some virtual meetings, but there is still a high demand for in-person meetings."

When asked what specific problems the shortage of conference-room space created, Amanda answered, "You wouldn't believe it. You should see those angry faces. One group is in the conference room running a little late, and the next group is knocking on the door or trying to barge into the meeting and take over the space. Some of our people conduct their meetings at a Starbucks, McDonald's, or Dunkin' Donuts. We have found small groups of people conducting brief meetings in the building lobby or even under a stairwell.

"When one group can't find a place to meet, we get all sorts of angry e-mails and intranet posts directed at me and other department heads. We spend far too much time fighting about conference-room space. We are wasting a lot of time that should be spent serving customers."

When asked what Belmont Travel has done so far to deal with the meeting-room shortage, Amanda said, "We are using online calendars to allocate space, but the results can be ugly. Some group gets scheduled for a meeting at 7:30 a.m. on a Monday, which doesn't go over very well. Neither does a meeting set for 4:45 p.m. on a Friday. Then you've got the problem of deception and trickery. A few groups book space just in case they might have a meeting. It's like booking a second airplane flight just in case there will not be space available with one carrier.

"I asked the CEO if he would consider keeping a trailer in the parking lot for meetings, but he said it would look too crude for a travel agency. Whatever we decide to do, my job is to reduce some of this timewasting and stressful conflict."

Questions

1. How can conflict about conference rooms exist in this age of high technology?
2. How should Amanda go about resolving the conflicts mentioned in this case? (You might want to consult the methods of conflict resolution described in Chapters 9 and 10.)
3. What's wrong with company employees meeting at a nearby coffee shop or restaurant?

Associated Role Play

One student plays the role of Amanda, who decides to hold a dinner meeting at 5:30 p.m. in a private room at a restaurant one block away from Belmont. She advises the four department heads who will attend the meeting that before dinner, they will discuss the conference-space problem. Four other students play the roles of the department heads, who are angry about the conference-room struggle. Observers will provide feedback about how much progress the five people have made toward resolving the conflict about conference-room space.

Notes

1. Yuhyung Shin, "Conflict Resolution in Virtual Teams," *Organizational Dynamics*, 4 (2005), p. 332.

2. Literature reviewed in Fatemeh Shoa Sharg, Mansour Soufi, and Mohammad Ali Dadashi, "Conflict Management and Negotiation," *International Research Journal of Applied and Basic Sciences*, No. 5, 2013, pp. 538–543; Suzanne C. de Janasz, Karen O. Dowd, and Beth Z. Schneider, *Interpersonal Skills in Organizations* (New York: McGraw-Hill Higher Education 2002), p. 243; Stephen P. Robbins and Timothy A. Judge, *Organizational Behavior*, 16th ed. (Upper Saddle River, NJ: Pearson, 2015), pp. 401–402.

3. Jinseok S. Chun and Jin Nam Choi, "Members' Needs, Intragroup Conflict, and Group Performance," *Journal of Applied Psychology*, May 2014, pp. 437–450.

4. Ruchi Sinha, et al., "Skewed Task Conflicts in Teams: What Happens When a Few Members See More Conflict than the Rest?" *Journal of Applied Psychology*, July 2016, p. 1046.

5. Joann Ellison Rodgers, "Go Forth in Anger," *Psychology Today*, April 2014, p. 76.

6. Zak Mustapha, "Managing Conflict in the Workplace," *Business.com*, February 22, 2017, p. 2.

7. Nathan A. Bowling and Terry A. Beehr, "Workplace Harassment from the Victim's Perspective: A Theoretical Model and Meta-Analysis," *Journal of Applied Psychology*, September 2006, pp. 998–1012.

8. Mary Ann Von Glinow, Debra L. Shapiro, and Jeanne M. Brett, "Can We *Talk*, and Should We? Managing Emotional

Conflict in Multicultural Teams," *Academy of Management Review*, October 2004, pp. 578–592.

9. M. Sandy Hershcovis, et al., "Predicting Workplace Aggression: A Meta-Analysis," *Journal of Applied Psychology*, January 2007, pp. 228–238.

10. H. Lee Murphy, "Back to Work in Aurora, as Shooting Still Echoes," *Reuters*, February 22, 2019, pp. 1–5.

11. "UAW Sues General Motors to Stop Plant Closings in Michigan, Ohio, Maryland," *The Associated Press*, February 26, 2019, p. 1.

12. Julie Bennett, "Balancing Work and Home Life Is Not Only a Woman's Issue," Society of Human Resource Management supplement appearing in *The Wall Street Journal*, June 20, 2012, p. B9.

13. Christoph Nohe, Laurenz L. Meier, Karlheinz Sonntag, and Alexandra Michel, "The Chicken or the Egg? A Meta-Analysis of Panel Studies of the Relationship between Work–Family Conflict and Strain," *Journal of Applied Psychology*, March 2015, pp. 522–536.

14. Survey reported in Greg Keller, "NYC Bill Would Shield Workers from After-Hours Calls, Emails," *The Commercial Appeal*, May 20, 2018.

15. Virginia Smith Major, Katherine J. Klein, and Mark G. Ehrhart, "Work Time, Work Interference with Family, and Psychological Distress," *Journal of Applied Psychology*, June 2002, pp. 427–436.

16. Leslie B. Hammer, Talya N. Bauer, and Alicia A. Grandey, "Work–Family Conflict and Work-Related Withdrawal Behaviors," *Journal of Business and Psychology*, Spring 2003, pp. 419–436.

17. Andreas Hirschi, Kristen Shockley, and Hannes Zacher, "Achieving Work–Family Balance: An Action Regulation Model," *Academy of Management Review*, January 2019, pp. 150–171.

18. American Management Association survey reported in Joann S. Lublin, "When #Me Too at Work Becomes Catch-22," *The Wall Street Journal*, January 25, 2018, pp. B1, B7.

19. Lauren Weber, "Harassment Claims Still Bring Retaliation," *The Wall Street Journal*, December 13, 2018, p. B6.

20. Vanessa Fuhrmans and Julian Steinberg, "When the Client Is a Harasser," *The Wall Street Journal*, July 7–8, 2018, pp. B1, B2.

21. Colleen Ammerman and Boris Groysberg, "Why Sexual Harassment Persists and What Organizations Can Do about It," *Harvard Business Review*, December 21, 2017, p. 2.

22. Andrew Slobodien and Elizabeth Peters, "Beyond Harassment Prohibitions: Don't Just 'Set and Forget' Anti-Harassment Policies," *HR Magazine*, November 2012, p. 76.

23. Vanessa K. Bohns and Lauren DeVincent, "To Reduce Sexual Misconduct, Help People Understand How Their Advances Might Be Received," *Harvard Business Review*, April 26, 2018, p. 2.

24. Jonathan A. Segal, "Strengthen Your Harassment Complaint Process," *HR Magazine*, April 2018, p. 65.

25. Quoted in Brendan L. Smith, "What It Really Takes to Stop Sexual Harassment," *Monitor on Psychology*, February 2018, p. 38.

26. "What Firms Can Do to Prevent Sexual Harassment," *Knowledge@Wharton* (http://knowledge.wharton.upenn.edu), November 28, 2017, p.3.

27. Sue Shellenbarger, "Harassment Training Gets a Revamp," *The Wall Street Journal*, December 20, 2017, p. A15.

28. Annette Simmons, *Territorial Games: Understanding and Ending Turf Wars at Work* (New York: AMACOM, 1998); Robert J. Herbold, *The Fiefdom Syndrome* (New York: Currency Doubleday, 2004).

29. Quoted in Amy Gallo, "How to Navigate at Turf War at Work," *Harvard Business Review*, September 27, 2017, p. 2.

Basic Techniques for Resolving Conflict

CHAPTER 9

Source: fizkes/Shutterstock.

Chapter Outline

Five Steps to Workplace Conflict Resolution

The Traditional Conflict-Resolution Styles

A Variety of Techniques for Resolving Conflict

Confrontation and Problem Solving

Win–Lose Conflict Resolution

Confront, Contain, and Connect for Anger

Reframing through Cognitive Restructuring and Asking Questions

Five Rules for Dealing Effectively with Organizational Conflict

Additional Behaviors and Attitudes for Resolving Conflict

Learning Objectives

After reading and studying this chapter and doing the exercises, you should be able to:

1. Identify five steps to workplace conflict resolution.
2. Summarize the traditional conflict-resolution styles.
3. Be prepared to apply a variety of techniques for resolving conflict.
4. Pinpoint several additional behaviors and attitudes for resolving conflict.

Workplace conflict is inevitable, and leaders and managers spend an estimated 20 percent of their time resolving conflict. An understanding of and skill in resolving conflict are therefore success factors for leaders and managers as well as corporate professionals and business owners. An important general consideration is to face conflict rather than letting conflict slide or glossing over it. Ignoring or glossing over conflict does not resolve the real causes of conflict and seldom leads to a long-term solution.

In this chapter we describe a variety of approaches to resolving workplace conflict. A description of one conception of five steps to workplace conflict resolution is followed by a summary of the five frequently quoted traditional conflict-resolution styles. We then describe several basic techniques for resolving conflict, followed by a list of useful behaviors and attitudes suited to conflict resolution.

Five Steps to Workplace Conflict Resolution

Many different approaches to resolving conflict in the workplace are possible, including the techniques described in this chapter, along with Chapters 10–12. Conflict specialist Patricia Lotich has developed a five-step model for conflict resolution in the workplace. The model is presented here because it integrates several well-accepted ideas about negotiation and managing conflict. Lotich also recommends intervening in the conflict at its beginning rather than allowing it to fester and become too difficult to resolve.[1]

Step 1: Separate the people from the problem, and focus on the process. The conflict is about the process, not the person. Focus on the issue, and avoid linking the issue to a particular individual or group. Most conflicts are about limited resources, such as different groups wanting a bigger chunk of the budget. If the conflict is about limited resources, investigate how the resources are allocated, rather than focusing on the individuals or groups competing for those resources. For example, it might pay to investigate why the marketing group receives so much money in comparison to the logistics group rather than frame the budget dispute as being between the heads of marketing and logistics. If the conflict is emotionally charged, establish a cooling-off period before attempting to resolve the issue or issues.

Step 2: Identify a mediator. When conflict is intense, it might warrant a neutral party to help mediate. The mediator could be a manager when the conflict is between two subordinates, or it could be a mediation specialist. The mediator will help the parties in conflict to discuss the issues. Among the mediator's activities would be establishing specific guidelines for interacting with each other, as well as identify underlying issues that contribute to the conflict. In the example of the marketing group versus the logistics group, one of the underlying issues might be that the role of logistics in getting products to market is underappreciated.

Lotich presents her own example of identifying underlying issues. She had an employee who was promoted to supervisor and was having a difficult time managing a person who was formerly a coworker. The underlying issue was about dealing with the resentment of the employee who felt that she was bypassed for promotion.

Step 3: Clarify the problem. An essential part of resolving conflict is to take the time to listen to all of the concerns and to attain a clear understanding of the nature of the problem. It is helpful to work toward identifying each party's interests more than

Source: wavebreakmedia/Shutterstock

When conflict is intense, it might warrant a neutral part to help mediate.

their positions in relation to the conflict. Understanding another person's interests (why it is important to him or her) contributes to separating the person from the problem. For example, if there are limited resources to support a team project, and you are the manager, listen to the concerns of the parties involved about meeting employee goals. Budget constraints, such as not having the right equipment, can hamper goal attainment.

Step 4: Explore all options. A standard technique is to brainstorm ideas for ways of resolving the problem that would result in a win–win solution. An ideal goal of conflict resolution is to achieve a positive result for all parties, as in negotiation. Achieving this goal will sometimes involve establishing criteria for determining the fairness of the outcome. In the marketing-versus-logistics conflict, one criterion might be that any division of the budget should not force either group to lay off staff.

Step 5. Agree on a resolution. The parties in the conflict should be part of the process to find and agree on a settlement of the conflict. The two sides might reach a spoken agreement that the proposed resolution is the best solution to the problem. At other times, a written agreement might be necessary. The marketing group in question might scrutinize its advertising expenses and find that certain types of advertising might have such low yield that the expense is not justified. These funds could then be shifted to the logistics group in the next budget cycle.

A justification for pursuing the five steps is that organizations that have mastered the art of conflict resolution have a competitive advantage. This is true because positive conflict outcomes decrease performance barriers and enable organizations to more easily reach corporate objectives.

The Traditional Conflict-Resolution Styles

Before describing specific methods of resolving conflict, it is useful to understand the five widely cited styles of handling conflict. As shown in Figure 9.1, the five styles are based on a combination of satisfying one's own concerns (assertiveness) and satisfying the concerns of others (cooperativeness).[2]

1. *Competitive.* The competitive style of managing conflict is a desire to achieve one's own concerns or goals at the expense of the other party or to dominate. A person with a competitive orientation is likely to engage in win–lose power struggles, such as trying to get a rival for a promotion fired. The competitive style is also referred to as *forcing.*

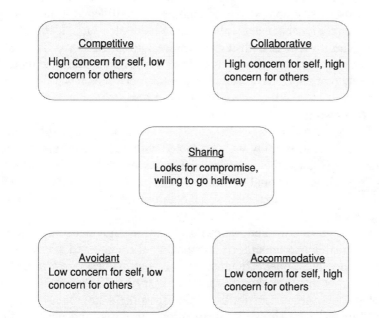

FIGURE 9.1 The Five Traditional Conflict-Management Styles

The competitive style of managing conflict is a desire to achieve one's own concerns or goals at the expense of the other party, or to dominate.

2. *Accommodative*. The accommodative style favors appeasement or satisfying the other's concerns without taking care of one's own. People with this orientation may be generous or self-sacrificing just to maintain a relationship. A dissatisfied employee might be accommodated with a larger-than-average pay increase just to calm the employee down and obtain his or her loyalty.

3. *Sharing*. The sharing style is halfway between domination and appeasement. Sharers prefer moderate but incomplete satisfaction for both parties, which results in a compromise. The phrase "splitting the difference" reflects this orientation and is commonly used in such activities as negotiating a budget or purchasing equipment. A compromise between an open-space office plan and cubicles might be an open-space plan but with cubicles readily available when privacy is needed.

4. *Collaborative*. In contrast to the other styles, the collaborative style reflects a desire to satisfy the needs of both parties. It is based on an underlying philosophy of win–win, the belief that after conflict has been resolved, both sides should gain something of value. (You will recognize win–win as the integrative approach to negotiation). A win–win approach is genuinely concerned with arriving at a settlement that meets the needs of both parties or that at least does not badly damage the welfare of either side. When a collaborative approach is used, the relationship between the parties improves. An example of a win–win approach would be for a manager to permit a call-center employee to work from home provided that his or her productivity increased enough to pay for the equipment needed to set up a work station at home.

   A study was conducted with 139 working adults about the link between the use of the collaborative style and emotional intelligence when working in teams. The results consistently showed that individuals with high emotional intelligence preferred to seek collaborative solutions when facing conflict.[3] These results make sense because a key component of emotional intelligence is the ability to build constructive relationships, and collaboration facilitates such relationships.

5. *Avoidant*. The avoider is both uncooperative and unassertive. He or she is indifferent to the concerns of either party. The person may actually withdraw from the conflict, rely on fate, or try to suppress the conflict. A manager sometimes uses the avoidant style to stay out of a conflict between two team members, who are left to resolve their own conflict.

   The five styles of management conflict have implications for other aspects of workplace behavior. A study was conducted with 320 public service workers from five states in Nigeria that explored the relationship between conflict-resolution strategies and organizational citizenship behavior (OCB). Such behavior reflects a willingness to work for the good of the organization even without the promise of a specific reward.

   The public service workers were chosen for the study because, at the time, many public enterprises had undergone organizational change and restructuring in order to improve organizational efficiency and competitiveness. As a result, there was a retrenchment of many workers in the public service. The retrenchment had serious psychological consequences for both laid-off workers and the layoff survivors who remained on the job. The strike negotiations, protests, and pleas of the workers'

win–win The belief that after a conflict has been resolved, both sides should gain something of value.

union halted the government from continuing with the retrenchment. It appeared likely that managers at most government ministries and firms used a combination of conflict-resolution strategies to resolve the conflicts that arose. Layoff survivors experienced job insecurity, lowered morale, decreased loyalty, distrust, and reduced productivity. Other negative consequences of the layoff included less creativity, organizational commitment, job satisfaction, and OCB.

A major finding of the study was that the avoiding style (including forcing a solution and withdrawing) was negatively related to OCB on the part of subordinates. The more the managers used forcing, or withdrawing, to end the conflict, the less the subordinates developed OCBs. An explanation for these findings is that when subordinates feel they have been denied the opportunity to share and exchange information on a conflict issue, they will feel unfairly treated. In exchange, the workers may not develop high OCB. Instead, they may feel aggrieved and frustrated and not bother going beyond their job responsibilities to help coworkers or the organization.

The study also found that confronting, compromising, and smoothing strategies were positively associated with OCB. An additional finding was that employees who scored high on a test of emotional intelligence were more likely to develop OCB. One rationale offered for this finding is that workers with high emotional intelligence are able to adopt effective coping strategies to deal with the stress caused by unfair treatment by superiors. Consequently, it is easier for them to develop organizational citizenship behaviors.[4]

These five styles of managing conflict provide useful cornerstone knowledge about the subject. Yet these styles are cited so frequently, some readers are prompted to think that these styles represent the only way to manage and resolve conflict. In reality, conflict resolution in particular encompasses many different techniques.

The accompanying self-quiz provides you an opportunity to think through your basic approach to management and resolving conflict.

A Variety of Techniques for Resolving Conflict

Styles of dealing with conflict are closely related to methods of resolving conflict. For example. a collaborative style is a way of managing and resolving conflict. In this section we present a sampling of basic conflict-resolution methods. The methods of conflict resolution presented in Chapter 10 might be considered more advanced, but the distinction between basic and advanced should not be considered as absolute.

Confrontation and Problem Solving

A widely applicable approach to resolving conflict is confrontation and problem solving, a method of identifying the true source of conflict and resolving it systematically. The confrontation approach is gentle and tactful rather than combative and abusive. Reasonableness is important because the person who takes the initiative to resolve the conflict wants to maintain a harmonious relationship with the other party. Resolving a conflict involves emotion, such as being angry with the other side. The best results will be attained if the emotion is expressed in a reasonable yet assertive manner rather than being explosive. A reasonable expression of emotion might be, "I am upset that this problem has lingered so long. I want to resolve it today."

During the confrontation, one person decides to work cooperatively and confronts the second person. At this point, the person confronted may indicate a willingness to accept the confrontation or may decide to gloss over its seriousness. The conflict is often resolved at this step, particularly if it is not serious or complicated. An example might be conflict about how much an executive is spending to entertain customers visiting the company.

After the confrontation, the two parties discuss their own opinions, attitudes, and feelings in relation to the conflict, attempting to identify the real issue. For example, the real cause of conflict between a team leader and a team member might be that they have a

confrontation and problem solving A method of identifying the true source of conflict and resolving it systematically.

Collaborative versus Competitive Styles of Conflict Management and Resolution

Answer on a scale of 1 to 5 how well you agree with each of the following statements: disagree strongly, disagree, neutral, agree, and agree strongly.

Statement about Conflict	Disagree Strongly	Disagree	Neutral	Agree	Agree Strongly
1. After a conflict is over, there is one winner and one loser.	5	4	3	2	1
2. Very little besides winning is important when attempting to resolve conflict.	5	4	3	2	1
3. When you root for one team in an athletic contest, it is natural to hate the other side.	5	4	3	2	1
4. I like the idea of shaking hands or bumping fists with the other side after a conflict has been resolved.	1	2	3	4	5
5. The ability to resolve conflict is an important skill for many types of workers.	1	2	3	4	5
6. The winner should take all.	5	4	3	2	1
7. If I lose an argument with someone, I will hold a grudge against him or her.	5	4	3	2	1
8. I like the idea of tournaments in which the first-round losers receive another opportunity to play.	1	2	3	4	5
9. Nice people usually finish last.	5	4	3	2	1
10. The other side in a conflict should be regarded as an enemy rather than a partner.	5	4	3	2	1
11. The other side in a conflict should be regarded as a partner rather than an enemy.	1	2	3	4	5
12. If I lost (or were to lose) a conflict with another person, I would seek revenge.	5	4	3	2	1
13. Being nasty and insulting toward the other side is an effective way of resolving conflict.	5	4	3	2	1
14. I think that labor unions should find a better way than calling a strike to settle a dispute.	1	2	3	4	5
15. I like the idea of social groups rioting to try to get their demands met.	5	4	3	2	1

Scoring and Interpretation: Calculate your score by adding up the numbers circled:

60–75: You prefer a *collaborative* or *win–win* approach to resolving conflict. You tend to be concerned about finding long-term solutions to conflict that benefit both sides.

15–59: You prefer a *competitive* or *win–lose* approach to resolving conflict. You want to maximize gain for yourself, with little concern about the welfare of the other side. In an organization that emphasizes collaboration, this approach to conflict resolution would not be welcome. You might also develop the reputation of being overly aggressive during conflict resolution or negotiation.

different concept of what constitutes a fair day's work. After understanding the real issue, the parties attempt to develop specific means of reducing or eliminating the cause of the conflict.

If the cause cannot be changed (such as changing one's opinion of a fair day's work), a way of working around the cause is devised. In this example, more specific output goals might be jointly agreed on. If both parties agree on a solution, then the confrontation has been successful. After the solution has been implemented, both parties should check periodically to ensure that their agreements are being kept.

The collaborative style of conflict resolution meshes together confrontation and problem solving. A major outcome is that trust is built between two parties as they search for the real reason for the conflict. Both the collaborative style of conflict resolution and confrontation and problem solving are therefore designed to achieve win–win solutions to conflict.

Win–Lose Conflict Resolution

The opposite approach to win–win conflict resolution is *win–lose*, in which one side attempts to maximize gain at the expense of the other. As in negotiation, win–lose is also referred to as a *zero-sum game*, in which one side wins nothing and the other side wins everything. Many people believe that win–lose is the best approach to resolving conflict, contributing to the fact that so much conflict goes unresolved in the form of bankruptcies, voluntary turnover, involuntary turnover, and physical attacks in the workplace. A person with a competitive orientation is likely to engage in power struggles in which one side wins and the other loses. "My way or the highway" is a win–lose strategy.

If faced with an adversary who has a win–lose orientation, a plausible defense is to keep pointing out the benefits of finding a solution that fits both sides. Highland Hospital in Rochester, New York, developed such a consistently heavy patient load that it proposed erecting a new five-story building on the perimeter of its premises to accommodate more patients and enlarged medal services. Members of the town board attempted to block the construction of the new medical building because it did not fit the character of the residential neighborhood in which the hospital was located. Hospital officials emphasized how an expanded medical facility would help the community.

The two sides sat down for a two-hour meeting on a Monday among neighborhood representatives, hospital officials, and city staffers. Soon both sides reached a workable compromise on rezoning. The new building at the perimeter of the property would be three stories or 60 feet high and set as far back on the hospital property as architecturally feasible. Highland Hospital officials also agreed to cap future construction at 9 stories instead of 11 at the center of the property.[5]

If faced with an adversary who has a win–lose orientation, a plausible defense is to keep on pointing out the benefits of finding a solution that fits both sides.

Confront, Contain, and Connect for Anger

A variation of confrontation and problem solving has been developed specifically to resolve conflict with angry people, and it involves confronting, containing, and connecting. You *confront* by jumping right in and getting an agitated worker talking to prevent future blowups. The confrontation, however, is not aimed at arguing with the angry worker. If the person yells, you talk more softly. You *contain* by moving an angry worker out of sight and earshot. At the same time, you remain impartial. The supervisor is advised not to choose sides or appear to be a friend. Finally, you *connect* by asking open-ended questions, such as "What would you like us to do about your concern?" to get to the real issues behind an outburst.

Using this approach, one worker revealed he was upset because a female coworker got to leave early to pick up her daughter at daycare. The man also needed to leave early one day a week for personal reasons but felt awkward making the request. So instead of asserting himself in an explicit and direct manner about his needs, he flared up.

An important feature of the confront, contain, and connect technique is that it provides angry workers a place where they can vent their frustrations without embarrassing themselves. Mediator Nina Meierding says: "Workers need a safe outlet to talk through anger and not feel they will be minimized or put their job in jeopardy."[6]

The accompanying Negotiation and Conflict Resolution in Action feature describes how many workers throughout the world are attempting to deal with conflicts and other sources of stress in settings built for that purpose.

NEGOTIATION AND CONFLICT RESOLUTION IN ACTION

Rage Rooms for Dealing with Conflict

A woman from an information technology (IT) firm frustrated by the many conflicts and challenges she faced in work and personal life moved through a warehouse alternately swinging a baseball bat, a golf club, and a sledgehammer. Her aim was to destroy office equipment and glass bottles placed on a table. When the woman completed her rage episode, she was applauded and given a bottle of water by the owners of Smash the Rage—Kathy Barros, a human resources (HR) professional, and Massiel Reye, a recruiter. The two owners operate their rage room at night and on the weekends in Miami, Florida.

Smash the Rage is one of many "rage rooms" located in the United States and across the world. Patrons of these rooms are encouraged to vent their anger in an appropriate and controlled environment. A statement on the Smash the Rage website reads, "Your heart is pounding. You're clenching your fists. You're red in the face. You just want to smash." The Break Club, a rage room in Buenos Aries, Argentina, says that corporations send their employees to the club.

At Smash Therapy in Rochester, New York, patrons wear closed-toes shoes and head-to-head protective gear. They enter a room where they can lash out at glass items, electronics, and other breakables using a crowbar, baseball bat, or sledgehammer, "without consequences or public embarrassment." A Smash Therapy crew cleans up afterward and sends the debris for recycling. The Riot Room, also in Rochester, offers ax-throwing and has a bar in a separate area. Although bar patrons are able to use the rage room and the ax-throwing area, Riot Room employees are instructed to deny people access if they appear to be inebriated.

Workplace frustrations, usually stemming from conflict, are the primary reasons most patrons visit Smash Therapy. Barrios said that some are repeat customers, and many are referrals. A lot of retail employees come in and complain about customers. Other issues are people feeling frustrated with their workloads, their bosses, and their colleagues.

The low-end price is $30 for people who bring in their own box of items to smash during a 15-minute session. An "office smash" costs $100 for one person for 25 minutes. Similar to other rage rooms, patrons must sign a waiver and wear closed-toe shoes and protective gear, including a safety suit, a helmet with a safety shield, and goggles.

The proprietors of Smash the Rage source most of their materials for destruction through conducting bulk pickups from people wanting to discard items. After the rage session, the smashed items, including glass and metal, are sorted for recycling or disposal.

A disclaimer on the company website reads as follows: "Smash the Rage does not claim to be a mental help or medical facility. We do not treat, give diagnosis, or provide medical therapy of any kind. We are classified as entertainment only. If you feel that you have any mental or medical issues that need to be treated, please see a licensed physician or obtain a referral." A patron of Smash the Rage posted on Facebook: "Awesome experience. Definitely therapeutic."

Many mental health professionals question the value of rage rooms. According to Dr. Nelly Ali-Klein, a psychiatrist who specializes in aggression and intermittent explosive disorders, smashing objects to show anger is counterproductive in the modern world. "The police will call on you. You will lose your job. Your spouse will hate you. Your children will be afraid," said Alia-Klein. By destroying things when a given situation makes you angry, you are training your brain to go into "destroy mode" every time you feel that way.

Questions

1. If conflict at work or at school created considerable stress for you, would you consider going to a rage room to feel better and resolve the conflict?
2. What are your thoughts on companies offering rage-room benefits, perhaps even with a rage room on company premises?

Source: Original story based on facts and observations in the following sources: Carol Brzozowski, "Rage Rooms offer a Chance to Vent . . . and Smash Stuff," *Workforce*, March/April 2019, p. 10; Marcia Greenwood, "Rochester Rage Rooms Are All the Rage," *Rochester Democrat and Chronicle*, November 6, 2018; "New Businesses Let You Smash Your Way through Stress and Anger," Healthline (www.healthline.com), November 6 , 2013, pp. 1–6; "Miami's Very First Rage Room: Smash the Rage," *Smash the Rage* (www.smashtherage.com), pp. 1–4.

Reframing through Cognitive Restructuring and Asking Questions

Another useful approach to resolving conflict is to reexamine or *reframe* the conflict situation by looking at in a different light. Two practical approaches follow for reframing: one by searching for the positives in the situation, and the other by asking questions.

Reframing through Cognitive Restructuring

An indirect way of resolving interpersonal conflict is to lessen the conflicting elements in a situation by viewing them more positively. According to the technique of cognitive restructuring, you mentally convert negative aspects into positive ones by looking for the positive elements in a situation. According to cognitive-restructuring theory, people can cope better with difficult situations by changing the way they think about stressors.[7] How you frame or choose your thoughts can determine the outcome of a conflict situation. Your thoughts can influence your actions. If your search for the beneficial elements in the situation, there will be less area for dispute. Although this technique might sound like a mind game, it can work effectively.

Imagine that one of Samantha's coworkers, Gordon, has asked her repeated questions about how to get approval to authorize a discount for a customer. Samantha is about ready to tell Gordon, "Go bother somebody else. I am not paid to be a trainer." Instead, she looks for the positive element in the situation. She says to herself, "Gordon has been asking me a lot of questions. This does take time, but answering these questions is a valuable experience. If I aspire to become a manager, I will have to help group members with problems."

After having completed this cognitive restructuring. Samantha can then deal with the situation more positively. She might say to Gordon, "I welcome the opportunity to help you, but we need to find a mutually convenient time. In this way, I can better concentrate on my own work."

cognitive restructuring
A way of resolving interpersonal conflict by mentally converting negative aspects into positive ones by looking for the positive elements in the situation.

Reframing by Asking Questions

Another way to use reframing is to step back, take a deep breath, and then ask all or some of the following questions about the conflict situation arising within the work group:

- Do I fully understand the situation?
- Is the person really angry at me or just worried and anxious?
- Do I have all the facts?
- What is the real issue here?
- How would I want to be treated if the situation were reversed?

By taking such an approach, you are more likely to communicate effectively and constructively with work associates when conflict situations arise. You carefully talk through the issues rather than becoming explosive, defensive, and argumentative. A useful scenario for reframing through questioning would be when a coworker or customer accuses you of negligence.[8]

Five Rules for Dealing Effectively with Organizational Conflict

A supplement to using techniques for resolving conflict is to apply basic rules to facilitate effective conflict management. As formulated by Jeffrey Pfeffer, a professor of organizational behavior at the Graduate School of Business, Stanford University, these rules can sometimes substitute for using a specific technique.[9]

1. *Stay focused on the most essential objectives.* Conflicts in organizations often involve side issues, such as the other side being rude or making petty demands. It is best to not pay too much attention to these issues and instead focus on your major objective. Assume that Janice, a vice president, is in conflict with other executives about the advisability of outsourcing the company call center. She thinks that the call center should be staffed with company employees in order to have better control

of quality. Janice should stay focused on this objective rather than getting sidelined by minor issues, such as the décor of the call center. In the words of a school system leader, "Figure out what winning looks like. If the conflict were over and you found that you had won, what would that look like?"

2. *Do not fight over things that do not matter.* An extension of the first rule is to not bother fighting about things that are not particularly important. In Janice's situation, one of the executives might insist that if the company staffs its own call center, about one-fifth of the agents should be allowed to work from home in order to save on real estate. Janice does not think this is a good idea, but opposing the idea is not worth the fight if it could mean losing the conflict about whether to outsource the call center.

3. *Build empathy for other people's points of view.* As in negotiation, empathy helps resolve differences. During conflict resolution, it helps to understand the objective and measures of the other side. This requires looking at the world through their eyes and not presuming evil intent. For example, a frequent struggle in the software industry centers on when to release a product. Software developers often want to delay a product release in the pursuit of perfection because the final software reflects the quality of their work. In contrast, sales executives are rewarded for generating revenue and might prefer to sell as soon as possible, then release software patches later on if necessary. Each side is pursuing objectives they think are reasonably consistent with their rewards and professional education—not intentionally trying to be difficult.

4. *Adhere to the adage "keep your friends close and your enemies closer."* It is difficult to follow this advice because most people prefer pleasant interactions with others and avoid discomfort. As a result, we tend to avoid people with whom we are having disagreements. The problem with this standard approach is that you will not know what others are thinking or doing if you do not interact with them. In the case of Janice, she might be aware that another company executive disagrees with most of her opinions and therefore will oppose her plan to keep the call center in house. Janice should therefore do what she can to build an amicable relationship with the executive who opposes her through such means as asking for his input on certain issues and sending him a congratulatory text if warranted.

5. *Use humor to defuse difficult situations.* As mentioned in relation to negotiation, injecting humor into the situation can help defuse tension and build good relations during the time spent in face-to-face or online conflict resolution. Janice might say during her presentation about the value of keeping the call center in house, "Maybe I have a hearing problem, but has anyone else present had difficulty understanding the tech support person from an overseas call center when you tried to resolve a computer issue?"

Pfeffer concludes that workplace conflict is unavoidable. Yet if you keep these simple, but difficult-to-implement, rules in mind you will be able to navigate conflict with better outcomes.

Additional Behaviors and Attitudes for Resolving Conflict

A wide variety of basic behaviors and attitudes are helpful in resolving conflict in addition to those already described in this chapter. The following list of approaches to resolving conflict is based on research from the Program on Negotiation at Harvard Law School, as well as the observations of other sources.[10] A theme of most of these approaches is that it is necessary to overcome the tendency to think that the other side in the conflict is wrong and that the conflict can be resolved by convincing the other side of that fact.

1. *Recognize that all of us have biased perceptions of what is fair.* Our sense of what constitutes a fair conflict resolution is biased by *egocentrism*, the tendency to see things our way and not understand the other side. Research conducted by Carnegie

Mellon University professors Linda Babcock and George Lowenstein indicates that when we are embroiled in a conflict, we need to overcome our egocentric viewpoint of what is fair. A mediator can sometimes help us develop a better understanding of the other side's point of view.

2. *Pause, breathe, and figure out the next steps.* A conflict situation is often stress-provoking, so we need to calm down on the spot. Deep breathing is often an effective instant approach to dealing with stress. After calming down, you might be able to figure out what to do next, such as the best way to deal with a client who threatens to terminate your business relationship. If the solution to the problem is complex, you will need more time to develop a resolution plan. For example, if the client wants to terminate the relationship because of what he or she perceives as poor technical support, you will need time to work on the problem with management.

3. *Look beneath the surface to identify deeper issues.* Many workplace conflicts arise over money, such as a labor union wanting higher wages and benefits for its members or a retail executive wanting more money for enlarging the company's online presence or renovating physical stores. Yet disputes over money often involve deeper sources of conflict, such as the feeling that one is being overlooked or disrespected. For example, a worker who thinks that his or her work is outstanding might want a bonus for financial reasons but also as a form of recognition. When a conflict does arise about money, listening closely to the other's grievances may help resolve the true cause of the conflict. To satisfy the worker in question, a small bonus might be sufficient if it were accompanied by another form of recognition, such as an outstanding performance evaluation.

4. *Assign high priority to building a good relationship.* Many workplace conflicts take place between and among work associates. Maintaining and strengthening the relationship should therefore be as important as winning or getting your way with someone in your organization. Relationships with other stakeholders, such as suppliers and government regulators, are also important. (Yet again, the negotiating strategy of "Allow for face saving" surfaces.)

5. *Avoid escalating tensions with threats and provocative moves.* A poor tactic in terms of its long-term consequences is to threaten the other side, such as threatening to sue to get your demand met or making nasty posts about the person on social media. Litigation may be necessary if the issue cannot be resolved through other means, such as in some patent disputes. Based on the human tendency to reciprocate, the party who receives the threat will often respond in kind, thereby escalating the conflict.

6. *Overcome an "us versus them" mentality.* Intergroup competition can lead to conflict in which suspicion and hostility toward another group arise. As a result, groups in conflict might develop a distorted perception of each other's views and regard the other side's position as more extreme than the true position. It is best for the groups in conflict to look for an identity they can share. Conflict-resolution efforts might begin by emphasizing the common goal of reaching a fair and equitable agreement. Assume that the marketing group in a credit-card company thinks that the credit-evaluation group is using algorithms that reject too many creditworthy applicants. During the first conflict-resolution session, the head of the marketing group might emphasize that both groups should share the goal of wanting the credit-card company to increase revenue and prosper.

7. *Decide on the most appropriate medium for dealing with the conflict.* The traditional way of resolving conflict is an in-person discussion. Yet other media are possible, such as telephone calls, videoconferences, e-mail, text messaging, chat, and intranet. Resolving conflict outside the office, such as at a restaurant, is another possibility. The more serious and complex the conflict, the more that in-person meetings are advised, such as settling trade disputes between countries. Whatever medium is chosen to resolve the dispute, it is important to have a meaningful discussion rather than a quick exchange of complaints.

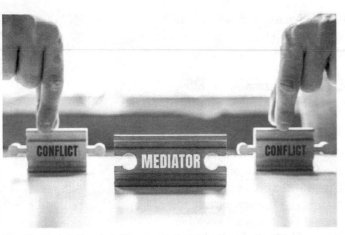
Source: BOKEH STOCK/Shutterstock

Conflict resolution is only complete when the parties find an acceptable way forward.

8. *Make effective use of nonverbal communication skills.* A good deal of information exchanged during conflicts and disputes is communicated nonverbally. Paying attention to the other side's nonverbal signals, such as rate of breathing and movements or posture, might help you figure out what the person really wants or dislikes. For example, suddenly sitting up straight accompanied by a smile might indicate agreement with your proposal. Nonverbal signals are also useful in calming down the other side during a heated exchange. Among the most effective of these signals are a calm tone of voice, a friendly hand wave, and a smile.

9. *Separate sacred from pseudo-sacred issues.* Conflict resolution can be intractable when core values that negotiators or others in conflict believe are sacred, or nonnegotiable, are involved. Sacred issues include religious attitudes, belief in the profit motive, or prohibitions against smoking or drinking alcoholic beverages at an in-house company party. At times, a sacred attitude might only be sacred under certain conditions. For example, a CEO might ease up on the demand that a new product or service earn a profit within the first year if he or he were assured that profits would be forthcoming within two years.

10. *Create an opening for communication so that all parties involved have a voice.* Whether the conflict is being approached in person or digitally, all the players in the conflict should have the opportunity to provide input about the problem. The parties involved should have the opportunity to express their understanding and feelings about the situation. At a telecommunicates company, the head of customer support decided that field technicians should communicate with central staff only through texting. Considerable conflict arose because many technical problems are more readily resolved through spoken conversations than via texting. A few field supervisors along with a few technicians were given the opportunity to express their concerns fully. A compromise was then reached about which types of problems were better suited for resolution by text messages alone versus phone conversations.

11. *Repeat back (paraphrase) your understanding of the issues.* A key component of active listening is to restate or paraphrase what you think you heard the other side say on key issues. In this way, the other side is likely to feel that you understand, and you have also demonstrated empathy. Many conflicts continue to fester because one or both sides do not think the other side understands the problems that he or she is facing. Getting back to the conflict between the field technicians (a.k.a. electronics repair workers), here are two examples of paraphrasing:
    - *Home office service manager to field technician supervisor:* "I understand that you find it difficult to adapt to exchanging some text messages about technical problems. You would prefer to resolve a lot of issues by speaking over the phone."
    - *Technician supervisor to home office service manager:* "I get it. The home office has found that you can save a lot of time in getting repairs done if the technicians attempt to resolve tough technical issues over the phone. You are trying to raise the productivity of the field technicians."

12. *Use "I" statements instead of "you" statements to clarify your position on the major issues.* "I" statements are a major contributor to conflict resolution. By framing your thoughts and reactions around yourself, you avoid placing blame on the other party or focusing on his or her emotions and reactions. This approach helps to stick to the facts around an issue. To illustrate, you might ask a subordinate, "Why were you late to this morning's client meeting? You know how important it was." A better

approach is to frame the statement around your own emotions and reactions surrounding the subordinate's tardiness. Using this approach, you might say, "I felt frustrated that I could not begin our client meeting at the scheduled time. I promised him that we would all meet this morning."

13. *Find the way forward.* Conflict resolution is only complete when the parties find an acceptable way forward. Carefully examine the options and decide jointly what to do next. Perhaps a comprise can be reached that is acceptable to both sides. If a compromise cannot be reached, figure out what can be done to prevent the conflict from escalating. Make sure that both sides understand their role in keeping the conflict resolved. Consider the recurring issues of whether to close a particular factory. A resolution might be reached that the factory can stay afloat for two more years, provided it is profitable. Factory personnel might be responsible for finding ways to cut costs by eliminating waste and not replacing all the workers who retire or quit voluntarily. For their role, corporate management will look for additional useful work for the factory, such as subcontracting some work from other companies and allocating any new work to the factory that fits its unique capabilities.

Summary

One five-step approach to conflict resolution is as follows: (1) Separate the people from the problem, and focus on the process; (2) identify a mediator; (3) clarify the problem; (4) explore all options; and (5) agree on a resolution.

The five traditional conflict-resolution styles are based on a combination of satisfying one's own concerns (assertiveness) and satisfying the concerns of others (cooperativeness). The styles are competitive, accommodative, sharing, collaborative, and avoidant. The collaborative style leads to win–win. The five styles have implications for other aspects of workplace behavior, such as the avoiding (including forcing) style being negatively related to organizational citizenship behavior among subordinates.

Techniques for resolving conflict include the following: confrontation and problem solving; win–lose conflict resolution; confront, contain, and connect for anger; and reframing through cognitive restructuring and asking questions. Five rules for dealing effectively with organizational conflict are (1) stay focused on the essential objectives, (2) do not fight over things that do not matter, (3) build empathy for other people's points of view, (4) adhere to the adage "keep your friends close and your enemies even closer," and (5) use humor to defuse difficult situations.

A few additional behaviors for resolving conflict are (1) recognize that all of us have biased perceptions of what is fair; (2) pause, breathe, and figure out the next steps; (3) look beneath the surface to identify deeper issues; (4) assign high priority to building a good relationship; (5) avoid escalating tensions with threats and provocative moves; (6) overcome an "us versus them" mentality; (7) decide on the most appropriate medium for dealing with the conflict; (8) make effective use of nonverbal communication skills; (9) separate sacred from pseudo-sacred issues; and (10) create an opening for communication so that all parties involved have a voice.

Key Terms and Phrases

Cognitive restructuring, p. 137
Confrontation and problem solving, p. 133

Win–win, p. 132

Discussion Questions and Activities

1. Explain which one of the techniques or approaches to conflict resolution presented in this chapter you think would be the most useful for you.
2. Given that so much has been researched and written about conflict resolution, why do so many conflicts go unresolved?
3. How might effective conflict-resolution skills of employees enhance company profits?
4. Suppose a team leader is accused of hostile-environment sexual harassment against several team members and is confronted by his manager about the problem. What possible collaborative solutions to this conflict could be reached?
5. Give an example of a couple of nonverbal signals a person can use to show the other side that he or she

is searching for a collaborative way to resolve the conflict.

6. Imagine that you are in conflict with your manager about your work attire being far too informal. What kind of statement could you make to help build a relationship with your manager in order to resolve this conflict?

7. How effective is the current president of the United States in resolving conflict? Provide some evidence for your answer.

8. Imagine that a food truck is given a permit to operate one block from a sit-down restaurant, and the restaurant experiences a decline in revenues. How might the restaurant owner go about resolving this conflict?

9. Think back to a hockey game you have watched that involved a fight between the players, or find a video of a hockey game that includes a fight. Why do you think the referee lets the players fight for a couple of minutes before intervening to stop the conflict?

10. Ask a person with at least a few years of work experience what he or she thinks is the best way of resolving workplace conflict. How well does the answer fit with the information in this chapter?

Skill-Building Exercise: Cognitive Restructuring for Reducing Conflict

The purpose of this exercise is to develop skill in reframing negative situations into positive ones through cognitive restructuring. Reframe each of the following negative statements in a positive way.

Negative: One of my clients, Sebastian, is really bugging me. He sends me far too many texts asking about his account or our services. Some of his texts are simply silly observations not directly related to his account.

Positive:

Negative: Mandy is so obsessed with sports that it is hurting my productivity. Where does it say in the employee handbook that I have to spend 30 minutes on Monday listening to Mandy's comments on her favorite team's weekend performance? Doesn't she know that I have a job to do and that I just don't care about her team?

Positive:

Negative: Our new CEO Baxter has developed a business strategy that I don't think will work. He thinks that if we get rid of all our low-price offerings, we will become a more upscale company. I think that if we follow Baxter's strategy, we will be out of business in two years. We are no longer the upscale company that Baxter thinks we are.

Positive:

Negative: You have just been demoted from project manager to project team member, and you have been transferred to a less prestigious project. The rationale offered to you is that you are too much of a team player and therefore not a good leader. You feel frustrated, and your ego is a little deflated.

Positive:

CASE PROBLEM 9A: Is Maxwell a Victim of Age Discrimination?

Maxwell, age 56, has worked for an automotive parts manufacturer for 25 years in a variety of capacities. He current job title is senior business analyst, and he has also worked as a procurement specialist, a supply-chain technician, and a project manager during his time with the company. The only salary increases Maxwell has received in the last 10 years have been company-wide cost-of-living adjustments.

During his last two performance evaluations, Maxwell asked his immediate manager, Estella, why he has not been assigned a project manager role in five years. Estella said, "When we find a project manager assignment that we think fits you well, we will give you serious consideration. But as you know, Maxwell, project managers these days have to be on top of the new technology."

Maxwell responded that his computer and automotive technology skills were as up to date as those of most of the project managers in the company. Estella said that she would take his comments into consideration. She also added, however, that project managers must be highly creative in today's competitive environment. Maxwell replied, "Maybe I haven't invented a new battery or a way to reduce shipping costs by 50 percent, but I have good job creativity. Just ask my coworkers." Estella said she would make note of Maxwell's comments.

Maxwell remembers leaving that performance-evaluation session with the feeling that he was being discriminated against because of his age. He reflected, "I think that Estella was using the usual euphemistic expressions to cover up for age discrimination. She said that a project manager needs to have the latest technology skills. That usually means a person must be under 35 to have good technology skills. Little does she know that most of the CEOs of Silicon Valley firms are around my age. Then she hits me with the stereotype that job creativity is a function of youth. Doesn't company leadership know that some of the most creative ideas in the automotive industry come from executives in their late 50s and early 60s?"

Maxwell went to the career section of the company's website to gather more insight into whether age discrimination existed, particularly for project managers and technical personnel. He came across a few terms in job descriptions that prompted him to think that age discrimination existed in subtle ways. When he found the term *digital native*, he recognized that nobody over 45 could really be a digital native because they acquired computer technology skills later in life.

In the same job description, Maxwell noted the term *high energy*, prompting Maxwell to think that somebody in the company assumes that younger people are more likely to have high energy. Maxwell noted that the company did not want to hire someone who was *overqualified* for a customer support position. It made him think that because experience is positively related to age, older applicants would be less likely to be hired.

At this point, Maxwell thought he was most likely being discriminated against based on his age. He pondered whether to look for a job outside the company or attempt to resolve any age discrimination problems that were holding him back in the company.

Case Questions

1. Based on the facts reported in this case, what is your opinion about whether Maxwell is a victim of age discrimination?
2. How should Maxwell attempt to resolve his conflict with the company in reference to the perceived age discrimination?
3. Which approach to conflict resolution might Maxwell use to deal with his problem yet still preserve a good relationship with the company?

Source: A few facts in this case are from Kate Rockwood, "More than a Number," *HR Magazine*, February 2018, pp. 24–31.

Associated Role Play

One student plays the role of Maxwell, who, after a weekend of heavy thought, decides that he is indeed a victim of age discrimination and wants to resolve the conflict. He sends Estella a text message requesting an interview to discuss the possibility that his age is holding him back from good assignments in the company. Another student plays the role of Estella, who agrees to meet with Maxwell but personally dislikes people considering themselves to be victims of any type of discrimination. Run the role play for about 10 minutes, with observers providing feedback about the effectiveness of the conflict-resolution session.

CASE PROBLEM 9B: Niki Wants Credit for Her Ideas

Niki is a member of a product development team at the pet food division of large food manufacturer. She is becoming increasingly concerned that her boss, Phil, regularly approves of her best ideas, yet takes ownership for them.

Niki explains what she sees as the problem: "After a couple of weeks of intensive research, I came up with the idea of a dog biscuit that contains tooth whitener. If a dog chews on these biscuits for at least a month, the dog will have cleaner, whiter teeth. I know that a lot of dog owners dislike dog teeth that are stained green or brown. Phil really liked my idea and said he would present it at our next product-development meeting.

"At the next product-development meeting, Phil said that *he* had this breakthrough idea for a dog biscuit that contains a veterinarian-approved tooth whitener. Next, he said that he wanted to thank the team for stimulating his thinking about this potential new product. I figured that maybe Phil was so excited about the tooth whitener that he forgot where he got the idea.

"Three weeks later, I approached Phil with an idea that fit our nonfood products. I suggested that we sell collars for dogs and cats that contain a computer chip with a built-in GPS. When the dog or cat strays too far from home, the chip will send a text message to the owner's smartphone. I knew that we would have to work with a computer scientist to get the idea from fantasy to reality, but Phil said the idea seemed promising.

"One week later, Phil sent out an e-mail to our team and his boss talking about the possibilities of a pet collar with a built-in chip to help the owner locate the pet when it strays. Phil did not even mention my name."

Niki now feels that Phil has gone too far in not giving her credit for her ideas. She is so angry that she wants to scream at Phil, but she thinks to herself, "I want credit for my ideas so that I can advance my career. But if I trigger a rotten relationship with Phil, that could damage my career. I have to figure out what to do next."

Case Questions

1. How justified is Niki in wanting to receive credit for her ideas from Phil? Or is she just being a poor team player?
2. Recommend an approach Niki might use to resolve her conflict with Phil, yet not trigger an adverse relationship with him.

Associated Role Play

One student plays the role of Niki, who has now become intensely stressed that Phil has taken credit for a couple of her best recent ideas. The student writes a text message (displayed to the class) about her concerns. Another person plays the role of Phil, who receives the text message. He believes that a manager or team leader stimulates the thinking of team members, so he is partially responsible for any ideas developed in the group. Phil responds back to Niki. The role players engage in at least three text messages each, all displayed to the rest of the class, if technology permits. Feedback is welcome on the effectiveness of the attempt at conflict resolution.

Notes

1. Patricia Lotich, "Five Steps to Conflict Resolution in the Workplace," *Thriving Small Business* (www.thethrivingsmallbusienss.com), October 6, 2016, pp. 1–3.

2. Kenneth Thomas, "Conflict and Conflict Management," in Marvin D. Dunnette (ed.), *Handbook of Industrial and Organizational Psychology* (Chicago: Rand McNally College Publishing, 1976), pp. 900–902.

3. Peter J. Jordan and Ashlea C. Troth, "Emotional Intelligence and Conflict Resolution: Implications for Human Resource Development," *Sage Journals* (http://sagepub.com), February 1, 2002.

4. Samuel O. Salami, "Conflict Resolution Strategies and Organizational Citizenship Behavior: The Moderating Role of Trait Emotional Intelligence," *Social Behavior and Personality*, No. 1, 2010, pp. 75–86.

5. Brian Sharp, "City Council Oks Amended Rezoning Plan for Highland Hospital," *Rochester Democrat and Chronicle/USA TODAY NETWORK*, March 21, 2019, p. 2A.

6. The quote and technique are both from Kathleen Doheny, "It's a Mad, Mad Corporate World," *Working Woman*, April 2000, pp. 71–72.

7. Richard S. Lazarus, "Psychological Stress in the Workplace," *Journal of Social Behavior and Personality*, 6, 1991, pp. 1–13.

8. "Conquer Conflict with this Technique," *Manager's Edge*, September 7, 2005, as adapted from Maria Broomhower, "Dissolving Conflict through Reframing," *Work911* (http://www.conflict911.com).

9. Jeffrey Pfeffer, "Win at Workplace Conflict," *Harvard Business Review*, May 29, 2014, pp. 1–3. The example of "Janice" is not included in the reference.

10. Katie Shonk, "5 Conflict Resolution Strategies," *Program on Negotiation at Harvard Law School* (https://www.pon.harvard.edu), March 4, 2019, pp. 1–2; Natalie Semezuk, "The 10 Most Effective Conflict Resolution Strategies," *dpm* (https://the digitalprojectmanager.com), November 9, 2018, pp. 1–5; "Handling Conflict Situations," in *Business: The Ultimate Resource* (Cambridge, MA: Perseus Publishing, 2002), pp. 356–357; "Conflict Resolution Skills," Edmonds Community College (www.edcc.edu), 2019, pp. 1–3.

Advanced Techniques for Resolving Conflict

Source: sirtravelalot/Shutterstock.

Learning Objectives

After reading and studying this chapter and doing the exercises, you should be able to:

1. Specify several characteristics of an effective conflict-management system.

2. Describe three different advanced techniques for resolving workplace conflict.

3. Explain the nature of a conflict of interest and how the conflict might be resolved.

The effective resolution of workplace conflict requires many different approaches, depending on the type and context of the conflict. The approaches to and techniques of conflict resolution described in Chapter 9 will go a long way toward resolving the majority of conflicts found in the workplace. In this chapter we describe additional techniques that might be called into play to resolve conflicts. One such approach, the anonymous polling technique, relies on information technology to gather diverse opinions on a major issue facing the organization. We also take a close look at the resolution one of the most controversial types of conflict facing people in high places, a conflict of interest. The stage is set for the chapter, however, with a description of the characteristics of an effective conflict-management system.

Characteristics of an Effective Conflict-Management System

Effective approaches to resolving workplace conflict tend to be embedded in effective conflict-management systems. Professor David B. Lipsky at Cornell University and Ariel C. Avgar of the University of Illinois at Urbana–Champaign observe that research into integrated conflict-management systems has revealed five essential characteristics, as follows[1]:

1. *Broad in scope.* The system should provide options for all employees in the workplace, including hourly and salaried workers, corporate professionals, supervisors, and managers, to have a wide variety of issues considered. The open-door policy described later in the chapter is an example of one such option.
2. *A culture of toleration and early resolution.* The system should welcome or at least tolerate dissent and encourage early resolution of conflicts through direct negotiation. In this manner, a salaried worker who thinks that she deserves more than a cost-of-living adjustment in her annual salary could attempt to resolve the conflict with her supervisor and perhaps a human resources representative.
3. *Multiple access points.* Employees should be able to identify the individual, department, or other organizational unit within the organization that has the authority, knowledge, and experience to help them resolve their conflict. If the person or place contacted cannot help resolve the problem, the employee should at least receive an adequate referral. An ethics hotline or website sometimes fits this purpose. For example, an employee who thinks that his manager is stealing money from the company might want to know how this problem might be approached.
4. *Multiple options.* The system should have rights-based and interest-based options for employees to consider. Among the employee rights might be the right to work in a physically and psychologically safe environment. Physical safety would include avoidance of dangerously loud noises, noxious chemicals, and machinery that lends itself to accidents. Psychological safety would include freedom from sexual, racial, and ethnic harassment. Interests would include such factors as being able to resolve disputes over overtime pay and receiving fair consideration for promotion.
5. *Support structures.* Strong support structures should be designed to coordinate and manage the multiple access points and multiple options. As a result of these structures, conflict management and resolution should brought into the daily operations of the organization.

A conflict-management system with the five characteristics just described should help address conflict in a manner that is consistent with the broader goals and objectives of the organization and fit the organizational culture. For example, if a company is attempting to recruit and retain talented employees, the conflict-management system should be what such talented workers might expect—swift and fair.

A Variety of Advanced Conflict-Resolution Techniques

In this section we describe four approaches to conflict resolution that go beyond typical descriptions of how to resolve conflict. We include a description of the open-door policy for individuals who might need to go beyond their immediate manager to resolve a dispute. This section also describes briefly when it might be worth walking away from a conflict.

The Application of Structural Methods

A structural method of resolving conflict emphasizes juggling work assignments and reporting relationships so that disputes are minimized. One structural method for resolving conflict is for a manager to have direct control over all the resources he or she needs to get the job done. In this way, the manager is less likely to experience conflict when attempting to get the cooperation of people who do not report directly to him or her.

Conflict can often be reduced or prevented by one or more members from one organizational unit exchanging places with those of another unit. For example, a manager might shift from marketing to operations. Working in another unit can foster empathy. Reassigning people in this way can also encourage people to develop different viewpoints in the affected groups. As the group members get to know one another better, they tend to reduce some of their distorted perceptions of one another. (Cross-functional teams accomplish the same purpose.) Exchanging members works best when the personnel exchanged have the technical competence to perform well in the new environment.

The formation of committees comprising members of groups that are in conflict or might experience conflict in the future can be helpful in resolving and preventing conflict. As the different factions work together, they might resolve their conflicts informally during committee meetings. Assume that Crystal, the director of human resources, is placed on the same strategy committee as Garth, the director of finance. Crystal talks about proposing a four-day executive retreat in British Columbia to formulate strategy. Garth then expresses his concerns about such an expensive retreat. The two then agree that a retreat might be scheduled in a location that would involve lower travel and hotel costs, such as Detroit, Michigan, or Gary, Indiana.

In some firms, management maintains an open-door policy, in which any employee can bring a gripe to its attention without checking with his or her immediate manager. The open-door policy is a popular grievance procedure because it enables problems to be settled quickly. Another key use of an open-door policy is to promote positive communication between employees at all levels and managers. When every employee understands that he or she can have access to any manager or senior-level employee and talk about any work-related topic of his or her choice, an open-door policy exists.[2] A legal handbook suggests that the following phrase be included in the open-door policy:

> If something about your job is bothering you, or if you have a question, concern, idea or problem related to your work, please discuss it with your immediate supervisor, as soon as possible. If for any reason, you don't feel comfortable bringing the matter to your supervisor, feel free to raise the issue with any company officer.[3]

The "something bothering you" often relates to a conflict that the employee wants to resolve. Among the many examples would be a strong disagreement about a low performance evaluation, thinking that one is a victim of harassment or discrimination, or being excluded from good assignments based on favoritism.

The open-door policy can be classified as a grievance procedure, a topic covered in Chapter 12. The accompanying Negotiation and Conflict Resolution in Action feature describes the open-door policy in one of the world's largest technology companies.

open-door policy A policy in which any employee can bring a gripe to management's attention without checking with his or her immediate manager.

Hewlett-Packard (HP) Maintains an Open-Door Philosophy and Policy

Hewlett-Packard is a leading technology solutions provider for consumers and businesses, with the entity referred to as "HP" really being two companies. Hewlett-Packard spun off its enterprise products and services as Hewlett-Packard Enterprises in 2015. Hewlett-Packard retained the personal computer and printer businesses and was renamed HP Inc. Combined, the two companies have annual revenues surpassing $100 billion. HP is a market leader in essential components of business infrastructure, such as servers, storage management software, imagining and printing, personal computers, personal access devices, digital cameras, and handheld devices.

Leadership at HP is committed to creating a positive work environment, a place where every employee's voice is heard and where issues are raised close in time to when they arise and are resolved quickly. An easy flow of communication across all levels of the company is also encouraged. The company considers openness as essential to quickly resolve customer concerns and to recognize business issues as they surface. Openness is also important for addressing the changing needs of HP's diverse and global workforce.

The essence of HP's open-door policy is open communication in a work environment of trust and mutual respect that establishes a solid foundation for collaboration, growth, high performance, and success across the various units of HP. As perceived by company leadership, the open-door policy creates an environment where:

- open communication between managers and other employees is a daily business practice;
- employees are able to seek counsel, provide or solicit feedback, or raise concerns within the company;
- managers are responsible for creating a work environment in which employee input is welcome and advice is freely given; and
- issues are surfaced early and candidly shared without the fear of retaliation when this input is shared in good faith.

The open-door policy at HP includes a grievance process. An employee who feels that his or her rights have been violated is supposed to first discuss the problem with the managers in his or her chain of command. Yet if the employee is not comfortable with that approach for any reason, or if the conflict is not resolved, the employee is authorized and encouraged to contact the Ethics and Compliance Office at corporate. compliance@hp.com.

The two HP companies encourage employees to use the open-door policy when they feel that they have been victims of sexual harassment in these words: "Any employee believing that he or she has been harassed, or who has witnessed harassment, should exercise Hewlett-Packard Enterprise's Open Door Policy to report any such incident to his or her manager, the next level of management or Human Resources. Employees who in good faith report harassment are protected from retaliation."

Brian Armstrong, the CEO and cofounder of Coinbase, the world's largest digital currency exchange, knows HP well and made this comment: "A true open-door policy extends beyond the CEO to the directors and the chairman. An employee who has exhausted all other outlets should feel empowered to call directly on the board and receive a fair hearing."

Questions

1. How effective do you think the HP open-door policy might be in resolving conflict?
2. Why is it important that HP specify "good faith" in terms of employees bringing complaints through the open-door policy?

Source: Original story based on facts and observations in the following sources: HP, "Open Door Policy, *hp.com* (https://h20195www2 .hp.com), p. 1; Michelle Chan, "Open Door Policy—the HP Way," *LinkedIn* (https://www.linkedin.com/pulse/open-door-policy-hp-way-michelle-chan), November 6, 2017, p. 1; Brian Armstrong. "50 Lessons from HP's Company Culture," *Medium Leadership* (https://medium .com), August 14, 2018, p. 5; "Harassment-Free Work Environment Policy," *Hewlett Packard Enterprise* (https://hpe.com), 2019, p. 2.

Using Anonymous Polling to Help Resolve Employee Conflicts

Conflicts sometimes arise because of disagreements about organizational strategy or because of an operational change that affects employees. An example of a strategy change would be a company intending to shift from a consumer-products focus to a commercial-products focus. An example of an organizational change affecting employees would be a manufacturing plant changing from a 12-hour operation to a 24-hour operation.

To help resolve these conflicts, or potential conflicts, management might need to collect a full range of opinions on the issue.

Anonymous polling software is a method of asking questions or leading discussions by embedding questions into presentations and enabling employees to respond anonymously via a clicker or smartphone. Figure 10.1 provides an example of what anonymous polling software looks like, although this application is used to evaluate a presentation. The software instantly tallies responses and aggregates the results in a chart during the presentation.

According to technical experts, there are two ways to enable participants to respond while remaining anonymous. The first is not to ask participants to create screen names and to have them auto-generate IDs. This method protects identities but still enables the survey facilitator to gather data for reporting purposes and correlate responses across multiple questions. The second method is to make the poll completely anonymous, which can slightly limit reporting options. Anonymous polling software offers several advantages for resolving conflict[4]:

Anonymous polling gives employees a voice in the conflict or differences of opinion.

anonymous polling software A method of asking questions or leading discussions by embedding questions into presentations and enabling employees to respond anonymously via a clicker or smartphone.

1. *Anonymous polling software promotes open discussion.* Carefully crafted questions and the sharing of aggregate responses let everyone know what the issues are surrounding the conflict.
2. *Anonymous polling gives employees a voice in the conflict or difference of opinion.* Instead of the conversation being dominated by a few outspoken individuals, as in a town hall meeting, all members present have an equal opportunity to provide input. At the same time, some people are more willing to express extreme opinions

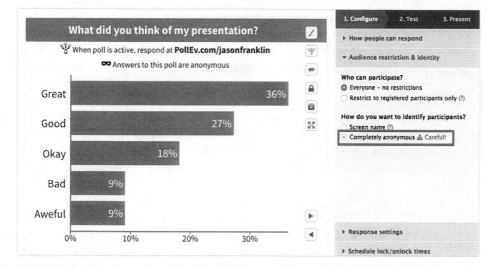

FIGURE 10.1 Anonymous Polling Software Used to Evaluate a Presentation

Important note: Again, if you choose to make activities completely anonymous, you will not be able to correlate anonymous responses from individual participants across multiple activities. Anonymous activities have limited reporting options as they can only be viewed in the Executive Summary.

Note to reader: The incorrect spelling of "awful" is in the original, probably because the person who designed the poll was thinking of the word, "awesome."

Source: Reprinted with permission from "Anonymous Polling," *Poll Everywhere* (https://www.polleverywhere.com/support/articles/response-settings/anonymous-polling).

anonymously than they would be to express them with attribution. (A problem, however, is the same one evident on social media: People are more willing to make senseless rants that exaggerate their negativity if they do so anonymously.)

3. *Anonymous polling enables all participants to know where the group stands on key issues.* During the heat of conflict, opinions often get skewed, and people lose sight of what the prevalent opinion is on the topic at hand. A system that enables people to respond anonymously to questions projected on a screen provides a quick snapshot of where participants stand on an issue. Input of this type is valuable for the managers attempting to resolve the conflict.

4. *Anonymous polling signals when consensus is reached.* Leaders who aspire to attain consensus on potentially divisive issues may benefit from accurate data about where people stand on an issue. More effective decision making may result from taking a baseline pulse at the start of the polling and then taking periodic polls to see how much progress has been attained in arriving at a resolution of the conflict.

Anonymous polling can be a valuable tool to help leaders resolve conflict. By facilitating open discussions, allowing a variety of employees to provide input, and enabling leaders to measure consensus, anonymous polling can get workers aligned on an issue or problem.

Resolving Conflicts within Self-Managed Work Teams

A dominant trend in job design and organizational structure is to organize workers into teams with considerable authority to direct and supervise themselves. A self-managed work team is a formally recognized group of employees responsible for an entire work process or segment that delivers a product or service to an internal or external customer.[5] Amit Maimon, a technology strategy consultant, observes that in a traditional team structure, the manager or team leader is typically asked to resolve conflicts. In contrast, self-managed teams must find ways to resolve their own conflicts. Self-managed teams are advised to focus on three attitudes and behaviors to resolve conflict[6]:

self-managed work team
A formally recognized group of employees responsible for an entire work process or segment that delivers a product or service to an internal or external customer.

1. *Encourage openness to productive conflict.* Self-managed work teams must openly commit to discussing their differences within the team. Conflict should not be perceived as an annoyance that creates anxiety and alienation but instead as an opportunity for growth and improved working relationships. Conflict resolution might be facilitated when it is introduced as an organized group activity. The group can arrive at an understanding about which conflicts can be resolved without involving others. To illustrate, the team might develop norms about what constitutes a low-risk decision and encourage team members to resolve low-risk decisions without team intervention. (A low-risk decision might be one that affects few people or in which the associated costs fall below a certain limit. For example, two team members might resolve their own conflict over who should take a business trip to represent the team at company headquarters.)

2. *Prioritize accountability over blame.* Self-managed teams should win and lose as a group. When problems arise, teams should not assign blame to the contributors closest to the source of the problem. Rather than digging for *who* was responsible, team members should investigate *why* the problem occurred. If the team feels comfortable speaking openly about conflict and setbacks, asking "How did this happen?" when conducting a postmortem will not lead to the blame game. Instead, it will point to the root cause.

   To further strengthen the blameless approach, a team might discuss the situation with several other teams within the organization. The discussion should be aimed at gathering multiple opinions regarding the root cause of the conflict and how it can be approached. Even if a unanimous opinion or clear plan of action does not emerge, the information-gathering process shifts the focus from the responsible parties and opens the resolution to several diverse ideas.

3. *Quantify the impact of the problem.* A team was experiencing conflict because a software developer preferred to work at night, which was inconvenient because the rest of the team worked during the day. The developer was absent from almost all the important meetings, which meant that his teammates had to spend time filling him in on everything he missed. The tension mounted until the team quantified the impact of the meetings he missed. For each 60-minute meeting missed, the team spent 30 more minutes recapping for him and listening to his thoughts. With six team members, the result was three hours of discussion attributed to the developer's insistence on working nights. Of note also, the software developer was missing about 10 meetings each month, meaning that the team was devoting more than 350 hours per year to these conversations.

Self-managed work teams must openly commit to discussing their differences within the team.

Instead of focusing on the symptoms of the conflict—having to spend extra time conversing with the developer—the team decided to develop a flexible schedule that worked for all team members. On meeting days, the team member who preferred to work at night could arrive in the afternoon, share a few hours of overlap with the rest of the team, and then resume his preferred work schedule.

Quantifying the impact of conflict provides several benefits. It encourages productive conversations, fosters an alignment around the gravity of the conflict, and unlocks creative solutions as team members identify the source and the impact of the conflicts.

The Resolution of Cross-Cultural Conflict

National culture can influence the choice of the most effective method of conflict resolution. Research provides some quantitative evidence that culture influences which method of conflict resolution a manager chooses and therefore thinks might be the most effective. Catherine Tinsley sorted conflict-resolution models into three types: resolving conflict by (a) deferring to status power, (b) applying regulations, and (c) integrating interests.

According to her observations, an individual's preference for a model, or method, is influenced by culture, which filters information and guides members toward a particular model. The 396 participants in the study were managers from Japanese, German, and American cultures. All participants had been educated by business programs in their cultures and were currently working for companies in their cultures. Participants completed surveys about resolving conflicts over different approaches to resolving a business problem.

A major finding of the study was that Japanese, German, and American managers tended to use different models when resolving workplace conflict. Half the variance (reason for something taking place) in choosing a conflict model could be accounted for by a manager's cultural group

National culture can influence the most effective method of conflict resolution.

membership. The Japanese participants preferred a status power model (using their authority). The German participants preferred a regulations model (appealing to rules and regulations), and the American participants preferred an interests (win-win) model.

Tinsley cautions that these cross-cultural differences may complicate the work life for expatriate managers who find themselves trying to resolve conflict in a foreign cultural system. A particular concern is that American managers may be surprised to learn that colleagues from Japanese and German cultures do not favor the interests (win-win) model.[7]

A study conducted in Asia provides additional evidence that cultural values could influence which approach to resolving conflict is the most effective. The two purposes of the research were to examine (a) how Chinese, Japanese, and Korean employees would resolve an interpersonal conflict with their supervisors and (b) how cultural factors might explain the differences in conflict-management styles. To obtain data, a survey was conducted of 275 employees in the three countries.

The study found that Korean employees, in comparison to Chinese and Japanese employees, were more likely to use compromise to resolve conflict with their supervisors. It was also found that Japanese workers, compared with their Chinese and Korean counterparts, were less likely to dominate and more likely to oblige their supervisors. A takeaway from the study is that the preferred approach to resolving interpersonal conflict is not the same in all East Asian countries. The study also reinforced the idea that cultural values influence individual approaches to conflict resolution. For example, the strong collective values among Korean employees might prompt them to compromise when resolving conflict.[8]

The Argument for Occasionally Walking Away from a Conflict

Workplace behavior specialist Amy Gallo cautions that not every conflict or disagreement on the job has to be resolved. Common wisdom is that the only way to manage a work disagreement is to resolve the issue immediately. Yet this advice is not always valid. Sometimes the best option is to do nothing, particularly if the disagreement is relatively minor. Doing nothing, or walking away from the conflict, is not a cop-out. Disregarding the minor conflict is a smart choice if you do not have the energy or time to invest in preparing for a difficult conversation. The same is true if you suspect that the other person might be unwilling to have a constructive discussion.

Dropping the issue will help maintain a stable relationship. Yet this approach will not work if you ruminate about the disagreement, making you more likely to have an outburst later. The approach will also backfire if you begin to act passive-aggressively toward your counterpart, such as ignoring that individual during the next several months. Doing nothing is effective only if you can put the conflict behind you.[9] Here are a couple of examples of disagreements that might be ignored:

- A team member says to the team leader, "I don't think you are happy with me this week. You haven't smiled at me yet."
- A front-desk receptionist says to the CEO while he is walking into the office, "I recommend that the company change its entire fleet of PCs to Apple computers. I'm an Apple fanatic."

Resolving Conflicts of Interest

intraindividual conflict
A situation that takes place when one person is faced with two incompatible goals.

Most of the conflicts described in this book are between and among individuals or between and among groups. Conflicts within individuals can also create problems that require resolution. Intraindividual conflict takes place when one person is faced with two incompatible goals. Role conflict is an intraindividual conflict because the two roles can be incompatible, such as a manager hiring a friend who is barely qualified for the position. The manager role demands that the manager hire the best person available for the position, whereas the friend role demands that he or she help a friend in need. Our focus in this section is on a special type of intraindividual conflict that is prevalent in various types of organizations, particularly government and business: conflicts of interest.

A **conflict of interest** occurs when an individual has competing interests or loyalties, and it is therefore a form of role conflict. A dual relationship is usually involved in a conflict of interest, such as an executive working for one company and being on the board of directors of another company that provides services to the first company. Two types of activities that usually create a conflict of interest are nepotism and self-dealing. *Nepotism* is giving favors to relatives and close friends, such as a CEO giving an unusually large bonus to a mediocre-performing staff member who is married to her sister. *Self-dealing* occurs when someone acts in his or her own interest rather than the interests of the organization, such as renting a luxury sports car with company money while on a business trip.[10]

conflict of interest When an individual has competing interests or loyalties and is therefore experiencing a form of role conflict.

Nepotism and self-interest do not inevitably create a harmful conflict of interest. A CEO might hire a close friend who performs well and receives no special favors. Renting the luxury sports car might be self-dealing, but it could also impress a customer prospect enough that a big sale is closed.

An important caution about conflicts of interest is that they are sometimes illegal and could lead to a civil lawsuit. For example, if a business organization has proof that a board member made outside profits from his or her role on the board, the board member has violated his or her duty of loyalty and could be sued. The term *outside profits* refers to the idea that board members are compensated for their membership, but they are not allowed to use board membership as a springboard for earning additional money. For example, if board member Rex is also a principal at a consulting firm, he is not supposed to funnel consulting contracts from the company in which he serves on the board to his consulting firm.

Board members can be accused of another type of conflict of interest referred to as *insider trading* if the board member is apprised of a development in the company that could impact the price of the company stock. If Rex learns that the company is about to land a major government contract and he immediately purchases 1,000 shares of the company stock, he could be accused of insider trading. A lengthier example of a potential conflict of interest follows:

The sole proprietor of a property management business that was experiencing rapid growth asked an ethics coach about whether he was involved in a conflict of interest. He said that he had several clients and managed more than 800 units. To complete maintenance and construction projects, he invited contractors to submit bids, but their response times were slow, and their prices were higher than he anticipated. The proprietor said he wanted to start a maintenance company so that he could improve the turnaround time and quality of work for his property management business. The new maintenance company was planned to be a separate entity for tax and liability purposes.

The proprietor wanted to know if what he planned to do was ethically acceptable. As the owner of both businesses, he would have an inside track on competitors' bids and make hiring decisions. He asked if he could source the work to another company he owns if he knew that he was providing better service at lower prices than they would otherwise get. He wanted to know if he should tell clients that he owned the other business or simply ask for forgiveness later. The proprietor was concerned that the new arrangement might be too self-serving and wondered whether he should avoid starting the company altogether.

The ethics coach responded that "self-serving" was an understatement and that he had described a huge conflict of interest. The proprietor was told to beware of the self-deceptive thinking that duped him into believing that he could make a bid and review competitors' bids objectively. The ethics coach advised that customers would not accept his deal, nor should they. He was told that, furthermore, his disclosure would not create an ethical playing field.

An attorney brought in to comment on the case suggested that the management company agree to perform maintenance and construction services for clients at a predetermined rate. The attorney said, "Rather than creating conflicts, this is simply another business arrangement with existing customers assuming that the two companies enter into agreement after full disclosure of all ownership interests."[11]

Types of Conflicts of Interest

Conflicts of interest in the workplace take a variety of forms, yet they can be categorized into four types:[12]

1. *Relational (family).* Family members are hired and favored over outside candidates or promoted over more qualified current employees.
2. *Relational (romantic).* An employee has a romantic relationship with a key person, such as a company manager or a major customer, and profits from that relationship. For example, if the CEO knows that a company employee, Mercedes, is romantically involved with an executive in a client organization, the CEO might give special treatment to Mercedes, knowing that she could readily influence the client.
3. *Financial.* An employee gains additional money beyond company-paid compensation in dealing with a customer, such as receiving a cash bonus for granting him or her a major discount.
4. *Confidential.* A worker has access to confidential information about the employer and uses it inappropriately, such as selling it to a competitor or using it to help a side business or the business of a friend or relative.

Figure 10.2 presents more examples of conflicts of interest.

How to Prevent or Resolve a Conflict of Interest

Allowing conflicts of interests to exist can have serious legal and financial consequences for the people or organization involved in the conflict. A recent example is that the premier consulting firm McKinsey & Co. agreed to pay $15 million to settle Justice Department allegations that the firm failed to fully disclose potential conflicts in three bankruptcy cases. According to the Justice Department, the payment represented "one of the highest

- Hiring an unqualified relative or friend as an employee or contractor
- Starting a company that provides products or services similar to those of your employer while still on the employer's payroll
- Arranging to work for a supplier or customer at a future date while still conducting business with the supplier or customer for your employer
- Offering paid products or services to a customer that compete with your employer, such as a heating, ventilation, and air-conditioning (HVAC) technician offering to repair a furnace at a customer's second home for a lower price than his employer offers
- Having a romantic relationship with a subordinate while he or she is still reporting to you
- Performing part-time work for a competitor
- Using a company database to find customers for a business you own or that of relative or friend
- A procurement manager hiring a brother-in-law to provide food-vending services for the company
- A management consultant working for two clients who are direct competitors and advising each on business strategy
- An employee working part-time for a company that competes directly with his or her primary employer
- An employee of a retailer with a substantial e-commerce operation setting up his own online retail store
- A paralegal working independently providing legal services for both the plaintiff and the defendant in an accident liability case without telling either side of her dual loyalty

FIGURE 10.2 Examples of Workplace Conflicts of Interest

Source: Several of the items in the list are adapted from these sources: "20 Examples of Conflicts of Interest in the Workplace," *Everfi* (https://everfi.com), March 24, 2016, pp. 1–3: Susan M. Heathfield, "Conflict of Interest," *thebalancecareers* (www.thebalancecareers.com), February 12, 2019, pp. 1–2; Rachel Blakely-Gray, "What You Need to Know about a Conflict of Interest in the Workplace," *Patriot Software* (www.patriotsoftware.com), September 25, 2017, pp. 1–5.

repayments by a bankruptcy professional for alleged noncompliance with disclosure rules."

A *Wall Street Journal* investigation found that in 7 of the 14 Chapter 11 cases in which McKinsey served in the role of advisor to the debtors, the firm had a financial interest in the outcome. According to the *Journal*, McKinsey named substantially fewer connections in each bankruptcy case it worked on than other advisers did. McKinsey did not admit to any wrongdoing but indicated that the settlement process had "provided additional clarity for the filing of future disclosures."[13]

Self-awareness is the starting point in resolving conflicts of interest.

Self-awareness is the starting point in resolving conflicts of interest. Most people who set up a situation in which a conflict of interest exists are probably smart enough to stop if they think through what they are doing. A manager might reflect, "Can I really recommend an objective performance bonus for a married woman in my department with whom I am having an affair?" Or a supervisor working for a consumer electronics company might say to herself, "Does it really make any sense for me to start an online business that sells knock-off consumer electronics products?"

A related approach to resolving a conflict of interest is to apply an ethics test similar to the one described in Chapter 7 in relation to evaluating the ethics of a negotiating tactic. Included in most approaches to evaluating the ethics of a decision is to ask a question such as, "How would I feel if my decision were made public or known to my loved ones?" If the contemplated conflict of interest or actual decision to engage in a conflict of interest does not pass this test, it should be abandoned. For example, the owner of a construction company might ask, "How would I like my spouse, children, and neighbors know that I received a contract to build this bridge based on my huge campaign donation?"

Company policy plays a key role in preventing and resolving conflicts of interest, as explained by business law writer Noreen Wainwright.[14] Company management should develop a clear policy on disclosure so that all employees and board members know what outside interests must be divulged. For example, a purchasing manager might not be aware that any personal relationships at supplier companies must be divulged. The policy should then be disseminated to all parties who might be directly affected by the policy. It might also be appropriate for the policy to be made public, such as a company advertising how it avoids conflicts of interests with all stakeholders.

The policy should be kept proportionate in the sense that the person with a conflicting interest should withdraw from making decisions in relation to the potential conflict. Usually, there is no problem with the person with the potential conflict making decisions on other organizational issues.

A clear policy needs to be developed for dealing with situations in which a person does not disclose conflicting interests. The conflict might be a serious issue, requiring disciplinary action. For example, an employee who starts a side business that competes with the primary employer might be told to terminate or sell the business to another person or he or she will be fired.

As with accusations of sexual harassment, suspected conflicts of interests should be carefully investigated before a conclusion is reached. When the potential conflict is brought to the attention of a manager, he or she should first establish the facts to determine if the conflict exists. If the conflict does exist, its seriousness should then be determined. The employee involved may not be aware that a conflict existed.[15] For example, a sales representative might declare, "Just because I purchased 1,000 shares of stock in that company, I didn't know that prohibits me from granting them a big discount on our maintenance service."

Summary

Five essential characteristics of an integrated conflict-management system are (1) broad in scope, (2) a culture of toleration and early resolution, (3) multiple access points, (4) multiple options, and (5) support structures.

A structural method of resolving conflict emphasizes juggling work assignments and reporting relationships so that disputes are minimized. A manager might have direct control over all the resources he or she needs to get the job done. Members from one organizational unit might exchange places with members of another organizational unit to understand the different viewpoints. Forming committees comprising members from groups that are in conflict or have the potential for conflict is helpful. In some firms, management maintains an open-door policy in which any employee can bring a gripe to its attention without checking with his or her immediate manager. Conflicts needing resolution are often brought forth in organizations with an open-door policy.

Anonymous polling is sometimes used to resolve employee conflicts when the conflict is about organizational strategy or because of an organizational change that affects employees. Anonymous polling software allows for the collection of the full range of opinions on the issue. Such software allows for open discussion, gives employees a voice on the issue, enables participants to know where they stand on the issue, and signals when consensus is reached.

Self-managed teams are advised to focus on three attitudes and behaviors to resolve conflict: (1) encourage openness to productive conflict, (2) prioritize accountability over blame, and (3) quantify the impact of the problem.

National culture can influence the choice and effectiveness of the method of conflict resolution. A study showed that half the variance for choosing a conflict model could be accounted for by a manager's cultural group membership. Japanese employees preferred using their authority, German employees preferred appealing to rules and regulations, and American employees preferred a win-win model.

Sometimes the best option is to do nothing about a conflict, particularly if the conflict is minor. Dropping the issue will sometimes maintain a stable relationship, but this approach will not work if you ruminate about the disagreement.

A conflict of interest exists when an individual has competing interests or loyalties, and it is therefore a form of role conflict. A dual relationship is usually involved in a conflict of interest. Nepotism and self-dealing usually create a conflict of interest. Conflicts of interests are sometimes illegal. Four types of conflicts of interest are (1) relational/family, (2) relational/romantic, (3) financial, and (4) confidential.

Preventing or resolving a conflict of interest can be accomplished in a variety of ways. Self-awareness is a starting point. A related approach is to apply an ethics test to the conflict or potential conflict. Company management should have a clear policy on disclosure, and the policy should be widely disseminated. A clear policy needs to be developed for dealing with situations in which a person does not disclose conflicting interests. Suspected conflicts of interest should be carefully investigated before a conclusion is reached.

Key Terms and Phrases

Anonymous polling software, p. 149
Conflict of interest, p. 153
Intraindividual conflict, p. 152

Open-door policy, p. 147
Self-managed work team, p. 150

Discussion Questions and Activities

1. Why should an organization worry about having an effective conflict-management system?
2. To help reduce conflict and develop empathy, organizations sometimes have key people switch positions with someone from another department. How might such a maneuver be an asset to a person's career development?
3. How might making use of the company open-door policy backfire on an individual?
4. What similarity do you see between the anonymous polling technique and the system of instructor evaluations at your school?
5. Give an example of how conflict might be productive within a team.
6. What is your opinion of the accuracy of the finding that American employees prefer a win-win solution to conflict?
7. Imagine that you are a team leader. What type of conflict do you think should be walked away from?
8. Provide an example of an intraindividual conflict that you have experienced in relation to work or school.
9. Carlos finds out that his company will soon be signing a $60 million contract to rebuild a highway, so Carlos quickly purchases 100 shares of his company stock. Is Carlos engaging in insider trading?
10. Why is it that so many politicians are accused of having a conflict of interest with construction firms?

Skill-Building Exercise: Identifying Potential Conflicts of Interest

For each of the following scenarios, identify the potential conflict of interest, and explain why you think there is a conflict of interest. If you do not see a potential conflict in one or more of the scenarios, explain why. Conduct the analysis individually or in a small group.

Scenario 1: The Final Exam and Girl Scout Cookies

The students enrolled in a capstone course, Business Strategy, are taking a difficult and complex two-hour final exam. As the students leave the exam room at the end of the allotted time, they notice that their professor has placed a sign on the table next to his desk, "Sign up here for purchasing Girl Scout Cookies from my daughter." To place the order, you must write down your name, e-mail address, and phone number. You are given the option of paying now or at the time of the delivery of the cookies. The smallest order allowed is two boxes, and you are able to purchase as many as two dozen boxes of various types of Girl Scout cookies.

Scenario 2: The Product Development Specialist with a Side Hustle

Harley works as a product development specialist at a consumer electronics company. She would like to have a higher income and satisfy her entrepreneurial urges at the same time. Harley's solution is to develop a *side hustle*, a part-time job to supplement the money she earns from her salary at the consumer electronics company. Harley decides to become a product-development consultant and contacts as many people in her network as possible to announce her new business activity. Through a referral by a network member, Harley is put in touch with Roger, the founder of a start-up consumer electronics company. During a business lunch with Roger, he tells Harley that he will pay her for a hot tip on a new consumer electronics gadget.

Scenario 3: The Referral to an Orthodontist

Alonzo is visiting the dentist office for a cleaning by the dental hygienist, which is accompanied by a brief exam by the dentist, Dr. Cartwright. The dental hygienist tells Alonzo that his teeth and gums look good but that he could do a better job of flossing and cleaning between the teeth with small brushes. She also comments that the slight overlapping of several of his teeth is creating problems in terms of plaque buildup.

After his five-minute exam, Dr. Cartwright tells Alonzo, "Your teeth and gums look pretty healthy. But I strongly recommend that you get braces; otherwise, your teeth will be a mess in a few years. They are already too crooked and overlapping. Here, let me give you the card of Dr. Tanya Menendez. She and her partners are among the best orthodontists in the area." Cartwright does not mention the fact that he and Menendez have been dating for two years.

Scenario 4: Jenna Recommends an Internet Service Provider

Jenna is the sales manager at a medium-size business that manufactures and sells windows and doors for residential and commercial properties. About 75 percent of the business is for replacement windows and doors. Jenna and the other members of the management team have heard repeated complaints about the Internet service provider (ISP) the company has used for years. After several meetings and frequent e-mail exchanges on the topic, company management thinks it would appropriate to find a new ISP with more reliable and less costly service.

Jenna recommends that the company switch to Starlight Communications, a small ISP, for two reasons: First, she knows from personal experience and favorable reviews on the Internet that the company provides excellent technology and customer support at a comparatively low price. Second, she has recently invested $100,000 of her own funds in Starlight and wants the company to prosper. In recommending Starlight to her colleagues, she emphasizes the quality and price of the service, but she does not mention her recent stock purchase.

In February 2019, a federal judge made a decision to delay a lawsuit involving a potential $10 billion cloud-computing contract Amazon.com was favored to win. The purpose of the delay was to wait while the federal government was investigating possible conflicts of interest in the procurement process. The investigation was about whether personal conflicts of interest impacted the integrity of the Joint Enterprise Defense Infrastructure (JEDI) cloud procurement.

The contract was expected to be awarded in the spring of 2019, but Amazon rival Oracle Corp. sued to halt the process until the government thoroughly investigated Oracle's claim of conflicts of interest. The claim centered on a former government employee, Deap Ubhi, who worked at Amazon before the procurement process and then returned to an executive position at Amazon. The Department of Defense (DoD) had mostly dismissed the conflict-of-interest claim earlier.

Pentagon spokesperson Elissa Smith later said, however, that "DoD can confirm that new information not previously provided to DoD has emerged related to potential conflicts of interest. As a result of this new information. DoD is continuing to investigate these potential conflicts." She added that she was currently considering whether the employment of Ubhi (and potentially others) by Amazon Web Services (AWS) created a conflict of interest that could not be dismissed.

The Oracle suit centers on Ubhi, who worked at Amazon before and after his 2016–2017 time as a DoD employee. Oracle contended that Ubhi played a heavy role in steering the procurement process to favor Amazon, which then rehired him. While at the Pentagon, Ubhi blogged that he was "currently leading the effort to accelerate adoption of the cloud for the Department of Defense." An Amazon spokesperson indicated that Ubhi worked for the AWS commercial division, not the public-sector division.

One of the major revelations of the Oracle lawsuit is that the DoD allowed multiple staffers with previous ties to AWS to adjust the proposal requirements so that only AWS met the requirements. Another person named in the lawsuit was Anthony DeMartino, who, as a consultant, had advised AWS on government contracting. He later took part in the JEDI drafting process as chief of staff to the deputy secretary of defense.

A judge accepted a motion from AWS to join a co-defendant in the suit. Amazon's proactive defense against Oracle's claim escalated the battle—a battle that could have major implications for the future of defense contracting, such as whether giant contracts should be granted to one supplier.

Amazon also dismissed allegations of a conflict of interest because Ubhi recused himself from JEDI discussion while working at the Pentagon. Oracle countered that he did not recuse himself until procurement for the cloud contract had reached advanced stages. Oracle lawyers claimed that Ubhi spearheaded the decision to adopt an approach that would give the entire cloud contract to one supplier. Oracle also noted that Amazon started negotiations about the company acquiring a start-up company in which Ubhi was a principal.

Amazon's federal lobbying expenditures exceeded $13 million in 2017. One source said that the company has reaped many benefits from its lobbying and that the JEDI contract would far exceed an earlier contract with the Central Intelligence Agency (CIA) for $600 million.

Questions

1. What does this case illustrate about the seriousness of conflicts of interests in obtaining a major government contract?

2. What could the leadership at Amazon have done to prevent charges of a conflict of interest in bidding on the cloud contract in question?

3. How might the lobbyists Amazon hired have contributed to the concern about conflicts of interest?

Source: Original case based on information in the following sources: John D. McKinnon and Kate O'Keefe, "Amazon Faces New Hurdle in Pentagon Job," *The Wall Street Journal,* February 20, 2019, p. A2; Aaron Gregg and Christian Davenport, "Pentagon to Review Amazon Employee's Influence over $10 Billion Government Contract," *Washington Post* (www.washingtonpost.com), January 24, 2019, pp. 1–4; Naomi Nix, "Inside the Navy Battle to Stop Amazon from Winning the Pentagon's Cloud Contract," *Bloomberg* (www.bloomberg.com), December 20, 2018, pp. 1–7; Tonya Riley, "Amazon's Bid on a $10 Billion Pentagon Contract Is Riddled with Conflict of Interest," *Mother Jones* (www.motherjones.com), December 28, 2018, pp. 1–5.

Associated Role Play

One student plays the role of Jeff Bezos, the CEO of Amazon.com and the world's richest man. Today he is defending himself and his company in court regarding accusations of a conflict of interest. Another student plays the role of the federal prosecutor, who is intent on getting to the truth and does not have a lot of sympathy for Bezos or Amazon. Observers will provide feedback about how well each side makes its case.

CASE PROBLEM 10B: The Struggle to Work Remotely

Casey is the leader of a team of nine health-benefits consultants in a human resources outsourcing firm. The health-benefits team helps small and medium-size businesses both establish and manage their medical insurance programs. Among the team's responsibilities are to choose the right package of benefits for the client's employees and administer the program. In this way, the clients do not need to have a health-benefits specialist on their payroll or have another manager or professional devoting time this activity.

Casey's team has ample work to perform as increasing numbers of companies decide to outsource the benefits aspect of human resources. For several years, team members have been able to work remotely, mostly from home, on two days per week. In recent months, CEO Bart has said that he would prefer that the professional staff spend more of their time on company premises. Bart's reasoning is that he wants the specialists to coordinate their work better and spark each other's thinking in face-to-face conversations. Bart also said that staff members are more likely to help each other solve problems when in the office rather than working remotely. Nevertheless, Bart did not prohibit remote work, and he left it up to the managers and team leaders to keep the amount of remote work in check.

Following Bart's demand to reduce the amount of remote work, Casey told her team members that they could work remotely a maximum of four days per month. After giving the new policy a try for two months, three team members had negative reactions to the cutback in working at home. Lola argued, "My aged and handicapped mother lives with my husband and me. I need to be home at least two days per week so that I can respond to her needs every once in a while even though I am getting my professional work done."

Kurt said that one of the reasons he chose to work at the company was the opportunity to work from home one or two days per week. He said, "I dislike commuting, and I am much more creative when I work from my den at home or at a café for a couple of hours. Besides, I have heard no complaints from my clients about my availability."

Serena also voiced her objection to the new policy, noting, "I've got a laptop and a smartphone. I can work from anywhere. As a single parent with two young children, being around the house at least one day per week is an asset in raising my children. I get a lot of work done after the children are in bed."

After processing these complaints and concerns, Casey decided to schedule a two-hour Tuesday morning meeting to resolve the conflict. "I dread this meeting," she thought, "but it is my responsibility as a team leader to keep morale high in the team and satisfy Bart's demands for less remote work."

Questions

1. How should Casey approach the attempt to find a resolution of the conflict about remote work?
2. What can Bart do to help resolve the conflict from an organizational standpoint?

Associated Role Play

One student plays the role of Casey at the Tuesday morning meeting. She is eager to resolve the conflict. Three other students play the roles of Lola, Kurt, and Serena, who would also like to resolve the conflict about remote work, but in their favor. Observers will comment on the progress in resolving the conflict.

Notes

1. David R. Lipsky and Ariel C. Avgar, "The Conflict over Conflict Management," *Dispute Resolution Journal*, No. 2–3, 2010, p. 39.

2. Susan M. Heathfield, "Open Door Policy Sample for the Workplace," *thebalancecareers* (www.thebalancecareers.com), August 7, 2018, p. 1.

3. "Sample Open-Door Policy." *Nolo* (www.nolo.com), p. 1.

4. Mike Broderick, "Using Technology to Help Resolve Employee Conflicts," *Training Industry* (https://trainingindustry.com), September 28, 2015, pp. 1–3; "How to Resolve a Conflict at Work," *Turning Technologies* (www.turningtechnologies.com), 2019, pp. 1–3; "Anonymous Responses," *Poll Everywhere* (www.polleverywhere.com), 2019, pp. 1–4.

5. Richard S. Wellings, William C. Byham, and Jeanne M. Wilson, *Empowered Teams: Creating Self-Directed Work Groups That Improve Quality, Productivity, and Participation* (San Francisco: Jossey-Bass, 1991), p. 3.

6. Amit Maimon, "How Self-Managed Teams Can Resolve Conflict," *Harvard Business Review*, April 17, 2017, pp. 1–5.

7. Catherine H. Tinsley, "How Negotiators Get to Yes: Predicting the Constellation of Strategies Used across Cultures to

Negotiate Conflict," *Journal of Applied Psychology*, August 2001, pp. 583–593.

8. Tae-Yeol Kim, Chongwei Wang, Mari Kondo, and Tae-Hyun Kim, "Conflict Management Styles: The Differences among the Chinese, Japanese, and Koreans," *International Journal of Conflict Management*, 1, 2007, pp. 23–41.

9. Amy Gallo, *The HBR Guide to Dealing with Conflict* (Boston, MA: Harvard Business School, 2017); "20 Examples of Conflicts of Interest in the Workplace," *Everfi* (https://everfi.com), March 24, 2016, pp. 1–3.

10. Jean Murray, "What Is a Conflict of Interest? Give Me Some Examples," *Business Law & Taxes Glossary* (www.thebalancesmb.com), October 31, 2018, pp. 1–4.

11. Gael O'Brien, "Inside Job: A Look at Conflicts of Interest and Personal Tasks," *Entrepreneur*, 2013, p. 68.

12. Rachel Blakely-Gray, "What You Need to Know about a Conflict of Interest in the Workplace," *Patriot Software* (www.patriotsoftware.com), September 25, 2017, pp. 1–5.

13. Gretchen Morgenson and Tom Corrigan, "McKinsey, U.S. Settle Bankruptcy Dispute," *Wall Street Journal*, February 10, 2019, pp. B1, B2.

14. Noreen Wainwright, "How to Resolve Conflict of Interest," *Bizfluent* (https://bizfluent.com), 2019, p. 1.

15. Pardip Singhota, "How to Manage Conflict of Interest in the Workplace," *Crispin Rhodes* (www.crispinrhodes.co.uk), April 2016, pp. 1–2.

Dealing with Incivility, Difficult People, and Criticism

Learning Objectives

After reading and studying this chapter and doing the exercises, you should be able to:

1. Describe how incivility is a major source of workplace conflict.

2. Identify at least six strategies and tactics for dealing with difficult people.

3. Understand how to resolve conflict through giving and receiving criticism.

Chapter Outline

Incivility as a Major Source of Workplace Conflict

> *Generalized Incivility*
> *Bullying*
> *Abusive Supervision*
> *Trash Talking*

Resolving Conflict with Difficult People

> *Implement a Strategy for Dealing with a Toxic Coworker*
> *Provide Constructive Feedback to the Difficult Person*
> *Listen and Respond*
> *Be Willing to Risk Small Public Confrontations*
> *Use Nonhostile Humor*
> *Give Recognition and Attention*
> *Use Tact and Diplomacy in Dealing with Annoying Behavior*
> *Avoid Creating Dependency on You*
> *Be Persistent in Dealing with a Narcissist*
> *Reinforce Civil Behavior and Good Moods*

Dealing with Conflict Surrounding Criticism

According to many business strategists, members of the executive suite and workers throughout the organization devote all their effort to achieving organizational goals and implementing the company vision. In reality, some of this important work gets sidetracked by interpersonal conflict stemming from the personality and behavior of workers who create problems for others. Unless these types of conflicts are resolved, or at least diminished, individual and organizational productivity are reduced. For example, a recent synthesis of the literature found that abusive supervision has negative implications for employee attitudes, performance, well-being, and productive behavior.[1]

The focus of this chapter is resolving conflict related to incivility, difficult people, and personal criticism. Collectively, these overlapping categories might be framed as negative workplace behavior that can impede individual welfare and organizational productivity.

Incivility as a Major Source of Workplace Conflict

Incivility also leads to a loss of focus, and decline in productivity.

Many instances of workplace conflict stem from the disposition of individuals as well as personality clashes. (A *disposition* is a characteristic attitude, similar to a personality trait.) People who are rude and uncivil or bully others readily enter into conflict. Incivility, employees' lack of regard for one another, has gained attention as a major source of workplace conflict. Many would argue that workplace incivility mirrors the decrease in civility in society.

A key point about what constitutes incivility depends on workplace norms and perceptions. Thirty years ago, if a male worker did not open a door for a female worker, he might have been regarded as uncivil. Today, a man who does not open doors for women (literally) would go unnoticed. However, the extreme contemporary view is that the man who opens doors for women is sexist and therefore a little uncivil! Ten years ago, a person who read text messages on his or her phone while conversing with a coworker might have been considered rude. Today, many people consider such multitasking to be acceptable behavior.

incivility Employees' lack of regard for one another.

Workplace incivility takes many forms. Here we examine incivility in four somewhat overlapping categories: generalized incivility, bullying, abusive supervision, and trash talking. The following section about dealing with difficult people might also be framed as resolving conflict caused by uncivil behavior.

Generalized Incivility

Incivility researcher Christine Porath says that if left unchecked, rampant incivility makes our days tenser. Incivility also leads to a loss of focus, a decline in productivity, a deliberate slacking off among disgruntled employees, and sometimes serious health problems. Another problem is that an organizational climate characterized by rudeness can result in aggressive behavior, high turnover, and lost customers. One of the many problems with incivility is that it can spiral, beginning with one party's perception of incivility and reciprocation with counter-incivility. The interpersonal conflict then intensifies as the two parties attempt to get even with each other, engaging in tit for tat. Being treated uncivilly by others often results in reciprocation by treating others who were not involved in the initial mistreatment in an uncivil manner. ("Act nasty to me, and I'll act nasty to somebody else.") Incivility often stems from a person experiencing heavy work pressure, but communication technology is another key factor. It is much easier to have misunderstandings when communication does not include tone of voice or facial expression.[2]

According to a Civility in America survey, 86 percent of respondents described their workplaces as civil and respectful. Despite this positive statistic, one-quarter of the 1,100 survey respondents said they quit a job because of an uncivil work environment.[3]

Research and observations about workplace incivility have advanced to the stage that theory has been developed to help explain the cause of the problem. Management professor Christopher C. Rosen and his colleagues developed and tested a model of incivility based on ego depletion theory. According to the model, when employees experience incivility, their self-control is reduced, putting them at risk for instigating incivility toward others. The reason is that the employees have diminished capacity to act in accordance with interpersonal norms. Being the victim of incivility leaves workers depleted because they must expend energy to understand how they were targeted with incivility and how to respond.

Making sense of what is happening is more complex in environments characterized by a high degree of organizational politics, in which intention and motives are ambiguous. Organizational politics strengthen the positive relationship between being treated uncivilly and diminished self-control. Nevertheless, workers can still counteract diminished self-control with a strong motivation to do otherwise. If workers think about how their behavior might reflect negatively on themselves, they are less likely to be uncivil, even if their attentional resources are somewhat depleted. (Attentional resources refer to the attention available to perform cognitive tasks that require considerable effort, such as developing a budget.) For example, most people really want to have cordial relationships with workplace associates.[4]

Incivility theory has been extended to explain why service workers sometimes sabotage or obtain revenge against customers who behave in an uncivil manner toward them. For example, anecdotal evidence suggests that because of dealing with rude and demanding customers, restaurant servers might sabotage customer food with some form of contamination, including expectoration. According to this new wrinkle in incivility theory, customer mistreatment ignites intuitive moral reactions on the part of employees. Employees respond with hostility that in turn leads to the moral disengagement mechanism of devaluing the targets. (Moral disengagement is the process by which an individual convinces him- or herself that ethical standards do not apply to him or her in a particular situation, given the extenuating circumstances.) The moral disengagement gives the badly treated employees the psychological freedom to sabotage customers. When employees perceive that the ethical climate in the organization is high, they are less likely to retaliate against customers.[5]

Some of the conflict stemming from incivility can be prevented by effective leadership. A study of cross-functional teams suggested that when leaders treated members of their team well and fairly, both individual and team productivity increased. Team members were also more likely to go above and beyond their job requirements.[6] A study about conflict resolution and incivility found that workers who use an integrative (collaborative or win–win) approach helped lessen the negative effects of incivility, such as lower job performance and commitment. Using an integrative conflict-management style was also associated with less intention to quit the job.

The accompanying Negotiation and Conflict Resolution in Action feature explains how the world's best-known soup company tackled the problem of incivility among employees.

Campbell Soup Feeds on Civility

Founder and CEO Douglas R. Conant of Conant Leadership was the CEO of Campbell Soup Company from 2001 until 2011. He believes strongly that the best way to win the hearts and minds of people and to generate huge profits for your enterprise is by leading with civility. Conant led a financial and employee engagement company turnaround with a conscious agenda to lead with civility. Conant took the helm of Campbell Soup when the company was struggling with respect to employee engagement, and he proceeded to revitalize the company.

Conant gives considerable credit to *touchpoints*, the idea of being tenderhearted with people, yet tough-minded on results. He held people accountable for attaining high performance but maintained these high standards in a way that showed he had a genuine concern for people. During his time as CEO, Conant handwrote 30,000 thank-you notes to employees whom he believed made a difference in employee engagement and morale. Conant would visit different Campbell sites around the world and see his notes posted on walls and bulletin boards. The notes set a good example for other company leaders in terms of actions they could take to reinforce good behavior.

When Conant began his tenure as CEO at Campbell Soup, the company had just lost 50 percent of its market value, sales were declining rapidly, and the organization was suffering from a series of layoffs. A Gallup poll indicated that employee engagement was among the worst for a Fortune 500 company. One of Conant's initial actions was to visibly set expectations for how he intended to create a more civil culture based on respect. He worked with his leadership team to establish the Campbell Promise: "Campbell valuing people. People valuing Campbell."

Conant supported the promise throughout the entire organization with a 10-point pledge to the senior leadership, laying out a clear and brief plan of how he intended to lead. The core of the pledge was a guarantee that Conant would conduct himself with integrity and honor. Promise number one in the pledge was, "We will treat you with respect and dignity." The promise set the tone for the company turnaround and sent the message to company leaders that a commitment to civility was critical and urgent.

Conant and his leadership team made "inspire trust" the number one leadership competency. Managers were told that they were expected to build trust with employees by honoring them and following through on the Campbell Promise. Civility on the part of the leader involves spending a substantial amount of effort in acknowledging people's contributions, actively listening, respecting the time of employees, and making employees feel valued.

The leadership team, including Conant, surveyed the organization every year to see how civil and respectful employees were really being. During performance evaluations, managers talked about how they were using the Campbell leadership model, centering on "inspire trust," to increase employee engagement. In the early years of the turnaround, hundreds of the top 350 leaders who were unable to or would not demonstrate their willingness to adapt their approach were dismissed and placed in other roles. Replacing those leaders with people who were committed to civility changed the culture and improved financial results.

Conant and his team reinforced civility with the Influence and Honor Award. Leaders who were chosen for the award were models of the behavior they were celebrating and were also high performers. The behavior in question was tough-minded on standards and tenderhearted with people.

Questions

1. What similarity do you see between "tough-minded on standards and tenderhearted with people" and one of the key principles of negotiation?
2. How civil was it to fire managers who did not buy into the desired civil approach to leadership?
3. Where might creating a breakthrough soup or other food product have fit into a turnaround for the Campbell Soup Company?

Source: Original story based on facts and observations in the following sources: Christine Porath and Douglas R. Conant, "The Key to Campbell Soup's Turnaround? Civility." *Harvard Business Review*, October 5, 2017, pp. 1–8; Mary Kaylor, "#Nextchat: Creating a Culture of Civility in the Workplace," *SHRM* (Blog.SHRM.org), October 29, p. 3; Gael O'Brien, "Can Civility Be Saved? Should It Be? *Business Ethics* (business-ethics.com), August 26. 2018, p. 1.

Bullying

bully A person who tries to control his or her victim through fear and intimidation.

Bullying behavior contributes to substantial interpersonal conflict in the workplace. One reason the problem of bullying continues to attract so much attention is that parents who deal with school bullying recognize that the same problem can happen in the workplace. A bully is a person who tries to control his or her victim through fear and intimidation.

Among the behaviors of workplace bullies are interrupting others, ranting in a loud voice, excessive teasing, hostile glances, and making threats. A bullying boss will often demand that a subordinate do things in his or her way or find another job.

A review of research grouped workplace bullying behavior into five categories, all of which are likely to trigger conflict:

- Threat to professional status (e.g., belittling the opinion of a worker and public humiliation)

- Threat to personal standing (e.g., name-calling, insults, and intimidation)

- Isolation (e.g., preventing access to opportunities and withholding of information)

- Overwork (e.g., undue pressure, unrealistic deadlines, and unwarranted interruptions)

- Destabilization (e.g., failure to give due credit, assignment of meaningless tasks, and setting up to fail)[7]

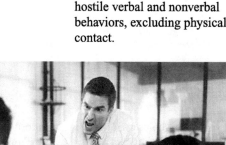

Bullying behavior contributes to substantial interpersonal conflict in the workplace.

Research suggests that the most likely victims of supervisory bullying are those workers with less power, especially those working in personal service roles such as housekeepers, nannies, and office assistants.[8] Bullying is often triggered by a person facing considerable pressure, such as a sales manager attempting to attain a sales goal.

As with sexual harassment, bullying behavior leads to conflict because a worker's demands for tranquility on the job are incompatible with the demands of the harasser or bully. Bullied workers complain of a variety of psychological ailments, such as anxiety, sleeplessness, panic attacks, and low self-esteem. The verbal-abuse aspect of bullying leads to a hostile environment that can drive many people to leave an employer.[9] Bullying is also associated with racial discrimination because the bully will often insult another worker based on his or her ethnicity.

A study conducted with 942 workers suggested that a problem-solving approach to conflict resolution provides some help in controlling bullying behavior.[10] If the worker being bullied attempts to resolve the problem causing the bullying, the aggressive behavior might decrease. For example, the bully might be so nasty because he or she is not getting enough attention from other group members.

Abusive Supervision

Nonphysical aggression by supervisors has received considerable research attention as a form of workplace bullying. **Abusive supervision** is defined as the perception by subordinates of how much their supervisors engage in the sustained display of hostile verbal and nonverbal behaviors, excluding physical contact.[11] A study conducted with working MBA students found that supervisors were more likely to abuse subordinates when the supervisors felt that their employer did not live up to their expectations. In other words, the supervisors engaged in displaced aggression.[12]

Another study with working adults provides more insight into when a supervisor is likely to be abusive. Supervisors are the most likely to be abusive in response to poor performance by the subordinate. Supervisors with a tendency toward being hostile combined with limited self-control are the most likely to be abusive. The study also suggested that supervisors who are mindful of their feelings of hostility are less likely to have hostile outbursts.[13] The use of surface

abusive supervision The perception by subordinates of how their supervisors engage in the sustained display of hostile verbal and nonverbal behaviors, excluding physical contact.

Supervisors are the most likely to be abusive in response to poor performance by the subordinate.

acting (fake polite behavior) to deal with angry customers is another factor that appears to trigger abusive supervision. A study found that this type of surface acting weakened a supervisor's self-control, leading to incidents of bullying of subordinates.[14]

According to a recent study conducted in two settings, supervisors will sometimes be abusive simply because they think that abuse will enhance performance. The abuse tends to backfire because it prompts counterproductive behavior on the part of subordinates rather than enhancing performance.[15] Abusive supervision therefore prompts more conflict in an organization.

The negative impact of abusive supervision on job performance can sometimes be reduced by the traits and behaviors of the subordinate. Two studies conducted with professional workers in India found that employees who scored high on the trait of conscientiousness were better able to maintain high performance when verbally abused by their supervisors. Equally important is that when employees took an active role in dealing with the abuse, they were less likely to experience lower performance than their counterparts who avoided conflict.[16]

Trash Talking

trash talking Uncivil remarks or aggressive communication that is expressed between opponents.

A form of uncivil behavior stemming from sports, and now frequent in organizational life, is trash talking—uncivil remarks or aggressive communication that is expressed between opponents. Trash talk usually includes boasts about oneself and insults about the competition. Trash talking has been conceptualized as competitive incivility. For example, when Dan Akerson was the CEO of GM, he announced that GM was going to launch a rear-wheel-drive automobile that would compete directly with the Mercedes C Class. When asked what he thought about Mercedes, he said, "They call it C class because it's very average."[17] For many workers, trash talk is not perceived as uncivil but as mirthful and in the spirit of competition. A representative piece of trash talk would be, "Our team completed its project under budget and in 10 days. I doubt your team could even come close to that."

A series of studies conducted at the Wharton School of the University of Pennsylvania found that targets of trash talking became very motivated. Yet trash talking can be disruptive and distracting, particularly when individuals are completing a creative task. Trash talking is better suited for revving up the opponent in a competitive task but can harm performance in a creative task.[18]

Resolving Conflict with Difficult People

A challenge facing all workers face from time to time is dealing constructively with workers who appear intent on creating problems and therefore creating conflict. The conflict often has to be resolved in order to establish harmony in the workplace. For a variety of reasons, these difficult or counterproductive people perform poorly themselves or interfere with the job performance of others. A difficult person is an individual who creates problems for others, yet has the skill and ability to do otherwise. A worker is classified as difficult if he or she is uncooperative, disrespectful, touchy, defensive, hostile, or even very unfriendly. The difficult person often meets or exceeds performance standards, yet annoys coworkers and superiors.[19]

difficult person An individual who creates problems for others yet has the skill and ability to do otherwise.

The number of difficult employees appears to be increasing in recent years, as indicated by the number of managers referring such individuals to employee assistance programs. Counselors who specialize in dealing with behavioral problems are affiliated with employee assistance programs. Plausible reasons for the increased number of difficult people in the workplace are that job stress has increased and that society is breeding more narcissistic personalities.[20]

The bully mentioned in reference to incivility is an example of a difficult person. Another, of many possible examples, is the "yes person" who will agree to any commitment and promise any deadline but will rarely deliver. Some well-known business executives are sometimes difficult people in their interactions with work associates. Another difficult or toxic coworker is the person who is quick to "throw others under the bus." These individuals are quick to assign blame to others when problems arise.[21] Psychiatrist Jody Foster (not the actress!) notes that when workers act in inappropriate ways (e.g., bullying, excessive micromanaging, or displaying narcissistic tendencies), the results can be devastating for the entire workplace.[22] A few difficult people can substantially lower the performance of a team or organization. It takes time to deal with the problems difficult people create, and their distracting behavior is often contagious.[23]

The techniques described in the following paragraphs and listed in Figure 11.1 have wide applicability for resolving conflict with difficult people and helping them change to more constructive behavior.

Implement a Strategy for Dealing with a Toxic Coworker

Consultant Abby Curnow-Chavez and her colleagues studied thousands of teams and collected data across industries, sectors, and countries to analyze what makes some teams high performers versus failures.[24] Their research suggested that the most important factor contributing to team success or failure is the quality of interpersonal relationships within the team. A major finding was that 70 percent of the variance between the lowest-performing teams and the highest-performing teams correlated with the quality of team relationships. All intrateam relationships are important because one toxic team member can hamper the performance of the team.

The toxic behaviors noted in the study included the following: backstabbing, criticizing, and blaming; gossiping and spreading negative rumors; agreeing to do something in a meeting but not following through; hoarding information; purposely undermining other team members; and caring only about personal agendas. Toxic team members create unnecessary drama and distraction that can diminish productivity. They also erode the *team brand* by creating a negative impression of the team throughout the organization. A team with toxic members can also undermine the values of the leader and the company be devaluing teamwork. Toxicity can degrade the team culture because other team members soon disrespect the toxic team member. They also treat that person with disrespect and gripe about him or her frequently.

The strategy for reducing conflict with the toxic team member involves four steps, as follows:

1. *Hold an honest, candid conversation with the person.* It is unlikely that the toxic person will change his or her behavior spontaneously, making constructive feedback about the negative behavior essential. The research in question suggested that high-performing teams are 106 times more likely to give each other feedback than are low-performing teams, even when the feedback is difficult.
2. *Elevate your own game, and be a role model.* Instead of being dragged down by the toxic team member, maintain your focus on your individual goals and those of the team. Make yourself a role model for how the rest of the team should act by setting a standard that supports collaboration and open dialogue rather than retaliation. The research found that members of high-performing teams were 55 times more likely to show a commitment to each other's success in comparison to low-performing teams.
3. *Talk with your immediate manager.* Proactively suggest to the manager that the team hold a meeting to establish team norms and start to address some of the toxic behavior within the team. A desirable outcome of the meeting or meetings should be to gain insight into each other's perspectives, set clear team norms, and increase peer-to-peer accountability.
4. *Take care of yourself.* It is important to not allow conflict with toxic coworkers to damage your physical and emotional health. Frame negative interactions with toxic people as work problems to be resolved rather than as personal attacks. Engage in your most effective approaches to stress management, such as physical exercise, meditation, or completing items on your to-do list.
5. Coworkers who irritate you rarely do annoying things on purpose. Tactful actions on your part can sometimes take care of these annoyances without having to confront

1. Implement a strategy for dealing with a toxic coworker.
2. Provide constructive feedback.
3. Listen and respond.
4. Be willing to risk small public confrontations.
5. Use nonhostile humor.
6. Give recognition and attention.
7. Use tact and diplomacy in dealing with annoying behavior.
8. Avoid creating dependency on you.
9. Be persistent in dealing with a narcissist.
10. Reinforce civil behavior and good moods.

FIGURE 11.1 Techniques for Resolving Conflict with Difficult People

the problem. For example, point to the phone in your hand if noisy workers are gathering outside your cubicle or next to your work table. Tact and diplomacy are useful for dealing with a variety of disrupters, such as coworkers who consistently talk about their personal interests, including sports or favorite restaurants and TV shows, while you are trying to focus on work.

When subtlety does not work, it may be necessary to proceed to the confrontation tactics described in Chapter 9. Tact and diplomacy can also be incorporated into a confrontation. In addition to confronting the person, you might point out a positive quality of the individual, such as the coworker's ready availability to answer questions.

Provide Constructive Feedback to the Difficult Person

You cannot assume that a person who is annoying you continually will suddenly change for the good. Make a sincere attempt to provide constructive feedback to the individual, a core tactic mentioned earlier in relation to toxic coworkers. During the feedback session, ask for feedback in return about what you might be doing wrong in the work relationship.[25] For example, you might say, "It is difficult for me to get my point across when you talk over my voice every time we work on a problem together. Is there anything I am doing wrong that makes work difficult for you?"

Feedback can also be useful in dealing with a bully by pointing out how you recognize the bullying and how you find it to be unacceptable. For example, "You have insulted me three times this morning. Maybe you want to lower my self-confidence, but it isn't working. I find most of your criticism to be pointless and mean-spirited."

Another application of feedback is in reducing the conflict created by the know-it-all. A know-it-all will often attempt to monopolize in-person or remote meetings by professing master knowledge of the problem at hand. To deal with a know-it-all coworker, a good starting point is to ask permission: "May I talk to you about something?" Talk about your direct observations, placing emphasis on your coworker's expertise and the consequences of flaunting it: "We all know that you are knowledgeable, but ours is a team effort. You didn't give anybody else at the meeting a chance to suggest a solution. Did you notice that?" As advised by career coach Priscilla Claman, the technique just described works best when you have already established a relationship of trust with the person you consider to be a know-it-all.[26]

The know-it-all has also been referred to as the *office soapboxer*, a person who is convinced that his or her view is the only view and does not hesitate to vocalize this belief. The term *soapbox* refers to an improvised platform used by a self-appointed spontaneous or informal speaker. Perhaps in yesteryear, soapboxes were strong enough to stand on. When a subordinate or coworker gets on a soapbox during a meeting, the situation can be annoying. Listen to the opinion expressed, and then refocus the group on the task of jointly making a decision. To reduce the conflict, avoid getting wrapped up in your emotional response to the person's behavior. Instead, remain focused on the work the team needs to accomplish, which will help you stay grounded and clear-minded.

During the meeting, be an example of decorum and respect for the opinion of others. If the soapboxer tries to grab the stage again, respond with a comment such as, "We heard that point already, and we are now considering other opinions." If the person in question claims to have the support of a key person outside the meeting, do not accept the maneuver. Explain that as a group, you have to move forward with the opinion of those physically present at the meeting.[27]

Listen and Respond

Closely related to giving feedback are the tactics of listening and responding. Give the difficult person ample opportunity to express his or her concerns, doubts, anger, or other feelings. Face the person directly and maintain eye contact. Then acknowledge your awareness of the difficult person's position.[28] For example: "You tell me that management expects us to work at an unreasonable pace all the time and that we should have a more relaxed environment." After listening, present your viewpoint in a manner such as this: "Your take on the situation may be valid based on how hard you prefer to work. Yet I have not found the work pace demanded of us to be unreasonable." This exchange of viewpoints is less likely to lead to failed communication than if you use a judgmental statement, such as "You shouldn't have such a negative attitude."

Be Willing to Risk Small Public Confrontations

A particularly devious type of difficult person is the manipulator—an individual who makes untrue statements or fakes certain behaviors to achieve a personal advantage. The manipulator might even resort to blackmail with a statement such as, "If you give me credit for the business-process-improvement suggestion you developed, I will probably forget about the fact that you accepted a rather generous gift from one of our suppliers." Another form of manipulation is to name drop to get one's way, such as saying, "I was talking with Noreen, our CEO, this morning, and she will be very happy if you get this spreadsheet analysis done for me by tomorrow morning."

manipulator   An individual who makes untrue statements or fakes certain behaviors to achieve a personal advantage.

Conflict resolution specialist Liz Kislik explains that sometimes the most effective way of exposing a manipulator's maneuverings is to confront him or her at the moment. If you have the moxie to confront the manipulator in an individual or group setting, it puts him or her on notice that the behavior in question has been exposed and will not be tolerated.[29] In the example about the reference to the CEO, the manipulation target might respond, "I would be proud to do a spreadsheet analysis that Noreen wants in a hurry. Might you please have her send me a text confirming her request?"

Use Nonhostile Humor

Nonhostile humor can often be used to help a difficult person understand how his or her behavior has affected others. Also, the humor will help defuse conflict between you and that person. The humor should point to the person's unacceptable behavior, yet not belittle the person. Assume that you and a coworker are working jointly on a report. Whenever you turn over a portion of your work for review, the person finds some fault. You point out lightly that striving for perfection is admirable but that you are developing stress symptoms based on your quest.

Give Recognition and Attention

Counterproductive or difficult people, like misbehaving children, are sometimes crying out for attention. By giving them recognition and attention, their behavior will sometimes cease. If their negative behavior is a product of a more deeply rooted problem, recognition and attention will not work. Other actions will need to be taken, such as referring them for counseling, either directly or by consulting with the manager and human resources professional. Two office bully specialists, Kathi Elster and Patricia Barnes, observe that an effective tactic for dealing with a mean bully is to befriend that person.[30] If feeling liked by others, the person might have less need to get attention by intimidating coworkers.

Use Tact and Diplomacy in Dealing with Annoying Behavior

Coworkers who irritate you rarely do annoying things on purpose. Tactful actions on your part can sometimes take care of these annoyances without the need to confront the problem. For example, point to the phone in your hand if noisy coworkers are gathered outside your cubicle. Tact and diplomacy are useful for dealing with a variety of disrupters, such as those coworkers who consistently talk about their personal interests, such as sports and favorite restaurants, while you are trying to focus on work. When subtlety does not work, it may be necessary to proceed to the confrontational tactics described earlier. Tact and diplomacy can also be incorporated into confrontation. In addition to confronting a person, you might point out the individual's good qualities.

Avoid Creating a Dependency on You

high-maintenance person
An individual who requires so much assistance, special attention, and extra help that it bothers and fatigues coworkers.

A trap to avoid with many difficult people, especially the high-maintenance person, is to let them become too dependent on you for solutions to problems. A **high-maintenance person** requires so much assistance, special attention, and extra help that it bothers and fatigues coworkers. In your desire to be helpful and supportive to a coworker, you run the risk of creating a dependency. A difficult person might be pestering you to regularly help solve some of his or her most challenging work problems.

The high-maintenance worker might ask you to verify a fact via a search engine, reboot a stalled computer, or help recharge a dead automobile battery. You may want to be a good organizational citizen, yet you also need time to concentrate on your own work, and you do not want to create a dependency relationship with a coworker.[31] As an antidote to the problem, make frequent statements such as, "You know how to use Google or Bing"; "You must know how to reboot a computer"; "Perhaps you should call your roadside service provider. They specialize in recharging batteries."

Be Persistent in Dealing with a Narcissist

narcissism An extremely positive and inflated view of the self, combined with limited empathy for others.

Narcissism refers to an extremely positive and inflated view of oneself, combined with limited empathy for others. The narcissist is self-absorbed, self-adoring, and self-centered and has a grandiose preoccupation with his or her importance. With a reasonable dose of narcissism, a person can be productive in a high-level position, such as a charismatic leader being self-confident, self-promoting, and flamboyant.[32] In many situations, however, narcissists are difficult people. As a result of their perception of others being highly interested in them, workplace narcissists often discuss their ideas in self-important ways while being indifferent to the ideas of others. When coworkers attempt to express their views, the narcissist will frequently become impatient with the conversation and is often oblivious to the discomfort that his or her lack of concern causes the coworker.

Confrontation about how the narcissist annoys you is a starting point in dealing with this type of difficult person. It is also necessary to persist in your demands to be listened to and to be able present your perspective on or a solution to a joint work problem. In discussing a joint work problem, the narcissist's default position is to talk about how he or she typically handles the problem. An example of a persistent response is "You have explained your position clearly several times, but I want the opportunity to also express my viewpoint."

Professional counselor Les Carter offers a couple of suggestions for dealing with the conflict created by narcissists that fit the theme of being persistent. One suggestion is to *choose your own path*. It is best not to be intimidated by a controlling narcissist. Do what you think is best, and do not worry about not accepting the advice, opinion, or demands of the narcissist. Tact and diplomacy, however, are beneficial in terms of preserving a good working relationship with the hyper-controller.

Another suggestion is to *establish boundaries and consequences*. A narcissist will often make demands on a coworker that will inconvenience the latter, such as insisting that he or she stay late once again to help the narcissist with a work project. The boundaries in this conflictual situation refer to the limits to which one coworker should be obliged to help a coworker regularly.[33] A consequence could be linked to the frequent demand to stay late to help the narcissistic coworker. The coworker subject to the demand might say, "If our good working relationship depends on my helping you after hours so frequently, I will have to back out of our good relationship."

Reinforce Civil Behavior and Good Moods

In the spirit of positive reinforcement, when a generally difficult person behaves acceptably, recognize the behavior in some way. Reinforcing statements would include, "It's enjoyable working with you today," and "I appreciate your professional attitude." Reinforcing civil behavior and good moods is another application of the motivation adage, "Catch the person doing something right." Instead of focusing your efforts on bringing unacceptable behavior to the attention of the difficult person, you make positive statements when the person engages in constructive behavior—a direct application of the theory of behavior modification.

The tactics for resolving conflict with difficult people described in this section require practice to be effective. Also, you may have to use a combination of the 10 tactics described to deal effectively with a difficult person. The point of these tactics is not to out-manipulate or subdue a difficult person but to minimize the conflict in order to establish a cordial and productive working relationship.

Reinforce civil behavior and good moods.

Dealing with Conflict Surrounding Criticism

Criticism, or negative feedback, is almost inevitable in a results-oriented work environment. As already described, negative feedback is often necessary to deal with difficult people. Yet it is challenging to give someone serious performance or behavioral feedback in a way that does not make that person defensive, thereby instigating conflict.

To soften the possible conflict resulting from delivering negative feedback about another person's behavior, it is important not to make judgments, generalize, or interpret what their behavior means. Instead, use neutral observations, such as "I observed that you used an expletive in talking with our chief marketing officer, and she was quite taken back." It is also helpful to frame your feedback in terms of personal growth. If you are the manager, you might begin the conversation with something like, "I often look for ways to help my team members develop, and I have some thoughts for you. When would it fit your schedule for us to talk?"[34]

The recipient of negative feedback can also play a major role in minimizing the potential conflict in the situation. In addition to becoming defensive, the recipient of criticism might engage in denial, play the role of the victim, or blame the circumstances. Conflict specialist Peter Bregman recommends a positive approach. No matter what the feedback or whoever is giving it, a better way to respond is, "I really appreciate you taking the time and effort to tell me. Thank you." This simple response communicates that the person being criticized is willing to listen and perhaps work on the problem that is causing conflict.[35]

Saying "thank you" in response to criticism is a variation of a recommended technique for dealing with criticism when the criticizer holds a power advantage over you and also has a valid criticism. If you deny that you have made a mistake, the criticism and conflict intensify. **Disarming the opposition** is a method of conflict resolution in which you disarm the criticizer by agreeing with his or her criticism of you. The technique assumes that you have done something wrong. *Disarming* refers to the idea that the armament the person was using against you was the personal attack, which is taken away when you accept the reason for the attack. Disarming the opposition generally works more effectively than counterattacking the person with whom you are in conflict.

disarming the opposition
A method of conflict resolution in which you disarm the criticizer by agreeing with his or her criticism of you.

Another reason that disarming the opposition is effective is that it implies that you are apologizing for a personal mistake or error. An apology often gets the other person on your side or at least softens the animosity. By offering an apology and regretting your mistake, you are likely to gain sympathy from the person who disapproves of what you have done or whom you have wronged. Agreeing with the criticism also offers the advantage of asking the person with more formal authority than you to help you improve your performance.

Assume that Margot is being criticized by her boss for regularly making overoptimistic sales forecasts for her territory. Margot might disarm the opposition by stating, "I am also concerned that I have been overshooting my forecasts by about 20 percent recently. What do you suggest I do to become a little more pessimistic about my sales prospects for the upcoming quarter?"

Summary

Incivility is a major source of workplace conflict and can lead to a loss of focus, a decline in productivity, a deliberate slacking off among disgruntled employees, and sometimes serious health problems. Incivility can spiral. According to an incivility model (or theory), when employees experience incivility, their self-control is reduced, putting them at risk for instigating incivility toward others. Organizational politics strengthen the positive relationship between being treated uncivilly and diminished self-control.

A related theory is that customer mistreatment leads to employee hostility that in turn leads to the moral-disengagement mechanism of devaluing the target (customer). Some of the conflict stemming from incivility can be prevented by leaders treating group members fairly, as well as employees using an integrative style of conflict management.

Bullying contributes to substantial interpersonal conflict in the workplace. Bullies interrupt others, rant in a loud voice, tease excessively, give hostile glances, and make threats. The most likely victims of bullying are workers with less power, especially those working in personal service roles.

Abusive supervision involves nonphysical aggression perpetrated by supervisors. Supervisors are more likely to be abusive when disappointed by their employers and when employees perform poorly. Abuse can also take place when supervisors think such behavior will enhance performance. Conscientious employees and those who actively deal with the abuse are less likely to experience lowered performance. Uncivil behavior can also take the form of trash talking, defined as uncivil remarks or aggressive communication between opponents.

The techniques described here for resolving conflict with difficult people are (1) implement a strategy for dealing with a toxic coworker, (2) provide constructive feedback, (3) listen and respond, (4) be willing to risk small public confrontations, (5) use nonhostile humor, (6) give recognition and attention, (7) use tact and diplomacy in dealing with annoying behavior, (8) avoid creating a dependency on you, (9) be persistent in dealing with a narcissist, and (10) reinforce civil behavior with good moods.

Criticizing others often makes them defensive, thereby leading to conflict. When criticizing others, is it helpful not to make judgments, generalize, or interpret what their behavior means. Instead, use neutral observations. To reduce conflict, it is helpful to express appreciation for the criticism. Disarming the opposition is a method of conflict resolution in which you disarm the criticizer by agreeing with the criticism.

Key Terms and Phrases

Abusive supervision, p. 165
Bully, p. 164
Difficult person, p. 166
Disarming the opposition, p. 171
High-maintenance person, p. 170

Incivility, p. 162
Manipulator, p. 169
Narcissism, p. 170
Trash talking, p. 166

Discussion Questions and Activities

1. What have you observed to be the most frequent form of uncivil behavior in the workplace?
2. How might having a civil work environment give a company a competitive advantage?
3. Many customer-contact workers become frustrated by a customer who texts or talks on the phone while the worker is attempting to serve him or her. How might the customer-contact worker resolve this conflict?
4. Have you ever been bullied by a boss? If so, what form did the bullying take?
5. Explain whether you would classify environmental sexual harassment as a type of bullying.
6. Why would surface acting by a supervisor in response to a nasty customer prompt the supervisor to abuse employees?
7. Under what circumstances do you think trash talking leads to increased job satisfaction rather than conflict?
8. Provide an example of toxic behavior that you have observed in a work team or a sports team.
9. What example of a high-maintenance coworker, or fellow student, have you observed?
10. Get the opinion of two experienced workers as to whether difficult people create morale and productivity problems in the workplace.

Skill-Building Exercise: Dealing with Criticism

In each of the following three scenarios, one worker is the recipient of criticism from a work associate. Your task is to develop a response to the criticism that you think is justified on the part of the recipient of the criticism. As part of your response, keep in mind that it is probably in the best interest of the person being criticized to maintain an adequate working relationship with the criticizer.

Scenario 1: The Caustic Boss

Tony, a project manager at a construction company, is displeased with several of the cost estimates for constructing temporary fences prepared by Shana, a cost estimator at the company. Tony says to Shana, "Did you fail your accounting courses in college? Do you understand that we cannot build fences at a loss? I can't understand how a cost estimator could be so far off in coming up with an accurate cost. What is your problem?"

How should Shana respond to Tony?

Scenario 2: The Nit-Picking Teammate

Coleen is a member of a patient-experience team at a large medical center. The mission of the team is to improve the experience of patients who visit the medical center's several hospitals and many clinics throughout the region.

Coleen prides herself on her ability to candidly express her opinions and let work associates know if what they are doing bothers her. During a lunch break with teammate Sean, Coleen says, "Sean, let me be frank with you. That new non-tuck-in shirt you are wearing looks very unprofessional. You probably think that you look cool, but to me, you look like you forgot to tuck in your shirt. Also, while I'm trying to be helpful, I wish that you would not start at least half of your sentences with 'You know.'"

How should Sean respond to Coleen?

Scenario 3: The Irate Customer

Chester is the service manager at a major car dealership for a luxury brand of German vehicles. He places an online order for six alternators at an average price of $550 that the dealership needs in a hurry. When the alternators arrive the next day, Chester observes that they are for the wrong vehicle. Chester is furious and asks to speak to Missy, the inventory specialist who shipped the order. He shouts at Missy, "I see why you are named Missy. You missed this order completely. Our customers have paid about $65,000 each for their cars. Now there will be a delay for a key repair while we wait for the correct alternators. Are you stupid or something?"

How should Missy respond to Chester?

CASE PROBLEM 11A: Avery Uses Commitment as an Excuse

Avery works as a price estimator in the division of a large electronics company that manufactures and sells security systems to homes and businesses. She holds a degree in electronics technology and has extensive knowledge about security systems. Up until several years ago, the company was prospering because of heightened concerns about security.

Although concerns about security remain high, two factors have reduced sales. One problem is that the market for security systems in her area has become saturated. Virtually every business firm and house has a security system. Another problem is that many homeowners are now purchasing security systems that are administered online or through smartphone apps. New business for the division stems mostly from getting businesses and homeowners to switch to the company or from security-system upgrades for existing customers.

As a result of the security-system business having stabilized in the geographic area, the atmosphere in her office has become tense. Workers have become less

calm and pleasant than previously. Avery, who has had a volatile personality since early childhood, has become tenser than her coworkers. During a recent proposal to upgrade the security system at a pharmaceutical distribution center, her company's sales representative accused Avery of providing a price estimate that was too high to clinch the deal. Avery replied, "You are a sad [expletive] sales rep. You will tell a prospective customer anything to close a sale. So long as you get your commission, you don't care if the company loses money on the project." Avery offered no apology for her outburst.

A week later at a department meeting to discuss goals for the year, Avery said to the group, including the manager, "Goal setting for me is a dumb [expletive] idea. I will have no work to do unless this time-wasting, expense-hogging sales group gets off its butt and makes some sales."

Horrified, the manager said to Avery, "You are being totally unprofessional. Please apologize to the sales group."

Avery responded, "Okay, maybe I shouldn't be so truthful in what I say. I can't help it. I'm a committed person who wants the company to succeed. I take the company's success personally."

Questions

1. To what extent does Avery's comment about being "committed" justify her expression of anger toward coworkers?
2. What do you recommend that Avery's manager and coworkers do to make her a less difficult person in the office?
3. What career advice might you offer Avery? (Or does she need any advice?)

Associated Role Play

One student plays the role of the sales representative, who accuses Avery of providing a cost estimate that is too high to clinch the deal with the pharmaceutical distribution center, and another student plays the role of Avery, who lashes back at the sales rep. The goal of the sales representative is to be treated in a more civil manner by Avery. The rep also wants Avery to get into a problem-solving mode. Avery, in turn, thinks that the rep is more interested in closing the sale than making money for the company. Observers should focus on the sales representative's ability to effectively deal with Avery's anger and hostility and then provide feedback on their observations to the role players.

CASE PROBLEM 11B: Candid Manager Blake

Blake is the manager of the mortgage department at the downtown headquarters of a bank. He has seven direct reports, including three mortgage consultants. Although these consultants work full-time hours at the bank, they are classified as contractors who work only on commissions, without any salary or benefits. A consequence of this compensation arrangement is that the mortgage consultants are under considerable pressure to sell home mortgages to bank customers. Until a mortgage is approved, the consultant receives no financial compensation.

Roxanne, a 29-year-old mortgage consultant, asked for an appointment to speak to Blake about her recent problems in finalizing mortgages. Blake was eager to meet with Roxanne because he was also under pressure for the mortgage department to secure more mortgages. A partial transcript of their meeting follows:

Roxanne: I've come to you for help. For several months, I haven't been closing enough mortgages to make a living. My husband and I have three children, and we can't pay all our expenses on his salary alone. Is there any way the bank can put me on salary? Or maybe give me a few months' worth of advance commissions? I've been a great producer in the past.

Blake: Grow up, Roxanne. When you took this job, you knew it did not include a salary and that the bank does not allow advances. We need you to produce, but we can't change the bank rules. We are not a small community bank.

Roxanne: Do you know how brutal it is out there? Home sales are down 10 percent in our area. I don't have enough warm leads coming into the bank to pursue for a mortgage. More potential bank customers are taking out mortgages online. Besides that, our mortgage approval committee has been shooting down too many deals on me lately.

Blake: Wake up, Roxanne—the mortgage business has changed in recent years. We can't add any more high-risk loans to our portfolio. It is very difficult to sell those mortgages to other institutions.

Roxanne: Okay, then what do you suggest I do to generate more mortgage applications that the committee will approve?

Blake: Do what you do best. You're a professional. Just bear down harder on good mortgage prospects who visit your desk. Be persuasive. Turn up the heat. Do something good, or be gone.

Roxanne: I'm trying. I want my commissions just as much as the bank wants its mortgages.

Blake: Just keep trying, and get back to me with results, not excuses.

Questions

1. What is your evaluation of the usefulness of Blake's criticism of Roxanne?
2. How should Roxanne respond to the criticism she is receiving from Blake?
3. To what extent do you think that Blake is being an abusive supervisor?

Associated Role Play

One student plays the role of Blake, who may seem like he is heartless or showing "tough love," but perhaps the role player can make him a little more encouraging. Another student plays the role of Roxanne, who is discouraged about her sales performance but wants to close more mortgages. Observers will look to see if the criticism offered by Blake offers any promise of motivating Roxanne and pointing her in the right direction. About eight minutes should suffice for this role play.

Notes

1. Trevor Watkins, Ran Fehr, and Wei He, "Whatever It Takes: Leaders' Perceptions of Abusive Supervision," *The Leadership Quarterly*, April 2019, p. 260.

2. "Why We Need to Kick Incivility out of the Office" (interview with Christine Porath), *Knowledge@Wharton* (knowledgeharton.upenn.edu), June 20, 2017; Christie Porath, "How Business Stops People from Working Together," *Harvard Business Review*, January 20, 2017, p. 2; Christopher C. Rosen, Joel Koopman, Allison Gabriel, and Russell E. Johnson, "Who Strikes Back? A Daily Investigation of When and Why Incivility Begets Incivility," *Journal of Applied Psychology*, November 2016, pp. 1620–1634; Lynne M. Andersson and Christine M. Pearson, "Tit for Tat? The Spiraling Effect of Incivility in the Workplace," *Academy of Management Review*, July 1999, pp. 452–471.

3. Leslie Gaines-Ross, "Offices Can Be Bastions of Civility in an Uncivil Time," *Harvard Business Review*, July 14, 2017, p. 2.

4. Rosen et al., "Who Strikes Back," p. 1629.

5. Yu-Shan (Sandy) Huang, Rebecca L. Greenbaum, Julena M. Bonner, and Cynthia S. Wang, "Why Sabotage Customers Who Mistreat You? Activated Hostility and Subsequent Devaluation of Targets as a Moral Disengagement Mechanism," *Journal of Applied Psychology*, April 2019, pp. 495–510.

6. Christine Porath, "How Rudeness Stops People from Working Together," *Harvard Business Review*, January 20, 2017, p. 4.

7. Helen Cowie, Paul Naylora, Ian Riversb, Peter K. Smith, and Beatriz Pereira et al., "Measuring Workplace Bullying," *Aggression and Violent Behavior*, No. 7, 2002, pp. 33–51.

8. Vincent J. Roscingo, Steven H. Lopez, and Randy Hodson, "Supervisory Bullying, Status Inequalities, and Organizational Context," *Social Forces*, July 2009, pp. 1561–1589; Dana Wilkie, "Where the Bullies Are," *HR Magazine*, March 2016, p. 52.

9. Arthur H. Bell, *You Can't Talk to Me That Way* (Franklin Lakes, NJ: Career Press, 2005).

10. Elfi Baillien and Hans De Witte, "The Relationship between the Occurrence of Conflicts in the Work Unit, the Conflict Management Styles in the Work Unit and Workplace Bullying," *Psychologica Belgica*, 49-4, 2009, pp. 207–226.

11. Bennett J. Tepper, "Consequences of Abusive Supervision," *Academy of Management Journal*, April 2000, p. 178.

12. Jenny M. Hoobler and Daniel J. Brass, "Abusive Supervision and Family Undermining as Displaced Aggression," *Journal of Applied Psychology,* September 2006, pp. 1125–1133.

13. Lindie H. Liang et al., "Why Are Abusive Supervisors Abusive? A Dual-System Self-Control Model," *Academy of Management Journal*, August 2016, pp. 1385–1406.

14. Kai Chi Yam et al., "Out of Control: A Self-Control Perspective on the Link between Surface Acting and Abusive Supervision," *Journal of Applied Psychology*, February 2016, pp. 292–301.

15. Watkins, Fehr, and He, "Whatever It Takes," pp. 260–272.

16. Amit K. Nandlkeolyar et al., "Surviving an Abusive Supervisor: The Joint Roles of Conscientiousness and Coping Strategies," *Journal of Applied Psychology*, January 2014, pp. 138–150.

17. "How Trash-Talking Affects Performance," *Knowledge@ Wharton* (http://knowledge.wharton.upenn.edu), July 5, 2017, p. 2.

18. "How Trash-talking Affects Performance," pp. 1–6; Jeremy A. Yip, Maurice E. Schweitzer, and Samir Nurmohamed, "Trash-Talking Competitive Incivility Motivates Rivalry, Performance, and Unethical Behavior," *Organizational Behavior and Human Decision Processes*, January 2018, pp. 17, 25–144.

19. Peggy Drexler, "The Value of 'Office Disrupters,'" *The Wall Street Journal*, February 15–16, 2014, p. C3.

20. Jennifer Schramm, "The Rise of the Difficult Employee," *HR Magazine*, June 2012, p. 144.

21. Eric Titner, "Signs Your Coworker Might Be Toxic," *Career Opportunities, the Job network* (www.thejobnetwork.com), March 11, 2018, p. 1.

22. Cited in, "How Disruptive Behavior by Employees Can Devastate a Workplace," *Knowledge@Wharton* (http://knowledge.whrton.upenn.edu), March 27, 2013, p. 1.

23. Robert Sutton, "How a Few Bad Apples Ruin Everything," *The Wall Street Journal*, October 24, 2001, p. R5.

24. Abby Curnow-Chavez, "4 Ways to Deal with a Toxic Coworker," *Harvard Business Review*, April 10, 2018, pp. 1–4.

25. Curnow-Chavez, "4 Ways to Deal with a Toxic Coworker," p. 4.

26. Priscilla Claman, "How to Deal with the Know-It-All in Your Office," *Harvard Business Review*, October 25, 2017, pp. 1–6.

27. Alicia Bassuk, "How to Deal with an Office Soapboxer," *Harvard Business Review*, August 30, 2016, pp. 1–5.

28. "Master Dealing with Difficult People," *Manager's Edge*, March 2009, p. 8.

29. Liz Kislik, "How to Work with a Manipulative Person," *Harvard Business Review*, November 6, 2017, pp. 1–6.

30. Kathi Elster and Patricia Barnes, "Field Guide to Office Bullies," *Bloomberg Businessweek*, November 26–December 2, 2012, p. 95.

31. Lin Grensing-Pophal, "High-Maintenance Employees," *HR Magazine*, February 2001, p. 89.

32. Emily Grijalva and P. D. Harms, "Narcissism: An Integrative Synthesis and Dominance Complementarity Model," *Academy of Management Perspectives*, May 2014, pp. 108–127.

33. Les Carter, *Enough about You: Let's Talk about Me* (San Francisco: Jossey-Bass, 2005), p. 47.

34. Rebecca Knight, "How to Help an Employee Who Rubs People the Wrong Way," *Harvard Business Review*, September 21, 2017, p. 2.

35. Peter Bregman, "The Best Response to Negative Feedback Is a Simple One," *Harvard Business Review*, April 9, 2019, pp. 1–5.

Third-Party Resolution of Conflict

Source: stockfour/Shutterstock.

Learning Objectives

After reading and studying this chapter and doing the exercises, you should be able to:

1. Explain how a manager goes about mediating conflict, including using a five-step process and applying confrontation and problem solving.
2. Describe how arbitration is applied to resolving workplace disputes.
3. Describe how the grievance procedure is applied to resolving workplace disputes.
4. Describe how outside mediation is applied to resolving workplace disputes.

The previous 11 chapters have emphasized how two parties interact between themselves to resolve conflict through negotiation and other approaches to conflict resolution. From an overall perspective, conflict-management systems (CMSs) consist of three types of conflict-management options: rights-based processes, interest-based processes, and negotiated processes.[1] Using this framework, negotiated processes cover efforts by individual parties to resolve conflict for themselves, without the benefit of third-party interventions—the major subject of the previous 11 chapters.

The focus of this chapter is rights-based processes and interest-based processes. Right-based processes, particularly grievance procedures and arbitration, involve third parties in determining or facilitating the outcome of a conflict. The third party will often rely on laws, contracts, or behavioral norms to arrive at a judgment or decision. Interest-based processes, such as mediation, include third parties that help parties reach agreements without determining outcomes for them.

alternative dispute resolution (ADR) The use of any form of mediation or arbitration as a substitute for the public judicial or administrative process to resolve a dispute.

Arbitration, the grievance procedure, and mediation by company outsiders are part of **alternative dispute resolution (ADR)**, defined as "the use of any form of mediation or arbitration as a substitute for the public judicial or administrative process to resolve a dispute." In short, you resolve conflicts out of court. Many organizations have implemented ADR because it is usually a means of circumventing the expensive, time-consuming features of conventional litigation. Lawyers are often involved in arbitration and mediation, but the judicial process is not involved. ADR offers the key advantage over litigation of providing a less expensive, faster, and often more efficient method of dispute resolution.[2]

The Manager's Role in Mediating Conflict

A manager often plays a key role in third-party resolution of conflict by acting as a mediator of the two or more people in conflict. To help two or more group member requires a high level of skill. Conflict specialist Patrick S. Nugent believes that being able to intervene in the conflicts of group members is a management skill that grows in importance. Such competencies are particularly useful in the new form of management based less on traditional hierarchy and more on developing self-management subordinates and teams. When the conflict is between two different groups, such as marketing and finance, a major goal of conflict resolution is to get the two sides to see the company's big picture.[3] An example of the big picture would be that the company is trying to provide an excellent service and earn a profit.

Much of the time a manager invests in conflict resolution is focused on assisting others in resolving their conflict. Often the conflict is between the heads of two different departments or divisions. A team leader will sometimes be placed in the position of having to resolve a conflict between two or more team members. Later in the chapter, we describe mediation from the standpoint of an outside third party who has no formal authority over the people in conflict.

Here we approach the manager's role in resolving conflict between subordinates from three perspectives. First, we provide more details about the manager's role as a mediator. Second, we present a five-step process for resolving conflict. Third, we show how a manager might use the technique of confrontation and problem solving to resolve conflict that was described in Chapter 8.

The Manager's Role as a Conflict Mediator

Management professors Jeanne Brett and Stephen B. Goldberg observe that when a disagreement erupts between two group or team members, it is tempting for the manager to jump in and make a decision about how to resolve the conflict. Such an approach might save time but does not involve the key players in making a decision. A manager should therefore assume the role of a mediator rather than exerting his or her authority. At times, a human resources (HR) professional will be asked to mediate conflict between individuals. The HR specialist might have more expertise in mediating conflict than the manager.

The first step for the manager in the mediator role is to understand the positions of both sides in terms of what they are claiming and rejecting. Understanding the interests of both sides, or why they are making the claims, is also important. For example, both sides might be claiming credit for an idea because each person is seeking a promotion. Initial meetings can be held separately or with the two sides present. An advantage of having the two people present at the same time is that the mediating sessions will be more transparent, and neither side can claim the other side is making a secret deal with the mediator.

The first meeting should be aimed at getting both sides to calm down enough to focus on the problem, and for the manager to show respect for the disputants.

The first meeting should be aimed at getting both sides to calm down enough to focus on the problem; to facilitate this, the manager should show respect for the disputants. Next, each side should have an opportunity to express his or her positions, interests, and priorities. In many cases, the people in conflict do not understand the terminology of "positions," "interests," and "priorities," yet they want to fully express their perception of the facts and their opinions.

In resolving a conflict, it is often more effective for the manager to seek a mediated solution rather than exerting authority because the two sides are more likely to accept a decision when they have been involved in its making. The mediator role is also helpful in facilitating the development of conflict-resolution skills of subordinates. If mediation fails, the manager will simply have to make an executive decision about how the conflict should be resolved.[4] Assume that two division heads are in conflict about whose division should be housed in a new office building leased by the company. Mediation gets nowhere, and the CEO finally decides that the more profitable division gets to transfer to the new building.

A Five-Step Process for Managing Conflict between Subordinates

According to the America Management Association, learning how to handle conflict efficiently is a necessary skill for all managers. Furthermore, resolving conflict between subordinates helps to keep conflict from hindering employee growth. Resolving interpersonal conflict can be accomplished through a five-step process[5]:

Step 1: Identify the source of the conflict. Identifying the origins of the conflict facilitates its resolution. To obtain the needed information, ask a series of questions to identify the cause. Examples include "What made you feel upset?"; "How did the incident begin?"; and "How much responsibility do you take for what went wrong?"

As a manager, supervisor, or team leader, it is necessary to give both parties the chance to tell their side of the story. Listening to both sides will give you the opportunity to gather more information, as well as demonstrate your impartiality. As you listen, make brief responses that encourage further talking, such as "I see," "I get it," or "Tell me more."

Step 2: Look beyond the incident. Sometimes it is the perspective on the situation rather than the situation itself that causes the anger, and perhaps the shouting. Perhaps one party in the conflict thinks that not asking for his or her input on a customer problem showed a lack of respect. The source of the conflict might be a minor problem that took place months previously. The level of stress, however, has reached a point that the two parties have begun personal attacks instead of addressing the real problem. In the calm of a conference room or private office, you might be able to get the two parties to look beyond the triggering incident to see the real cause. One such insight might be, "I guess we don't think each other really has the right experience or knowledge to solve the tough kind of problems we face."

Probing questions will again be useful in this second step to conflict resolution. Two such questions are, "What really happened here?" and "When do you estimate that the problem between the two of you began?"

Step 3: Request solutions. After you have gathered the viewpoint of both parties regarding the conflict, the next step is to look for how the situation might be changed. It is helpful to gather input from both parties with a question such as, "How can you make things better between you two?" Because you are assuming the role of a mediator in this situation, you have to attend to verbal nuances and also study the body language of the two parties, which will help you understand if any real progress is being made.

Your goal is to get the disputants to stop fighting and begin cooperating so that a constructive working relationship develops. To accomplish this, the parties must stop blaming each other and look to resolve the conflict.

Step 4: Identify a solution or solutions that both parties can support. As you are listening for the most acceptable course of action, provide input. Point out the merits of the ideas that emerge, not only from the perspective of both sides but also from the perspective of the organizational unit or total organization. For example, you might point out that more collaboration will lead to better teamwork in the group and will make the department more respected and valuable.

Step 5: Agreement. In your role of mediator, you want to get the two parties to shake hands or bump fists with respect to one of the alternatives chosen in step 4. You might go the extreme of having both sides provide a written description of their agreement. It will usually be sufficient to meet with the individuals together and have them respond to questions such as, "What action plans have you developed to prevent this type of action plan from arising in the future?" and "How will you resolve the same type of problem should it arise again?"

In the conflict about not respecting each other's experience or knowledge, the two might shift their emphasis to the results each one can attain. For example, "If Jud has an answer to a major problem facing a customer, I'll judge the solution on its own merits. I won't worry about his experience in solving this type of problem."

The Application of Confrontation and Problem Solving

Working in the mediator role, the manager can sometimes apply the technique of confrontation and problem solving described in Chapter 8. The manager sits down with the two sides and encourages them to talk to each other about the problem rather than talking to the manager. This approach is preferable to inviting each side to speak with the manager individually because then each side might attempt to convince that manager that he or she is in the right and perhaps exaggerate what the other disputant did wrong.

During the confrontation-and-problem-solving session, the manager is placed in a mediator role of being impartial and wanting both sides to come to an agreement. As shown in the following illustration, the core of this approach is *storytelling*, in which each worker describes how and why the conflict started and why it continues. Each side must allow the other side to talk, with the manager remaining impartial.[6] An abbreviated example is as follows:

Manager: I've brought you two together to see if you can resolve the problems you have about sharing the time of our office assistant, Tanya.

Isabelle: It pleases me that you did. Greg wants so much of Tanya's time that she doesn't have enough time to help me or the other team members.

Greg: What Isabelle really means is that she wants Tanya to take care of a lot of trivial tasks she should be taking care of by herself. For example, I have seen Isabelle ask Tanya to download software that she could easily download herself.

Isabelle: Look who's talking. I recently heard you ask Tanya to order lunch for you and a visitor to our team.

Manager: I think I understand what is happening here. Both of you are antagonistic toward each other, and you look for little problems to attack. With a little more mutual respect, you would be able to better appreciate the help each of you is asking from Tanya.

Greg: I guess that Isabelle isn't such a big resource hog. Next time Tanya is tied up carrying out a task for her, I will try to be more patient and compassionate.

Isabelle: Maybe I could be a little more of a team player by recognizing that we have an equal right to getting help from Tanya. I know that Greg can exaggerate problems from time to time.

An effective component to mediation through confrontation and problem solving is for the manager to ask each side to restate or paraphrase what the other person has said.[7] In the scenario just presented, Greg might say, "I heard Isabelle say that I hog too much of Tanya's time." Isabelle might say, "I heard Greg say that I ask Tanya to take care of a bunch of trivial tasks for me."

Arbitration

A standard way of resolving difficult disputes when the two parties cannot agree is to call in a third party to provide a settlement. Arbitration is the judicial resolution of a dispute by an independent third party. Arbitration clauses are frequently found in employment contracts, credit-card agreements, and retail contracts. An arbitration hearing usually involves an individual arbitrator but might also rely on a tribunal or panel. A tribunal may involve several arbitrators, although some legal systems require an odd number to prevent a tie. (The U.S. Supreme Court has nine justices.) The most common arrangement is one or three arbitrators. Arbitration is used instead of referring a dispute to a court, yet unlike mediation and negotiation, the arbitrator's decision is binding.[8]

arbitration The judicial resolution of a dispute by an independent third party.

Arbitration clauses are frequently found in employment contracts, credit-card agreements, and retail contracts.

Arbitrators are trained professionals with expertise in specific areas of arbitration, such as employment, labor, construction, commercial, and international disputes. The American Arbitration Association (AAA) maintains a list of qualified arbitrators that is available to potential users.

Steps in the Arbitration Process

As laid out by the AAA, here are the steps in the arbitration process[9]:

1. *Ruling and Initiation.* Arbitration begins when one party submits a demand to the AAA. The other party, the respondent, is notified by the AAA, and a deadline is imposed for a response.
2. *Arbitrator Selection.* The AAA helps in identifying an arbitrator who fits the criteria established by the parties, such as industry knowledge.
3. *Preliminary Hearing.* The arbitrator conducts a preliminary hearing with the parties to discuss the issues in the case and gather relevant information, such as names of witnesses.
4. *Information Exchange and Preparation.* The parties prepare their presentations and exchange information.
5. *Hearings.* At the hearing, the parties present their testimony and evidence to the arbitrator. When the case is unusually complex, more than one hearing might be necessary.

6. *Post-Hearing Submissions.* After the hearing, the arbitrator may allow for the submission of additional documentation by the arbitrator.

7. *The Award.* The arbitrator settles the case by issuing a decision, and an award if deemed appropriate.

An example of arbitration took place over a royalty dispute between the Monsanto division of German drugmaker Bayer and the Indian seed company Nuziveedu Seeds Ltd (NSL). By Monsanto's calculations, NSL, along with its two affiliates, owed the company close to $23 million. Monsanto's position was that it had patent protection in India and therefore had the right to collect royalties through bilateral contracts with the Indian seed companies. At the conclusion of the three-person arbitration panel, Monsanto said that it had received a favorable ruling, although the terms of the settlement were not revealed.[10]

Final-Offer Arbitration in Negotiation

A long-noted problem in adversarial negotiation is that the two sides rarely bring their most reasonable offer to the table. Instead, each side presents an offer or demand that is to its advantage and seeks to give up as little as possible. This is particularly true when either side does not implement the tactic of beginning with a plausible demand or offer. The typical approach to negotiation can be costly and inefficient. However, a type of arbitration exists that is helpful in producing a satisfactory outcome to negotiations.

final-offer arbitration
A method of settling negotiations by having an arbitrator choose the most reasonable offer if necessary.

High-profile professors Max H. Bazerman and Daniel Kahneman have developed a negotiation strategy that can efficiently lead to a fair and equitable agreement. Final-offer arbitration is a method of settling negotiations by having an arbitrator choose the most reasonable offer if necessary. One side presents an objectively fair offer and challenges the other side to make its own best offer. If the other side is unreasonable, the first side challenges the other side to take the competing offers to an arbitrator. The arbitrator then decides which of the two offers is more reasonable, rather than deciding on a compromise. The threat of losing in final-offer arbitration will usually make each side come up with a more realistic offer or demand.

The major insurance company AIG tested final-offer arbitration in an accident injury claims case and attained a rapid, fair settlement. AIG did not want to overpay on the claim but also did not want to appear unfair to its customer. Based on expert opinion, AIG made an offer of $850,000, whereas the claimant's attorney countered with $2.6 million, which he claimed was fair. The claimant's attorney understood that the final-offer arbitrator would choose between the two amounts and not offer a compromise. The two sides settled on $1.05 million in a few days.[11]

The Advantages and Disadvantages of Arbitration

Arbitration is gaining in popularity and offers many advantages. A major advantage is that arbitration usually saves time and money in comparison to litigation. Frequently, an arbitrator can be chosen with expertise in a particular industry or discipline. If the arbitration can be conducted properly without needing to hire legal counsel, this can cut costs. Yet if legal counsel is really needed, avoiding legal costs can backfire.

Arbitration also has some potential disadvantages. Formal evidence and discovery of facts are usually not included in arbitration. The decision of the arbitrator is binding and usually cannot be appealed as in lawsuits. Many companies insert arbitration clauses that favor the company over the employee in their employment contracts, including the prevention of class-action suits against the employer.[12]

Informal Arbitration

Many instances of workplace conflict are arbitrated informally by a manager. Instead of the people involved in conflict having a formal sit-down session with the manager acting as a mediator or judge, the two sides ask the manager who he or she thinks is right. When the manager makes the decision for the two parties, he or she is acting in the role of arbitrator. The manager might also proactively be an informal arbitrator when the manager observes that two group members are having a dispute.

By listening carefully to both sides and offering a solution to the conflict that should work, the manager is an informal arbitrator. Assume that division president Fred learns that the vice president of engineering, Rick, and the vice president of human resources, Niki, disagree about the subcontracting of design work. Rick believes that he should be able to subcontract whenever it fits the best interests of the division. In contrast, Niki dislikes subcontracting design work because she wants company executives to build a stable, permanent workforce. Fred decides that he has had enough of this bickering and issues the following order to Rick: "From now on you can only subcontract design work during bona fide peak workload emergencies."

Many instances of workplace conflict are arbitrated informally by a manager.

The Grievance Procedure

Another approach to appealing to a third party in order to resolve a conflict is the grievance procedure—the formal process of filing a complaint and resolving a dispute within an organization. In practice, the grievance procedure is a step-by-step process the employee must follow to get his or her complaint resolved, or at least addressed. During the process, the formal (written) complaint moves from one level of the organization to the next higher level. When employees are represented by a labor union, a union representative is included at each level. Figure 12.1 outlines the grievance procedure. Grievance procedures are almost always included in a collective bargaining agreement.[13]

grievance procedure The formal process of filing a complaint and resolving a dispute within an organization.

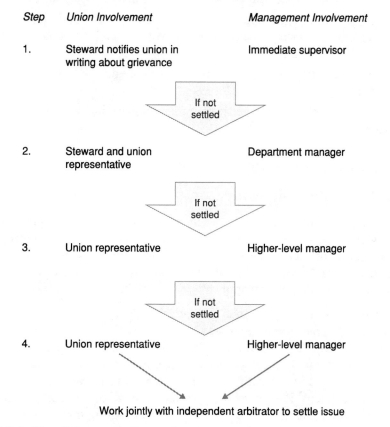

FIGURE 12.1 The Grievance Procedure

The grievance procedure provides for an internal judicial review of any action taken by management that could be in violation of the negotiated agreement. The employee, however, must file a grievance. As an effort is made to settle the grievance, the effort to resolve the problem moves up the chain of command of both company management and the union. If earlier attempts to resolve the grievance fail, the grievance moves to arbitration.

Classification of Grievances

A grievance occurs when an employee feels his or her rights have been violated in some way. The Office and Professional Employees International Union (OPEIU) uses the following classification of grievances:[14]

- *Wage Amounts*. Wage grievances involve a failure to pay an agreed-upon amount in areas such as starting pay, merit increase, shift premium, vacation pay, or bonus pay. An improper job classification can also lead to a wage grievance, such as the job being classified as too low.
- *Wage Inequities*. This type of problem is usually handled through the collective bargaining agreement.
- *Unreasonable Rate of Production or Excessive Workload*. In this case, a time or production standard might be violated, or a violation of the principle of a "fair day's work for a fair day's pay" might occur.
- *Assignment and Placement of Workers*. A worker might be given an improper transfer that violates a seniority clause or might be subject to an improper layoff or recall back to the job.
- *Improper Disciplinary Action*. Examples included penalties without just cause, employees not being properly notified of rule or penalties, or a disciplinary layoff.
- *Physical Working Conditions*. This could involve unsafe or unhealthy working conditions that are in violation of local, state, or federal safety laws.
- *Supervisory Practices*. A supervisor might abuse authority, intimidate or coerce, perform work that is supposed to be performed by members of the bargaining unit, discriminate, or practice favoritism.
- *Personal Rights and Privileges*. A supervisor might deny a leave of absence or discriminate by not treating employees equally.
- *Violation of Union Rights*. A supervisor might undermine the union or the grievance procedure.
- *Other Contract Violations*. Violations of contracts containing clauses not covered in the previous list items could also occur.

Suggestions for the Employer

The Advisory, Conciliation, and Arbitration Service (Acas) code of practice on disciplinary and grievance procedures recommends that managers or supervisors follow a five-step procedure for dealing with grievances professionally and responsibly.[15] Observe that these suggestions do not exactly follow the steps in the grievance procedure outlined in Figure 12.1, which is especially applicable when a labor union is present.

1. *Informal action.* If the grievance is relatively minor, the supervisor should have a discussion with the employee to see if it can be resolved informally. For example, a worker might say, "I was docked one hour of pay because I was late for work yesterday. It wasn't my fault; there was a major accident on the highway that blocked traffic." A quiet word will usually resolve a minor problem, yet the supervisor should record the incident. If a grievance is serious enough that it cannot be resolved by informal action, the grievance should be put in writing and submitted through a formal grievance procedure.

2. *Investigation.* Quickly after receiving a formal grievance, the employer should investigate the situation. The aim of the investigation is to establish the facts of the grievance before any decision is made. With many grievances, a couple of people should be interviewed. For example, if Lily says she was the only production technician who was denied overtime work last month, a couple of other employees might be interviewed to substantiate Lily's claims.

3. *Grievance meeting.* After the investigation is completed, the supervisor should hold a meeting with the employee so that he or she has an opportunity to explain the complaint. The employee's opinion should be sought on how the grievance should be resolved and the outcome he or she is seeking. The Acas code of practice states that an employee has the right to be accompanied by another person to the meeting.

4. *Decision.* After considering the evidence, the employer decides whether to uphold or reject the grievance. The decision should be communicated to the employee as soon as feasible. If the grievance is upheld, the employee should be informed of what action the employer intends to take and how the action will be implemented. The letter should also provide the employee with the right of appeal in case the grievance is rejected or the resolution seems inadequate.

5. *Appeal.* If a grievance is rejected, even partially, the employer should be prepared for an appeal. The appeal should be dealt with by an impartial manager or a more senior manager than the supervisor who first dealt with the grievance. After the hearing, the employee should be informed in writing of the outcome of the appeal.

Suggestions for the Employee

The Teamsters Union offers detailed advice for the employee and union steward who want to file a grievance. To begin, the worker should recognize that the first stages of filing a grievance are key, no matter what kind of grievance procedure the contract contains. At this point, facts are gathered and arguments are tested. The following suggestions are geared toward the steward but also should be useful for the employee who wants to meet with management to resolve conflict about a grievance:[16]

- Is your case documented? Both the employee and the steward can contribute to the documentation.
- Have you developed an evidence list, including the names of witnesses? Have the witnesses put their testimony in writing?
- Have you or the union made a written information request?
- Do you have management's side of the story? What type of evidence does management have?
- Have you identified the weak points in your case? Prepare in advance of management addressing the weak points.

The Teamsters Union also offers a roadmap for presenting a case, as follows: Look at the potential *problems* the grievance is attempting to address, and plan the order in which they will be presented. Make sure you have the *facts*, including witnesses and documents. Photos or videos could prove helpful. The *chronology* counts in terms of writing out the dates of events related to the grievance. Write out your *arguments*, and place them in the order you will want to present them. Discuss and be prepared to respond to the *remedies* that will solve the grievance.

The many steps recommended to the employer, employee, and union steward for dealing with a grievance underscore the complexity of the third-party resolution of conflict.

Mediation

Earlier in the chapter, we described how the manager can mediate conflicts. Similar to arbitration, mediation can also be a formal process, using an outside third party who helps the disputants resolve their conflict. The legal definition of mediation is the settlement

mediation The settlement of a dispute or conflict with the assistance of an independent person who intervenes between the two contending parties in order to aid in the settlement of the agreement.

of a dispute or conflict with the involvement of an independent person between the two contending parties in order to aid in the settlement of their disagreement.[17] The mediator works to find points of agreement and helps the disputants to arrive at a fair result. Unlike an arbitrator, the mediator does not make a judgment on what the outcome of the conflict should be or bind the parties to his or her decision. Similar to arbitration, mediation can save time and money. The cost of mediation is typically about 10 percent of the price of litigation, yet mediation results in no formal, enforceable ruling.[18]

Mediator Paul Holtzman recommends that the time to consider mediation is when a dispute first surfaces. Among the workplace problems that might benefit from mediation are termination, noncompete agreements, intellectual property rights, and patent infringement. With all such problems, it is best to make a rational assessment of the most likely costs and opportunities early in the case, before too much anger builds up, making mediation difficult.

The time to consider mediation is when a dispute first surfaces.

After each side has prepared to mediate, the mediation usually takes a few hours to one day to complete. Holtzman estimates that mediation has a success rate of between 70 and 80 percent. Mediation can capture the advantage of more accurate memories because waiting for a court settlement can take a long time. Also, potential witnesses to a dispute may no longer be available when the time finally arrives for a court settlement. What takes place in mediation is confidential, so facts do not have to be revealed to the public, such as the media.[19]

Mediation continues to find new business-related applications. For example, the Mortgage Modification Mediation program used in bankruptcy cases in Orlando, Florida, has been successful enough to spawn similar programs in Florida and across the United States. The novel program places lenders or loan-servicing companies and their legal counsel in the same virtual room as debtors and their counsel. The goal of the mediation is to determine if a loan modification can be achieved. About one-half of the time, a loan modification is agreed upon.

According to the format of the program, an individual or married couple has 90 days after filing for bankruptcy to file a motion for Mortgage Modification Mediation. The parties use a secure web portal to submit documents to begin the mediation. All correspondence is communicated through the portal. A mediator is selected from an approved list, and mediation must conclude within 150 days. Both lenders and debtors contribute $250 to pay for the mediator. The actual mediation is done by phone. If the parties reach a temporary accord, a temporary modification is established. After three to five payments have been made, the lender agrees to a final modification. The portal and the phone conferences enhance communication, enabling lenders or loan servicers to better understand the mortgagee's financial situation and ability to succeed in a modified loan.[20]

A behavioral perspective on mediation is that a key aspect is storytelling, as mentioned earlier in relation to mediation by the manager. Each employee or company representative explains how and why the conflict began and why it persists. While one disputant talks, the other party and the mediator listen intently. After storytelling, the key behavioral components of mediation come into play: acknowledgment, collaborative brainstorming, problem solving, and resolution of the conflict.[21]

The accompanying Negotiation and Conflict Resolution in Action feature illustrates how mediation was used to resolve conflict between a major airline and its mechanics' union.

Southwest Airlines and the Aircraft Mechanics Union Reach a Deal

Federal aviation regulators warned Southwest Airlines Co. and its 2,400 mechanics in 2019 that their labor dispute threatened to damage the airline's safety practices. The management at Southwest had complained that mechanics were citing minor maintenance issues, such as missing seat row numbers or broken coffee dispensers, to force flight cancellations. Canceled flights had surged to 62 per day in February 2019 from the previous average of 14, as stated in a lawsuit filed by Southwest. Union leaders countercharged with allegations of intimidation and undue pressure by airline supervisors to get the planes back in the air.

In response to a stern warning from the Federal Aviation Association (FAA), a Southwestern spokeswoman said, "We appreciate the FAA's oversight and maintain our dedicated focus on assuring the highest level of compliance and safety all times."

The lawsuit alleged that the Aircraft Mechanics Fraternal Association (AMFA) was conducting an illegal work slowdown aimed at pressuring the airline into agreeing to a new contract. The CEO of Southwest Airlines, Gary Kelly, said that the flight cancellations were costing the company millions of dollars. The aircraft mechanics union had countered with a lawsuit accusing Southwest and Kelly of defamation of character.

The airline carrier claimed that the mechanics had taken an abnormally high number of airplanes out of service in recent weeks, in a move seen as a negotiating tactic. Negotiations had broken down over the extent to which Southwest would be allowed to outsource maintenance. The mechanics cited safety concerns as justification for taking the aircraft out of service. In support of this contention, the union's national director issued a statement denying that the mechanics were improperly grounding any airplanes.

Harvey Harteveldt, the founder of a travel industry analysis group, said, "Southwest has a legitimate argument here, and is trying to strike a balance between keeping everything safe and not having the airplanes taken out of service for what could be considered extremely minor, noncritical matters." He explained that it would be acceptable for an airplane to fly with a broken coffee maker or a dead bulb in a passenger reading light.

In addition to hundreds of flight cancellations, the bitter, six-year-long dispute had raised safety concerns. One reason is that an angry airline mechanic might unintentionally not concentrate as well on potential safety problems. After working with a mediator, the AMFA and Southwest Airlines Negotiating Committees reached an Agreement in Principle that was mutually agreed upon by both parties. The agreement was reached after the FAA cautioned that the deteriorating relationship between the company and mechanics' union posed a threat to the airline's safety management system. The new five-year contract called for mechanics receiving a 20 percent salary increase, as well as $160 million in bonuses.

Toward the end of the dispute, both sides issued conciliatory statements without dictating how the tentative agreement reached might impact their respective lawsuits. The vice president of labor relations at Southwest, Russell McCrady, said, "Our mechanics certainly deserve a new contract, and this industry-leading agreement in principle addresses our employees' interests." Bret Oestreich, national director for the AMFA, commented, "I commend both sides for their hard work and tireless negotiating this past week."

Questions

1. Why might it have been preferable for Southwest Airlines and the AMFA to have negotiated their own resolution of the conflict rather than having the matter settled in court?
2. Southwest Airlines has a strong positive reputation for dealing with its customers. Why might it have been difficult to establish the same type of relationship with the mechanics' union?

Source: Original story based on facts and observations in the following sources: "Southwest and Its Mechanics Reach a Tentative Deal in Labor Dispute," *CNBC* (www.cnbc.com), March 18, 2019, pp. 1–2; "Southwest, Mechanics Reach Tentative Deal in Labor Dispute," *The Associated Press*, March 18, 2019, pp. 1–2; Zach Wichter, "Southwest Airlines Sues Mechanics in Labor Feud" *The New York Times*, March 2, 2019, p. B4; Andy Pasztor and Andrew Tangel, "FAA Raises Red Flag on Southwest Labor Dispute," The Wall Street Journal, March 9–10, 2019, pp. A1, A4; Diana Zoga, "Mechanics, Southwest Airlines Reach Breakthrough in Labor Dispute," *NBC Washington* (nbcwashington.com), March 17, 2019, pp. 1–4.

Summary

Arbitration, the grievance procedure, and mediation by company outsiders are part of alternative dispute resolution. A manager often plays a key role in third-party resolution of conflict by acting as a mediator of the two or more people in conflict. The first step for the manager in the mediator role is to understand the positions of both sides in terms of what they are claiming and rejecting. It is often more effective for the manager to seek a mediated solution rather than exerting authority to resolve a conflict because the two sides are more likely to accept a decision when they have been involved in its making.

A five-step process for managing conflict between subordinates proceeds as follows: (1) identify the source of the conflict, (2) look beyond the incident, (3) request solutions, (4) identify a solution or solutions that both parties can support, and (5) agreement. When working in the mediator role, the manager can sometimes apply the confrontation-and-problem-solving technique. During the session, the manager is placed in the mediator role of being impartial and assisting both sides to come to an agreement.

Arbitration is the judicial resolution of a dispute by an independent third party. An arbitration hearing usually involves an individual arbitrator but might also rely on a tribunal or panel. Arbitrators are trained professionals with expertise in specific areas of arbitration, such as employment or construction. The steps in the arbitration process are as follows: (1) ruling and initiation, (2) arbitrator selection, (3) preliminary hearing, (4) information exchange and preparation, (5) hearings, (6) post-hearing submissions, and (7) the award. Final-offer arbitration involves an arbitrator choosing the most reasonable offer in negotiation if the two parties cannot arrive at a negotiated solution on their own.

A major advantage of arbitration is that it saves time and money in comparison to litigation. Arbitration also has disadvantages, such as the decision of the arbitrator being binding, with no appeal possible. Many instances of workplace conflict can be arbitrated informally by a manager, with the manager choosing which side is right or imposing a compromise decision.

The grievance procedure is another approach to appealing to a third party to resolve conflict. During the process, the formal complaint moves from one level of the organization to the next higher level if not settled at the previous level. One classification of grievances is as follows: wage amounts; wage inequities; unreasonable rate of production or excessive workload; assignment and placement of workers; improper disciplinary action; physical working conditions; supervisory practices; personal rights and privileges; violation of union rights; and other contract violations.

A five-step procedure has been developed for dealing with grievances professionally and responsibly, as follows: (1) informal action, (2) investigation, (3) grievance meeting, (4) decision, and (5) appeal. Suggestions to employees for submitting a grievance include documenting the case, gathering evidence, and knowing management's side of the story.

Mediation can be a formal process, using an outside third party who helps the disputants resolve their conflict. The mediator works to find points of agreement and helps the disputants to arrive at a fair result. Unlike an arbitrator, the mediator does not make a judgment on what the outcome of the conflict should be or bind the parties to a decision. Mediation should be considered when a dispute first surfaces. Among the problems that might benefit from mediation are termination, noncompetitive agreements, intellectual property rights, and patent infringement. Mediation saves time and has a high success rate. Mediation continues to find new business-related applications, such as the mediation of mortgage modifications for bankrupt creditors.

Key Terms and Phrases

Alternative dispute resolution (ADR), p. 178
Arbitration, p. 181
Final-offer arbitration, p. 182

Grievance procedure, p. 183
Mediation, p. 185

Discussion Question and Activities

1. What would be an example of a "big picture" that a manager mediating a conflict might want both parties to see?
2. Why might mediating conflict be a cost-effective use of a manager's time?
3. What would you see as a potential problem of a manager mediating a sexual harassment dispute between two group members?
4. Why is it important for arbitrators to be highly ethical?
5. In what way does final-offer arbitration limit a negotiator from being too greedy?

6. What is the major difference between a manager assuming the role of a mediator versus an arbitrator in a dispute between two subordinates?
7. If you were a party in an arbitration dispute, what would you do to impress the arbitrator?
8. From the standpoint of office politics, how wise is it for an employee to file a grievance against his or her employer?
9. What type of grievance procedure exists for a student who feels that he or she has been unfairly suspended from the university for cheating or some other form of misconduct?
10. Suppose Microsoft discovers that a new company calls itself "Macrosoft" and sells software. Should Microsoft sue Macrosoft for trademark infringement? Or would it be better to have the issue resolved through arbitration?

Skill-Building Exercise: Resolving Conflict between Subordinates

The purpose of this exercise is to practice resolving conflict between two subordinates. The person attempting to resolve the conflict might pick up a couple of suggestions from the five-step process for resolving conflict described in the chapter. The person can play the role of a manager or team leader. Person A and Person B go beyond not getting along well with each other—their bickering interrupts work within the group.

One of the complaints Person A has about Person B is that "Person B never listens to me or anybody else. He (or she) just keeps blabbering away when we are working on a problem or in a team meeting. She (or he) wastes a lot of time by going into so much detail about goofy ideas." One of the complaints Person B has about Person A is that "Person A is so stubborn and pig-headed that she (or he) won't accept my best solutions to mutual problems. I think that she (or he) is suffering from the not-invented-here syndrome. I just don't know what to do with her (or him)."

Run the skill-building exercise for about 15 minutes to see what progress can be made in dealing with the difficult interpersonal conflict situation. The role players for the two workers in conflict can add details as to why they cannot get along.

CASE PROBLEM 12A: Katie Doesn't Like to Fetch

Katie is an administrative assistant at a craft brewery who reports to Floyd, the brewery CEO. Although the brewery is relatively large, most workers are expected to pitch in on occasional tasks that go beyond their immediate job description. Both office and brewery workers are represented by a union, and the contract allows for reasonably loose job descriptions within limits. For example, a brewer is not permitted to drive a delivery truck, and a truck driver is not permitted to brew beer.

As a high-level administrative assistant, Katie has a wide variety of responsibilities. She writes reports based on notes given to her by members of management, prepares spreadsheets about industry data, plans travel for members of top-level management, and occasionally conducts Internet searches. Although Katie reports directly to the CEO, she also carries out tasks for other members of the executive suite.

Katie is upset with one aspect of her interaction with Nate, the vice president of finance. When Nate wants Katie to gather information, such as conducting an Internet search on the returns on investment for other craft breweries, he often expresses his demand in these words: "Katie, please fetch me data on how many new craft breweries there are in the northern United States this year."

The first time Katie heard Nate use the term *fetch* in relation to her, she became upset. "Please don't ask me to *fetch* information again. I am not an office dog. My parents used to ask the family dog to fetch slippers or the newspaper." Nate shrugged his shoulders and laughed in amusement.

The next time Nate asked Katie to fetch information, she again responded angrily. Nate explained that the term *fetch* means "to gather and bring back" and that he was not demeaning her. Nate also explained that he reserved the right to speak English correctly in the office. He also accused Katie of being too worried about political correctness.

When Nate asked Katie to fetch data yet again, she complied but decided she'd had enough and decided to file a grievance under the "Supervisory Practices: Abuse of Authority" clause in the union contract. Katie submitted a written grievance to her union representative. In the grievance, she stated, "Nate Daniels, our vice president of finance, is deliberately humiliating me by asking me to fetch information. I warned him twice that I find that the word *fetch* when asking me to execute a task to be demeaning and insulting. Daniels must stop telling me to fetch information or face a penalty."

Questions

1. Does Katie have a legitimate grievance?
2. How might Katie and Nate have resolved their conflict other than through Katie filing a grievance?
3. Imagine that this grievance worked its way up to arbitration, and you were the arbitrator. How would you rule in this case?

Associated Role Play

The Katie and Nate grievance incident works its way up the grievance chain until an arbitrator is involved. One person pays the role of Katie, who feels more strongly than ever that she has been the victim of supervisory abuse because Nate keeps asking her to fetch data despite her request that he not use the term *fetch*. Another person plays the role of Nate, who feels strongly that he is a victim of the "political correctness movement" and that he has the right to use precise language in dealing with subordinates. A third student plays the role the arbitrator, who thinks that this grievance should be resolved as soon as possible. Observers might provide feedback about how well this grievance has been resolved.

CASE PROBLEM 12B: Uber Placates Drivers with $20 Million Settlement

Uber management and many of its drivers had been in a legal battle for years over whether the drivers are employees or independent contractors. To pursue their misclassification claims against Uber, drivers resorted to filing individual arbitrations in massive numbers. The contract Uber drivers have with the company prohibits class-action suits to settle any claims but allows for individual arbitration. Uber preferred an individual arbitration clause because it makes it difficult for employees to win big settlements in relatively low-value cases that might otherwise be ripe for aggregated litigation. Individual arbitration can also be expensive, time-consuming, and complicated, prompting many employees to abandon their claims.

Uber and its lawyers won key rulings from the 9th U.S. Circuit Court of Appeals that blocked the drivers' hope to litigate their claims in court or even to arbitrate their claims as a class action. The court ruled that the only way to challenge the company for alleged state and federal employment law violations was to file an independent arbitration claim. Between August and November of 2018, 12,500 Uber drivers decided to file individual arbitration claims despite the difficulties. The drivers claimed that Uber had failed to pay them the federally mandated minimum wage and also failed to pay them overtime. The thousands of drivers filed their arbitration demands through the arbitration group JAMS, as required in Uber contracts.

The individual arbitration process moved slowly. At one point, of the 12,500 arbitration demands filed by the Uber drivers, the company had paid the required JAMS initial filing fee in just under 300 cases. Furthermore, Uber had paid the arbitrator's $1,500 retainer fee in only six cases. (Under Uber's arbitration clause, it is up to the company to pay the initial arbitration fee.)

The drivers' lawyers claimed that Uber's hesitation to pay arbitration fees was evidence of company management's bad-faith negotiating. The lawyer also said, "Uber's actions make clear it does not actually support arbitration; rather it supports avoiding any method of dispute resolution, no matter the venue." Uber's failure to pay the filing fees prevented the start of arbitration.

The drivers' lawyers proposed an alternative to arbitrating thousands of individual cases at a minimum cost of $1,500 each. The suggestion was for the two sides to select nine cases to be arbitrated, with mediation to follow. Uber rejected that proposal in favor of four representative arbitrations with no mediation. Neither the proposal by the lawyers for the drivers nor the Uber proposal was accepted.

In 2019, management at the ride-hailing company agreed to pay the drivers $20 million but maintained their status as independent contractors. As independent contractors, drivers do not receive health-care benefits or other employee benefits from Uber, but they do have other perks, including flexible schedules.

An Uber spokesperson said the company had changed substantially since the lawsuit was originally filed in 2013. The company representative also said, "We're pleased to reach a settlement on this matter, and we'll continue working hard to improve the quality, security, and dignity of independent work." Shannon Liss-Riordan, an attorney for the drivers, expressed the opinion that the settlement was substantial. She estimated that the drivers would receive approximately 37 cents per each mile they had driven for Uber.

Questions

1. What influence might the demands by 12,500 Uber drivers for individual arbitration have had on their ability to reach an adequate financial settlement of their claim about being underpaid?
2. What is your evaluation of the drivers' lawyers' claim that Uber was not negotiating in good faith?
3. How might Uber have avoided all the negative publicity it received with respect to its labor–management relations?
4. Ask any Uber driver you know, including possibly yourself, whether or not Uber pays fair wages.

Source: Original case based on facts and observations in the following sources: Kate Conger, "Uber Settles Drivers' Lawsuits for $20 Million," *The New York Times* (www.nytimes.com), March 12, 2019, pp. 1–3; Bryan Menegus, "Uber's Arbitration Policy Comes Back to Bite It in the Ass," *GIZMODO* (https://gizmodo.com), December 5, 2018, pp. 1–4; Alison Frankel, "Forced into Arbitration, 12,500 Drivers Claim Uber Won't Pay Fees to Launch Cases," *Reuters* (www.reuters.com), December 6, 2018, pp. 1–11; Charlotte Garden, "Uber and Lyft Drivers Turn the Table on Individual Arbitration" *onlabor* (https://onlabor.org), January 8, 2019, pp. 1–6.

Associated Role Play

One student plays the role of an arbitrator trying to help Uber and its employees arrive at a reasonable settlement of their conflict. Another student plays the role of an Uber executive at the arbitration meeting, and a third student plays the role of a lawyer for the drivers who is also attending the meeting. Assume that a final settlement has not been reached on compensating the drivers for past underpayment or classifying them as employees or independent contractors. Run the role play for about 15 minutes. Observers will provide feedback on how well the arbitration of this historic case is proceeding.

Notes

1. Terms synthesized in Pekula Aula and Kalle Sira, "Organizational Communication and Conflict Management Systems," *Nordicom Review*, No. 1, 2010, p. 129.
2. David B. Lipsky and Ronald L. Seeber, "Resolving Workplace Disputes in the United States: The Growth of Alternative Dispute Resolution in Employment Relations," *Journal of Alternative Dispute Resolution in Employment*, No. 2, 2000, p. 37. The quote is from the same source.
3. Patrick S. Nugent, "Managing Conflict: Third-Party Interventions for Managers," *Academy of Management Executive*, February 2002, p. 152.
4. Jeanne Brett and Stephen B. Goldberg, "How to Handle a Disagreement on Your Team," *Harvard Business Review*, July 1, 2017, pp. 1–4.
5. "The Five Steps to Conflict Resolution," American Management Association (www.amanet.org), 2019, pp. 1–2.
6. Deb Levine, "Solutions: Advice from HR Knowledge Advisors," *HR Magazine*, October 2013, p. 18.
7. "What Is Arbitration?" *HR.com*, 2019, pp. 1–3.
8. Tamar Lytle, "Confronting Conflict," *HR Magazine*, October 2013, p. 18.
9. Jean Murray, "Learn How the Arbitration Process Works," *The Balance Small Business* (www.thebalancesmb.com), February 13, 2019, pp. 1–3.
10. Mayank Bhardwaj, "Exclusive: Monsanto Wins Arbitration Ruling over Royalties from Indian Seed Company," *Reuters* (www.reuters.com), February 11, 2019, pp. 1–3.
11. Max H. Bazerman and Daniel Kahneman, "How to Make the Other Side Play Fair," *Harvard Business Review*, September 2016, pp. 76–81.
12. Jean Murray, "Mandatory Arbitration Clauses in Business Agreements," *The Balance Small Business* (www.thebalancesmb.com), May 31, 2018, pp. 1–3.
13. "Grievance Procedure," *Business Dictionary* (www.businessdictionary.com), 2019, p. 1.
14. "Handling Grievances: Types of Grievances," *OPEIU Local 8* (www.opeiu8.org), 2019, p. 1.
15. Zeba Sayed, "Grievance Procedures: Five-Step Guide for Employers," *Personnel Today* (www.personneltoday.com), July 5, 2017, pp. 1–2; "Discipline and Grievance—Acas Code of Practice," *Advisory, Conciliation, and Arbitration Service* (www.acas.org.uk), March 2015, pp. 1–2.
16. "The Grievance Meeting: How to Present a Grievance to Management," *Teamsters for a Democratic Union* (www.tdu.org), 2019, pp. 1–2.
17. Deb Levine, "Solutions: Advice from HR Knowledge Advisors," October 2013, p. 18.
18. Paul Holtzman, "Why Litigate When You Can Mediate?" *HR Magazine*, September 2015, pp. 86–87.
19. Holtzman, "Why Litigate When You Can Mediate?" p. 87.
20. Daniel Gill, Orlando's Mortgage Mediation Program a Success Model for Others," *Bankruptcy Law News on Bloomberg Law* (www.bna.com), January 29, 2018, pp. 1–7.
21. Deb Levine, "Solutions," *HR Magazine*, October 2013, p. 18.

Glossary

Abusive supervision The perception by subordinates of how their supervisors engage in the sustained display of hostile verbal and nonverbal behaviors, excluding physical contact.

Alternative dispute resolution (ADR) The use of any form of mediation or arbitration as a substitute for the public judicial or administrative process to resolve a dispute.

Anonymous polling software A method of asking questions or leading discussions by embedding questions into presentations and enabling employees to respond anonymously via a clicker or smartphone.

Arbitration The judicial resolution of a dispute by an independent third party.

BATNA Best alternative to a negotiated agreement.

Bully A person who tries to control his or her victim through fear and intimidation.

Casual time orientation A cultural value prompting people to view time as an unlimited and unending resource; people with this orientation tend to be patient.

Cognitive restructuring A way of resolving interpersonal conflict by mentally converting negative aspects into positive ones by looking for the positive elements in the situation.

Collectivism A cultural value holding that the group and society receive high priority.

Compromise The settlement of differences by mutual concessions.

Conflict The opposition of persons or forces, giving rise to some tension or to a disagreement between two or more parties that are interdependent.

Conflict of interest When an individual has competing interests or loyalties and is therefore experiencing a form of role conflict.

Conflict management The adoption of a proactive approach to handling conflict by managers, supervisors, and union representatives.

Confrontation and problem solving A method of identifying the true source of conflict and resolving it systematically.

Cultural sensitivity An awareness of and a willingness to investigate the reasons why people of another culture act as they do.

Difficult person An individual who creates problems for others yet has the skill and ability to do otherwise.

Disarming the opposition A method of conflict resolution in which you disarm the criticizer by agreeing with his or her criticism of you.

Distributive negotiation A type of negotiation in which the basic task is to allocate a resource between two parties.

Downsizing The laying off of workers to reduce costs and increase efficiency.

Emotional intelligence The ability to monitor one's own and others' feelings and emotions, to discriminate among them, and to use this information to guide one's thinking and actions.

Empathy An emotional response focused on another person that allows one person to effectively connect with another.

Ethics The set of moral choices a person makes. An individual's beliefs about what is right and wrong, good and bad, are the basis for his or her ethics.

Face-negotiation theory The theory holding that differences in handling conflicts are part of maintaining face in society.

Final-offer arbitration A method of settling negotiations by having an arbitrator choose the most reasonable offer if necessary.

Formality A cultural value that attaches considerable importance to tradition, ceremony, social rules, and rank.

Grievance procedure The formal process of filing a complaint and resolving a dispute within an organization.

Haggle To bargain over the price of something, or to *dicker*.

High-context culture A culture in which societies or groups have close connections over an extended period of time.

High-maintenance person An individual who requires so much assistance, special attention, and extra help that it bothers and fatigues coworkers.

Impasse A situation that takes place when the two sides attempting to resolve a problem are unable to reach an agreement and become deadlocked.

Incivility Employees' lack of regard for one another.

Individualism A cultural value or mental set in which people see themselves first as individuals and believe that their own interests take priority.

Informality A casual attitude toward tradition, ceremony, social rules, and rank.

Integrative negotiation A type of negotiation in which both sides attempt to attain a mutually beneficial result.

Intraindividual conflict A situation that takes place when one person is faced with two incompatible goals.

Law of reciprocity Everyone expects to be paid back.

Leverage The power that one side in a negotiation has to influence the other side to accept his or her position.

Long-term orientation A long-range perspective prompting people to be thrifty and not demand quick returns on their investments.

Lowballing A negotiating tactic in which the other side gets you committed to the deal before revealing the actual total cost to you.

Low-context culture A culture where people have many short-term connections. In these societies and groups, cultural behaviors and beliefs may need to be spelled out explicitly.

Machiavellian A person in the workplace with a personality trait that compels him or her to ruthlessly manipulate others, often for his or her personal advantage.

Machiavellianism A personality trait that compels someone to ruthlessly manipulate others, often for his or her personal advantage.

Manipulator An individual who makes untrue statements or fakes certain behaviors to achieve a personal advantage.

Mediation The settlement of a dispute or conflict with the assistance of an independent person who intervenes between the two contending parties in order to aid in the settlement of the agreement.

Min–max Specifies the minimum the negotiator will accept as well as the maximum the negotiator will give away.

Mutual-gains bargaining A type of negotiation in which both sides attempt to attain mutually beneficial results.

Narcissism An extremely positive and inflated view of the self, combined with limited empathy for others.

Negotiation A situation in which two or more parties confer with each other to resolve their differences.

Nibble Just before closing an agreement, or immediately after, one or two parties in negotiation add a small demand that would not be perceived as a deal changer.

Open-door policy A policy in which any employee can bring a gripe to management's attention without checking with his or her immediate manager.

Personal-gains bargaining A situation in which the negotiator's aim is to win as much as possible for his or her side at the expense of the other side.

Political astuteness Understanding the lay of the land and using it to your advantage.

Power distance The extent to which employees accept the idea that members of an organization have different levels of power.

Practical intelligence Adapting the environment to suit an individual's needs; includes wisdom and common sense.

Principled negotiation A method of deciding issues on their merit rather than through a haggling process of what each side says it will and will not do, instead looking for mutual gains.

Relationship management A domain of emotional intelligence that includes the interpersonal skills of being able to communicate clearly and convincingly, disarm conflicts, and build strong personal bonds. Relationship management has also been defined as the ability to inspire, influence, and develop others while managing conflict.

Self-awareness A domain of emotional intelligence that allows people to know their strengths and limitations and have high self-esteem.

Self-managed work team A formally recognized group of employees responsible for an entire work process or segment that delivers a product or service to an internal or external customer.

Self-management A domain of emotional intelligence that helps prevent the negotiator from throwing temper tantrums when negotiations do not proceed as planned.

Self-monitoring The process of observing and controlling how we appear to others.

Sexual harassment Unwanted sexually oriented behavior in the workplace that results in discomfort and/or interference with the job.

Short-term orientation A demand for immediate results and a propensity not to save for the future.

Social awareness A domain of emotional intelligence that enables the negotiator to show empathy for the other side without totally neglecting his or her own needs.

Stalking-horse bid An initial bid on the debtor's assets.

Territorial disputes Protecting and hoarding resources that give one power, such as information, relationships, and decision-making authority.

Trash talking Uncivil remarks or aggressive communication that is expressed between opponents.

Urgent time orientation A cultural value prompting people to perceive time as a scarce resource; people with this orientation tend to be impatient.

Win–win The belief that after a conflict has been resolved, both sides should gain something of value.

Work–family conflict The situation that occurs when the individual has to perform multiple roles: worker, spouse, and often parent or guardian of a dependent parent.

Name Index

Organization Index

Subject Index